POLITICAL
ANTHROPOLOGY

POLITICAL ANTHROPOLOGY

AN INTRODUCTION

SECOND EDITION

TED C. LEWELLEN

BERGIN & GARVEY
Westport, Connecticut
London

Library of Congress Cataloging-in-Publication Data

Lewellen, Ted C., 1940–
    Political anthropology : an introduction / Ted C. Lewellen.—2nd
ed.
      p.   cm.
    Includes bibliographical references and index.
    ISBN 0-89789-289-5.—ISBN 0-89789-290-9 (pbk.)
    1. Political anthropology.   I. Title.
GN492.L48   1992
306.2—dc20   91–44660

British Library Cataloguing in Publication Data is available.

Library of Congress Catalog Card Number: 91–44660
ISBN: 0-89789-289-5 (hb.)
      0-89789-290-9 (pbk.)

First published in 1992

Bergin & Garvey, 88 Post Road West, Westport, CT 06881
An imprint of Greenwood Publishing Group, Inc.

Printed in the United States of America

The paper used in this book complies with the
Permanent Paper Standard issued by the National
Information Standards Organization (Z39.48–1984).

10 9 8 7 6 5 4

Contents

Foreword to the First Edition

In this succinct and lucid account of the sporadic growth of political anthropology over the past four decades, Ted Lewellen traces the development of its theoretical structure and the personal contributions of its main formulators. He makes available to the wider public of educated readers the issues, problems, perplexities, and achievements of political anthropologists as they have striven to make sense of the multitudinous ways in which societies on varying levels of scale and complexity handle order and dispute, both internal and external. He assesses the strength and probes the weaknesses of successive anthropological approaches to the study of political structures and processes, viewed both cross-culturally and in intensive case studies. The result is a commendable guide to the varied sources of this increasingly important subdiscipline, a guide which, as far as I know, is unique of its kind; his criticisms are sharp, his style genial, and his judgments just. As a student of the first generation of British political anthropologists of the structural-functionalist school, and a teacher of the medial generation of American political anthropologists, I can vouch for the accuracy and balance of Professor Lewellen's conclusions, and applaud the penetration of his criticisms, even when they are directed at positions promoted by those of my own theoretical persuasion.

Professor Lewellen states candidly that he has not written a textbook. Indeed, most textbooks are bulkier and overcharged with disparate materials, mainly descriptive. But this concise work is theoretically fine-honed and minutely integrated. It seems to be the introduction to political anthropology that we have all been waiting for, the prism which accurately segregates the significant constituents. Not only students but also seasoned scholars will find worth in it. It is at once a summation and a new start.

Victor Turner

Introduction

In a 1959 review article, political scientist David Easton charged that political anthropology did not really exist because the practitioners of this nondiscipline had utterly failed to mark off the political system from other subsystems of society. The judgment was then generally accepted with the humble mortification proper to a young science being criticized by one much older and wiser. It was not until almost ten years later that anthropologists had gained sufficient confidence to protest that Easton had completely misunderstood the nature of political anthropology and had construed its greatest virtue into a vice (Bailey 1968; A. P. Cohen 1969; Southall 1974). In the societies in which anthropologists have traditionally worked, politics cannot be analytically isolated from kinship, religion, age-grade associations, secret societies, and so forth, because these are precisely the institutions manifesting power and authority. In many societies government simply does not exist. This recognition, and the specification of the manner in which the idiom of politics is expressed through the medium of apparently nonpolitical institutions, may be the primary contributions of anthropology to the study of comparative politics. Recently, political anthropologists have carried this idea into the sacred domain of the political scientist by demonstrating that informal organizations and relationships may be more important than formal institutions even in such modern governments as those of the United States and Israel.

Two decades ago, Ronald Cohen (1970: 484) could still agree with Easton to the extent that "there are, as yet, no well-established conventions as to what [political anthropology] includes or excludes or what should be the basic methodological attack on the subject." This is less true today. Joan Vincent's *Anthropology and Politics: Visions, Traditions and Trends* (1990) offers a minutely detailed history, and an annual series, edited by Myron Aronoff, with the general title *Political Anthropology*, further helps provide an ongoing clarification of the subject. However, political anthropology, like anthropology as a whole, remains immune to precise definition. Cross-cultural studies of law and warfare may or may not be included (they are not included in this book). Numerous theoretical approaches compete with one another—cultural materialism, structuralism, various Marxisms, neo-evolutionism, feminist revision-ism, symbolic anthropology. . . . There are world-system perspectives and perspectives that examine the actions of individuals. Cross-cultural statistical analyses vie with historical studies.

Indeed, one problem with a book such as this is that it might give the reader the impression that the field is more coherent than is actually the case. Though a handful of researchers—notably Ronald Cohen, Abner Cohen, F. G. Bailey, Joan Vincent, Myron Aronoff, and Peter Skalník—are self-consciously political anthropologists, most articles in the field are by cultural anthropologists writing about politics. The result is that political anthropology exists largely through a potpourri of studies that can be classified within a few broad themes only with some effort and not a little artifice.

This said, a number of major thrusts of political anthropology can be legitimately delineated. First, in the past the classification of political systems was an important area of research. These studies, some of which are now under attack, provided political anthropology with a basic vocabulary and no few insights into the ways that systems work at different levels of complexity. Second, the evolution of political systems is a continuing fascination in the United States, though British and French anthropologists often like to pretend that evolutionary theory died with Lewis Henry Morgan. Third is the study of the structure and functions of political systems in preindustrial societies. This point of view was vehemently repudiated on both sides of the Atlantic because of its static and ideal nature. After the initial burst of revolutionary rhetoric, there emerged a general recognition that even the most dynamic of political processes may take place within relatively stable structural boundaries. In any case, political anthropology had its beginnings in this paradigm, and many of its enduring works are structural-functionalist. Fourth, for the last several decades the theoretical focus has been on the processes of politics in preindustrial or developing societies. Perhaps the most assertive trend of the 1970s was action theory, an outgrowth of the process approach with an emphasis not on changing institutions but on the manipulative strategies of individuals. Fifth, there is a wide and growing literature on the political response of formerly tribal societies to modernization. Sixth, world-system theory has given rise to a number of studies that interpret politics in the light of the spread of capitalism out of Europe beginning in the sixteenth century. Seventh, one dominant current theme is how subcultures embedded in state societies nonviolently and often quite subtly manipulate power to their own advantage. Finally, the feminist movement in academic scholarship as a whole has introduced a new and important voice into political anthropology, questioning basic assumptions about power and offering new data and interpretations.

Beyond these minimal themes, political anthropology shares a set of common values and assumptions rooted in the nature of anthropology itself.

THE ANTHROPOLOGICAL PERSPECTIVE

In their introduction to *African Political Systems* (1940), generally considered the foundation work in political anthropology, Meyer Fortes and E. E. Evans-Pritchard stated flatly, "We have not found that the theories of political philosophers have helped us to understand the societies we have studied and we consider them of little scientific value" (p. i). This sentiment might well have been the slogan of political anthropology in its developmental period. Until the mid-1960s, the theoretical framework of political anthropology, its methodology, its vocabulary, and its focus of interest owed little to political science, political sociology, or political psychology. In articles written before 1960, one might encounter an occasional reference to Friederick Hegel, Karl Marx, Talcott Parsons, or David Easton. By and large, however, anthropologists remained blissfully untrained in political science; their point of view was resolutely anthropological. This has changed as anthropologists turn increasingly to the study of modern nation-states and begin to assimilate systems theory and decision-models brought in from other disciplines. In many ways, however, political anthropology continues to be as much anthropology as political.

Above all, anthropology is based on field experience. Researchers working in intense interaction with individuals in their day-to-day setting seek to find, in the words of Ralph Nicholas (1966: 49), "order in the chaos of many people doing many things with many meanings." This disarmingly simple goal turns out to be tremendously complex. The closer one is to real people in natural settings, the harder it is to make generalizations about their behavior. This has led to a form of argument called Bongo-Bongoism: No matter what generalization is made, someone is always able to protest, "Ah, but in the Bongo Bongo tribe they do it differently." It is probably safe to say that there is always a Bongo Bongo tribe threateningly positioned at the periphery of every theorist's consciousness.

The result is that anthropology has been decidedly inductive and comparative. Ideally, general theory should evolve from field data and should be so stated that it can be cross culturally compared and analyzed. The founders of political anthropology believed that concepts emerging from studies of the United States or Western Europe had little application to hunting-gathering bands or horticultural tribes. More recently, however, it has become almost universally recognized that virtually all groups, no matter how remote, have been influenced by Western expansion, so that concepts drawn from history and economics are increasingly becoming part of the normal vocabulary of anthropology.

Culture remains a key concept of political anthropology. Though neither the British nor the French are particularly concerned with this rather ambiguous notion, and many American materialist and ecology-oriented theorists ignore it as much as possible, the concept is implicit in most political studies. Basically, the two broad ways of conceiving culture are to think of it as an adaptive system—that is, the ways that groups of people respond technologically and ideationally to the challenges of their environments—or to think of it as a system of subjective but socially shared symbols and meanings, including language, myths, rituals, political concepts of legitimization, and the like. So far, this latter definition has been most employed in political anthropology, because it provides the mental and social context within which political processes take place (Aronoff 1983).

Another important concept, deriving from early studies of peoples who had little specialization of labor or of institutions, is that societies are comprised of interwoven networks of relations, so that a change in one element affects the others. Although we no longer interpret this as rigidly as we did—the relative autonomy of some subgroups is well documented—the idea of society as an integrated system remains fundamental to the anthropological perspective. Because the experimental sciences have been using two-part causal models for so long, one sometimes gets the impression that the concept of system is a recent discovery. Yet since the mid-nineteenth century, anthropologists have consistently and unself-consciously studied societies as systems. It is true that the cross-cultural testing of hypotheses requires isolating discrete units from their cultural context, but in its statistical form this is a fairly late development, and it is generally used in a systemic framework. All the major paradigms in anthropology—evolutionary theory, the various functionalisms, French structuralism, process theory, decision theory, dependency theory, and so forth are basically systems theories.

Finally, the theme of evolution, while periodically banished from social anthropology with great fanfare, remains an implicit assumption underlying even timeless structural interpretations. The reason is that anthropology deals with societies representing a wide spectrum in technological and social development, and it is virtually impossible to view these except along some scale of cultural complexity. More recently, anthropologists have recognized the crucial role of the influence of Western capitalism on even the most preindustrial societies, so that history can no longer be ignored.

Induction, cross-cultural comparison, culture, system, and *evolution* are not really defining qualities of anthropology so much as various aspects of the anthropological way of looking at the world. Although these provide a unified point of view, it is at the same time replete with contradictions. Anthropologists seek no less than an understanding of the nature of humankind, yet they are suspicious of any generalization at all. They idealize a holistic view; yet, by the very complexity of the systems they confront, they are forced to isolate small subsystems. They demand precise classification, yet may argue that typologies distort more than they clarify. In sum, anthropologists are torn between diametrically opposed demands: to be true to the intense particularity of their field experience, and to give meaning to that experience by generalizing it to the world at large. This antithesis is a theme that runs through all of political anthropology.

This book is written for anyone seeking a relatively painless overview of one of anthropology's most fascinating areas of specialization. I emphasize painless because this book is not a scholarly monograph nor a state-of-the-art summary. Rather, I have written the introduction to the subject that I would have welcomed as a student in a class on political anthropology—a book that provides the background necessary to understand more focused ethnographic and theoretical accounts, as a stage setting might provide the context and meaning for a play's action. Even though this book may be read easily by undergraduates, professionals (including those outside the field of anthropology) should not be frightened off. I am offering here mostly other people's research; while the mode of presentation may be simplified, many of the ideas are both complex and insightful. If this book does no more than convey enough of the excitement of this frontier discipline to direct readers to the real thing, I will be satisfied.

Aside from some general updating, this second edition includes three entirely new chapters: "Women and Power," "Anthropology in the World System," and "The Power of the People." In addition, the chapter on religion has been almost doubled to include material on secular ritual and on revitalization movements. Work on this second edition was supported by a PETE (Program for the Enhancement of Teaching Effectiveness) summer grant from the University of Richmond.

Chapter One

The Development of
Political Anthropology

Though political anthropology as a specialization within social anthropology did not appear until as late as 1940, and did not really kick in, *1940* until after World War II, this is also true for most anthropological subject specializations. From its beginnings as a scientific discipline in the latter half of the nineteenth century to the middle of the twentieth, anthropology was relatively unified. The early evolutionists admitted no boundaries to their comparative method and blithely roamed through the world and through the farther reaches of history examining any subject that met their eye. Franz Boas, the father of American anthropology, was equally ready to analyze Eskimo art, Kwakiutl economics, or immigrant craniums. Whatever lines were drawn were theoretical: one was either an evolutionist, or a historical particularist, or a structural-functionalist, and so forth, but there was little sense that one might be a political anthropologist, an ethnolinguist, or an ecological anthropologist. The ideal of a holistic anthropology only began to break down through the 1940s as increasing data and increasing numbers of professional anthropologists forced specialization. The development of political anthropology was part of this general process, which continues today, with ever smaller subspecialties being delineated. Yet the comparative study of politics in preindustrial societies dates to the very beginnings of anthropology.

THE NINETEENTH-CENTURY EVOLUTIONISTS

Charles Darwin's influence dominated the development of cultural anthropology in the second half of the nineteenth century just as it dominated biology. Much of the evolutionary theory emerging from this period was as rudimentary as the societies it sought to make sense of: evolutionary schemas were rigid and simplistic; there were endless arguments over whether the earliest societies were matriarchal or patriarchal; ethnocentrism ran rampant as Christianity and the Aryan "race" were seen as the ultimate developments of human progress; customs were torn out of their cultural context and compared indiscriminately by armchair anthropologists who had never seen the "savages" that were their subjects. Yet it is easy to forget how perceptive many of these studies were. Whatever their faults, the evolutionists laid the foundation for modern scientific anthropology (see Figure 1).

Prior to this period, the tradition that reached back to Plato and ran through Aristotle, Thomas Hobbes, Jean-Jacques Rousseau, and most philosophers of politics until (but not including) Karl Marx described government and politics as products of civilization; lower stages were characterized by anarchy. One of the earliest to challenge this view with hard evidence was Sir Henry Maine, who, in *Ancient Law* (1861), postulated that primitive society was organized along the lines of kinship, was patriarchal, and was ordered by sacred proscriptions. Evolution was in the direction of secularization and organization based not on kinship but on territory—"local contiguity" formed the basis for political action.

Maine's important insight that kinship could be a primary sociopolitical structure was developed by Lewis Henry Morgan in *Ancient Society* (1877). Morgan had studied the Iroquois Indians of New York State first hand and had been fascinated by their kinship terminology, which was very different from that used in Western European countries but similar to that employed in other parts of the world. His description and categorization of kinship systems was itself a lasting contribution, but before these could gain recognition, they had to be couched in the theoretical framework popular at the time. Morgan developed an evolutionary sequence based on the mode of subsistence, the stages of which he termed *savagery*, *barbarism*, and *civilization*. These grossly connotative terms actually translate rather well into their modern equivalents, societies based on hunting-gathering, horticulture, and developed agriculture. Morgan, like others of his time, began with the "postulate of the psychic unity of mankind"—belief in a common origin and parallel development all over the world—though he was unable to follow the idea to its inherently antiracist conclusions and assumed that the Aryans were naturally "in the central stream of human progress" (Morgan 1877: 533).

With his considerable sophistication in the analysis of kinship, Morgan was able to elaborate Maine's inchoate ideas. Social organization began

Figure 1
Political Anthropology Family Tree

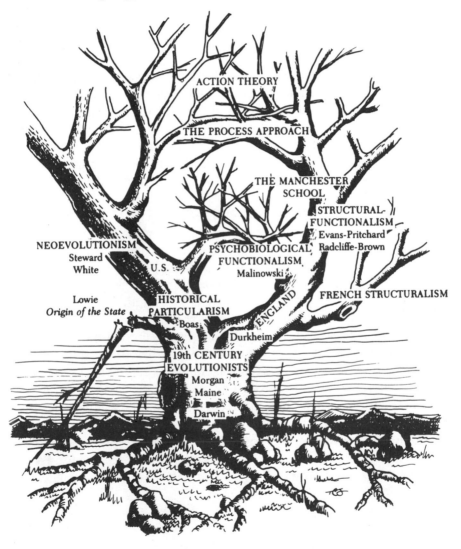

with the "promiscuous horde" that developed into kin-based units, organized along sexual lines—namely, intermarrying sets of male siblings and female siblings (this was an early insight into what is now called cross-cousin marriage). In emphasizing the role of exogamy (marriage outside the social group), he touched on the conception of intergroup bonds formed through marriage that would become the "alliance theory" of French structuralists three-quarters of a century later. Progressive restriction of marriage partners led to the development of gens (i.e., clans) which joined to create increasingly larger units up to a confederacy of tribes. Sociopolitical structure at this level is egalitarian and is based on sets of interpersonal relations. (With the exception of the promiscuous horde, this is not a bad description of the Iroquois confederacy, though there is little reason to generalize to a universal evolutionary process.) The specialization of the political sphere does not appear until the full domestication of plants and animals creates sufficient surplus to lead to urbanization and private property. True government, then, is based on territory and property.

Morgan is subject to most of the criticisms directed by later generations at the evolutionists (except, of course, that he was no armchair anthropologist, having studied the Iroquois first hand). Yet much of his thinking has been absorbed into modern anthropology. This is especially true in relation to politics. Though anthropologists no longer distinguish kin-based from territory-based groups (all people recognize territorial boundaries), Morgan's emphasis on kinship as a primary medium of political articulation at the subsistence levels of hunting-gathering and horticulture was justified. Equally important was Morgan's discovery of the gens as a corporate lineage in which decision making was confined within a group tracing common ancestry through either the male or the female line. Another lasting insight was his recognition of the egalitarianism of primitive society and the lack of a concept of private property. These latter ideas contributed to Morgan's most effective influence: They formed the basis for Frederick Engels' *The Origin of the Family, Private Property and the State* (1891), the Marxian view of the evolution of capitalism.

THE REACTION

Early-twentieth-century anthropology was characterized by two fundamental changes: the rejection of evolutionary theory and methodology, and a widening hiatus between the anthropologies of the United States and of England and France. In the latter countries, the immediate repudiation of evolutionism was relatively mild, but there was a significant shift in new directions. This shift was based on the work of Emile Durkheim—in France leading to an increasingly cognitive structuralism that would culminate with the works of Claude Lévi-Strauss; in England leading to an emphasis on social facts (and a corresponding disregard for the psychological aspect of culture) and a theoretical point of view dominated by the ideas of function and structure. Durkheim had little influence on U.S. cultural anthropology, where Franz Boas's "historical particularism" dominated. Boas was absolute, and often vehement, in his repudiation of the comparative method and of the vast generalizations that had emerged from it. He emphasized minute descriptive studies of particular cultures. Theory did not disappear altogether, but such orientations as diffusionism took on a very particularistic turn, with field anthropologists spending years collecting the most minuscule facts of daily life and charting them on enormous trait lists (one suspects this type of inquiry declined through sheer boredom). Though English anthropologists were turning increasingly to the study of kinship, not much was accomplished in the political dimension, aside from an occasional reference to Durkheim's mechanical and organic solidarity. In the United States, little in the way of theory separated out the political for analysis.

A major exception was Robert Lowie's *The Origin of the State* (1927). To find a framework to deal with the political, Lowie reached back to outmoded evolutionary theory. Fittingly enough, he started by rejecting the unilineal evolution of his predecessors; there was no evidence that all societies pass through similar stages of development. Maine's and Morgan's contention that primitive political order was maintained solely through personal relations was also rejected. Rather, the territorial bond, which Morgan saw as a characteristic of civilization, was universal and thus formed a bridge between primitive political organization and the state. In an earlier book, *Primitive Society* (1920), Lowie had recognized the political importance of associations in uniting otherwise disparate groups, and he saw these as forming the basis of the state because they weakened the blood ties of kin groups. Now he modified this view, showing how associations can also be as "separatistic" as kin relations. Thus associations, which are of their nature neither centralizing nor disruptive, require a supra-ordinate authority to achieve higher level integration.

Georges Balandier's (1970) contention that specific, explicit political anthropology developed during the 1920s is true only to a point. Here we find certain lasting ideas: that all societies recognize territory, that increases in population and in conflict lead to states, that class stratification is a key element in movement up the evolutionary ladder toward the state, and that the central element of the state is a monopoly of coercive power. Though these concepts were not developed in a systematic causal model, Lowie clarified a number of issues, asked a number of crucial questions, and presented anthropology with a fascinating challenge.

Unfortunately, the challenge was not taken up. The evolutionary phrasing of Lowie's book, despite his denials of unilineal development, must have seemed sadly anachronistic to his peers who had thought themselves done with this evolutionary nonsense once and for all. The beginning of political anthropology was also its end—until 1940.

THE BRITISH FUNCTIONALISTS

In England during the 1930s two brands of functionalism vied for dominance, the psychobiological functionalism of Bronislaw Malinowski, and the structural-functionalism of A. R. Radcliffe-Brown. Often considered the founder of modern fieldwork techniques for his extensive research in the Trobriand Islands, Malinowski sought to interpret cultural institutions as derived from certain psychological and biological needs. Though he contributed little to political anthropology per se, his studies of law, economics, and religion—as observed in ongoing, rather than historical, society—cleared the way for the type of specialization that would later become commonplace. Malinowski's participant observation method became the model for an entire generation of British field-workers whose intense analyses of African societies would establish political anthropology as a legitimate subdiscipline. However, Radcliffe-Brown's structural brand of functionalism ultimately came to predominate in England, where academic chairmanships at Oxford, London, or Manchester were close to the equivalent of theoretical fiefdoms. For Radcliffe-Brown, a society was an equilibrium system in which each part functioned to the maintenance of the whole (the obvious organic analogy was not avoided). Thus there was a sense that societies were to be described from high above, to be mapped to show how their various elements intermeshed. As we shall see, this approach is more atemporal than static; that is, it does not really postulate an unchanging society or a society without conflict, but rather its focus is on those norms, values, and ideal structures that form the framework within which activity takes place.

Feeding this theoretical orientation, and feeding on it, was the concentration of British research in colonial Africa. Much of the purpose of such research was to instruct colonial authorities on the social systems under their control, and this affected both the emphasis and the image of social anthropology. On the one hand, there was little recognition that the societies anthropologists were studying were severely changed by colonialism, and by the Pax Britannica imposed by English guns. Also, there was a tendency to study chiefdom and state systems, some of which, like the Zulu, had been integrated partially as a reaction to the British threat.

These two trends, structural-functionalism and the African experience, came together in 1940 in a work which, at a single blow, established modern political anthropology: *African Political Systems*, edited by Meyer Fortes and E. E. Evans-Pritchard. In their introduction, the editors distinguish two types of African political system: those with centralized authority and judicial institutions (primitive states), and those without such authority and institutions (stateless societies). A major difference between these types is the role of kinship. Integration and decision making in stateless societies is based on bilateral family-band groups at the lowest level, and on corporate unilineal descent groups at a higher level. State societies are those in which an administrative organization overrides or unites such groups as the permanent basis of political structure. Even though this typology was later criticized as much too simplistic, the detailed descriptions of how lineages functioned politically in several specific societies were lasting contributions. Social equilibrium was assumed, so that the major problem was to show how the various conflict and interest groups maintained a balance of forces that resulted in a stable, ongoing social structure. The integrating power of religion and symbol were also noted, especially the role of ritual in confirming and consolidating group values.

African Political Systems' introduction and eight ethnographic articles established the problems, the theoretical foundation, the methodology, and the controversy for more than a decade of research into the politics of preindustrial societies. The original typology was increasingly refined. For example, A. W. Southall in *Alur Society* (1953) challenged the assumption that segmentary systems—those in which authority was dispersed among a number of groups—were always uncentralized; he provided an example of a society in which segmentary lineage organization existed side-by-side with a centralized state. Others questioned segmentation as a factor for typing at all, since even centralized governments are segmented. Nor could lineages be the basis for all stateless societies, because age grades, secret associations, and ritual groups could cross-cut lineage divisions for purposes of political action. Jumping off from Fortes's and Evans-Pritchard's bare suggestion of types (the two editors did not seem to think their typology universal, or even very important), classifications were increasingly refined until political taxonomy became virtually an autonomous field of research. The static structural-functionalist paradigm maintained itself through a number of studies as the old guard—Evans-Pritchard, Raymond Firth, Daryll Forde, and Meyer Fortes—held, contemporaneously or successively, the princely academic chairs of British anthropology. This is not to say that the situation itself was static; there was constant ferment, as Malinowskian or Radcliffe-Brownian emphases alternated, and as conflict and change increasingly imposed themselves with the rapid demise of African colonialism.

THE TRANSITION

By the 1950s, after a decade of gradual chipping away, the edifice of structural-functionalism was showing cracks in its very foundation. There was little sense yet of a complete repudiation of this paradigm, but there was a quite self-conscious sense that fundamental modifications were being made.

A major contribution in this direction was Edmund Leach's *Political Systems of Highland Burma* (1954), which signaled the shift to a more process-oriented, more dynamic form of analysis. In the Kachin Hills area of Burma, Leach found not one but three different political systems: a virtually anarchic traditional system, an unstable and intermediate system, and a small-scale centralized state. The traditional system and the state were more or less distinct communities made up of many linguistic, cultural, and political subgroups, all somehow forming an interrelated whole. This whole could not be supposed to be in equilibrium; there was constant tension and change within and between the various subsystems. To make sense out of all this, Leach felt it necessary "to force these facts within the constraining mold of an *as if* system of ideas, composed of concepts which are treated *as if* they are part of an equilibrium system" (Leach 1954: ix). This was no more than the people themselves did, for they also had an ideal cognitive pattern for their society, expressed in ritual and symbolism. In reality, however, the people were hardly constrained to follow their own, and certainly not the anthropologist's, *as if* conception of their behavior. These ideas are similar to the mentalistic structuralism of Claude Lévi-Strauss (whom Leach would later help introduce into English-language anthropology), and there are suggestions of the cognitive mapping later to become central to American psychological anthropology. The immediate importance for the study of politics, however, was in the clear differentiation of abstract political structure from the on-the-ground political reality. Almost as crucial, Leach finally got political anthropology out of Africa and broke it free from the relatively cohesive, single-language societies to which it had been confined.

Meanwhile, Max Gluckman was also breaking new ground. In his chapter on the Zulu in *African Political Systems*, in *Custom and Conflict in Africa* (1956), and in *Order and Rebellion in Tribal Africa* (1960), Gluckman developed the theme that equilibrium is neither static nor stable, but grows out of an ongoing dialectical process in which conflicts within one set of relations are absorbed and integrated within another set of relations: Cross-cutting loyalties tend to unite the wider society in settling a feud between local groups; witchcraft accusations displace hostilities within a group in a way that does not threaten the system; apartheid in South Africa, while radically dividing white from black, ultimately unites both groups within themselves. The Roman maxim "divide and conquer" is cleverly restated as "divide and cohere." Politically, this is especially evident in African rituals of rebellion in which, periodically, the king must dress as a pauper or act the clown, is symbolically killed, or is subjected to open hatred and obscenities from his people. For Gluckman, such rituals are not merely catharsis; they are the symbolic reassertion of the priority of the system over the individual, of kingship over any particular king.

At this stage, both Leach and Gluckman are transitional figures, still rooted in the structural-functionalism of the 1930s and 1940s, developing ever more clever arguments in defense of equilibrium theory; yet at the same time they are taking a giant step toward a new paradigm. Gluckman, as founder and chairman of the anthropology department at Manchester University, was to see his ideas extensively elaborated by his students, known collectively as the Manchester School, a phrase that came to represent a new orientation to society based not on structure and function but on process and conflict.

THE NEO-EVOLUTIONISTS

Without a doubt, England dominated political anthropology during its first two decades. Meanwhile, in the United States, an incipient and quite different political anthropology was fermenting. Evolutionism, long banned by Boasian edict from the proper study of humankind, began a slow and not entirely respectable resurgence through the writings of

Leslie White and Julian Steward. White (1943, 1959) developed a complex sequence leading through agricultural intensification to private ownership, specialization, class stratification, political centralization, and so forth. Much of this was elucidated at such a high level of generality that it left White open to the charge of merely resuscitating nineteenth-century unilineal theory. Steward's (1955) use of the term *multilinear* evolution for his own theory only served to validate an unnecessary dichotomy. Actually, no serious evolutionist has ever held a truly unilineal theory (Harris 1968: 171-73). But the situation was not clarified until the unilineal/multilineal dichotomy was replaced with the complementary concepts of *general evolution* and *specific evolution*, the higher level referring to evolutionary processes such as increased specialization or intensification of production, the lower to the historic sequence of forms (Sahlins and Service 1960). This clarified, evolutionary anthropology was free to move, unfettered by a heavy load of semantic, rather than substantive, difficulties.

Thus, in contrast to their English colleagues, American political anthropologists started with the idea of change on a panoramic scale in a context that was fundamentally ecological and materialist. White measures evolution in energy efficiency and sees technology as a prime mover. Steward's cultural ecology focused on the "cultural core"—mainly, the subsistence and economic arrangements that largely determine social structure and ideology. The differences between British and American anthropology were vast but can be overemphasized. For example, one of the earliest American political ethnographies, E. Adamson Hoebel's 1940 study of the Comanche Indians, was neither evolutionary nor materialist. Throughout the 1940s and 1950s, and into the 1960s, there was a strong current of structural-functionalism in the United States. But that which was particularly American was vastly different from that which was particularly British, to the extent that there was often little communication between the two.

Political evolution quickly became almost synonymous with political classification. The two major evolutionary works of the period, Elman Service's *Primitive Social Organization* (1962) and Morton Fried's *The Evolution of Political Society* (1967), were more taxonomic and descriptive than causal; the emphasis was on the characteristics of different levels of sociocultural integration, rather than on the factors that caused evolution from one level to another. Causal theories were hardly lacking, but these derived from archaeology rather than cultural anthropology. Many notable archaeologists devoted their careers to the processes involved in the evolution of state societies. These two trends, the archaeological and the cultural, which originally ran parallel, came together in Service's *Origins of the State and Civilization* (1975). Political evolution remains an ongoing field of study, but it can no longer claim to be the major focus of American political anthropology—process and decision-making orientations have crossed the Atlantic from England.

PROCESS AND DECISION MAKING

Max Gluckman had tentatively experimented with the analysis of situations involving individuals, in contrast to the usual ethnographic focus on group norms and social structures. Elaborating on this experiment, Victor Turner, in *Schism and Continuity in an African Society* (1957), followed a single individual through a series of "social dramas" in which personal and community manipulations of norms and values were laid bare. To Gluckman and Leach's emphasis on process and conflict was added a new element—individual decision making observed in crisis situations.

The belated discovery that the world is in motion stimulated an enthusiastic disavowal of structural-functionalism, almost equal to that which had temporarily obliterated evolutionism at the turn of the century. *Structure* and *function* became unfashionable terms, to be replaced by *process, conflict, faction, struggle, manipulative strategy*, and the like. As Janet Bujra (1973: 43) succinctly expressed it,

For the early functionalist, the assumption was that social unity was the normal state of affairs, whereas conflict was a problematic situation which could not easily be incorporated into their theoretical framework. More recent studies of political behavior, however, seem to indicate that it is conflict which is the norm, and it is the existence of social unity which is more difficult to explain.

That conflict and accord, unity and disunity, might be two sides of the same coin, as Gluckman emphasized, was temporarily forgotten.

The change from structural theory to process theory had its correlate in the dissolution of the false stability imposed by colonialism in Africa. With the rise of postcolonial nation-states, and the incorporation of tribal societies within larger political organizations, new problems presented themselves. No longer could primitive politics be treated as though it existed in a closed system; the wider sociopolitical field replaced the more restricted concept of political system. On the other hand, the intensive study of particular situations gave rise to the more restricted concept of political arena, wherein individuals and political teams vie for power and leadership.

Though many of these ideas come together in such works as Balandier's *Political Anthropology* (1970) and Swartz, Turner, and Tuden's "Introduction" to their edited volume of the same title (1966), it would be a mistake to consider the process approach as a coherent theory. Many ethnographies that emphasize process continue to focus on the level of norms and institutions. The individual-focused, decision-making approach—often referred to as action theory—is a somewhat separate subdivision of the less cohesive process orientation.

Process theory opened the way for a cross-Atlantic dialogue that was muted, at best, during the heyday of structural-functionalism. Such American leaders of political anthropology as Marc Swartz and Ronald Cohen, who had shown only passing interest in evolution or evolutionary typology, joined the British in what constituted a truly international trend.

WOMEN, WORLD SYSTEMS, AND WEAPONS OF THE WEAK

While earlier perspectives and theoretical approaches continued throughout the 1980s and into the 1990s, three strong new trends were evident. Perhaps the most important development was the emergence of a distinctly feminist anthropology. Though not specifically political, virtually all of the writers in the field were examining the relative power of women. Not only has the assumption of universal male domination been challenged (and defeated) but also other anthropological myths, such as the model of Man the Hunter as the focus of physical evolution. In addition to the expected cross-cultural statistical comparisons, two important theoretical schools have developed within feminist anthropology, one analyzing the cultural construction of gender and the other, based on Marxist theory, examining the historical development of gender stratification.

Eric Wolf's *Europe and the People Without History* (1982) brought the world-system perspective and so-called dependency theory into the mainstream of anthropology. Wolf contends that all, or virtually all, cultures today can only be understood in relation to the expansion of European capitalism over the last centuries.

In a closely related development, many researchers are countering the natives-as-victims approach, which focused on the destruction of tribal cultures by the spread of Western civilization, with a new emphasis on the ways that indigenous peoples fight back, often quite subtly, against the dominant state, either to maintain their group identity or to create for themselves niches of independence and pride. Political scientist James Scott's *Weapons of the Weak* (1985) demonstrates how peasants resist— through gossip, slander, petty arson, and thievery—the marginalization that comes with large-scale capitalist agriculture.

Political anthropology may be as amorphous as ever, but from its rude beginnings it has become a firmly established subdiscipline of cultural anthropology.

SUGGESTED READINGS

Harris, Marvin. *The Rise of Anthropological Theory* (New York: Thomas Crowell, 1968). Harris' relentlessly materialistic orientation can be infuriating when applied to theories for which he has no sympathy. Nevertheless, this massive work is impressive in its scope and scholarship and entertaining even when one disagrees with the analysis. Though Harris does not deal separately with political anthropology, he provides the context within which political anthropology must be understood.

Kuper, Adam. *Anthropologists and Anthropology: The British School 1922–1972* (New York: Pica Press, 1973). Political anthropology had its origins in British structural-functionalism. I know of no book that presents a clearer overview of this school and its critics. Also, there are fascinating biographies and character portraits of such luminaries as E. E. Evans-Pritchard, E. R. Leach, and Max Gluckman.

Mair, Lucy. *Primitive Government* (Baltimore: Penguin, 1962). This book, which deals entirely with Africa, is one of the few works to attempt a general overview of politics in preindustrial societies from the point of view of British structuralism. However, the author's generalizations sometimes get lost in the myriad examples, which follow one on the other with confusing rapidity.

Vincent, Joan. *Anthropology and Politics: Visions, Traditions, and Trends* (Tucson: University of Arizona Press, 1990). An exhaustive and erudite history of political anthropology from the nineteenth century to 1990. Vincent rejects as ethnocentric the genealogical method of tracing the discipline through a family tree and attempts to include virtually everybody who ever wrote on the subject. The results are impressive, and sometimes difficult.

Traditional Eskimo society was made up of egalitarian bands that fluctuated in size according to seasonal availability of food.

Chapter Two

Types of Preindustrial Political Systems

No anthropologist is more open to the threat of Bongo-Bongoism than the one daring to classify. (As you will recall, whatever generalization is made in the field of anthropology, some researcher will be able to protest, "Ah, but in the Bongo Bongo tribe they do it differently.") It is safe to say that when it comes to creating typologies of social systems, such aberrant tribes abound. One noted British anthropologist, Edmund Leach, once relegated virtually all attempts at anthropological classification to the lowly status of butterfly collecting, on the grounds that the resulting typologies made no more sense than, say, grouping together all blue butterflies (Leach 1961).

Though a few political anthropologists might unhesitatingly agree, classification has been a major focus of research ever since politics was separated out as a subsystem worthy of specific attention. The results of forty years of the increasing refinement of political types will completely satisfy no one, but this is as one might expect when something as fluid and unpredictable as society is confined within a set of neat pigeon holes. Yet, surprisingly, a general system of classification has been more or less agreed on, as shown in Figure 2, and this system seems vindicated to some extent by quantitative cross-cultural testing. The synthetic classification shown in Figure 2 is based on means of political integration, access to leadership positions, and method of group decision making. Centralized systems seem relatively uniform by these criteria, but if other criteria are used, many subtypes are possible. A classification of early states based on degree of complexity appears as Table 3.

Such classification is possible because a society is no more just a collection of individual human beings than a house is just a conglomer-

Figure 2
Preindustrial Political Systems

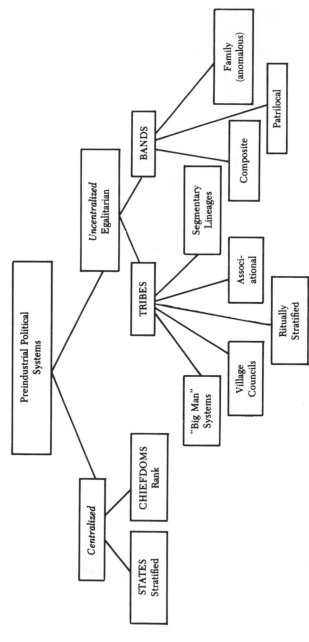

Sources: Eisenstadt 1959; Fried 1967; Service 1971.

ation of lumber, bricks, and nails. Two houses built of different materials but to the same floor plan are obviously much more alike than two houses of the same materials but very different designs (say, a town house and a ranch house). Similarly, we would not expect to find the same architecture in the arctic and in the tropics, nor among the pastoral Nuer of Africa and the modern industrial Swedes. In short, a house is defined by its organization, not its components, and that organization is influenced by its physical environment and the level of technology of the people who designed it.

The analogy can be strained, but it helps to keep some such idea in mind when dealing with any anthropological classification. If we are to place the Bushmen of the Kalahari Desert of Africa in the same political category (bands) as the nineteenth-century Shoshone Indians of Utah, it must be on the assumption that a hunting-gathering adaptation to an arid environment gives rise to particular social characteristics, such as egalitarian groups with no formal leadership and a system of economic exchange based on sharing. The relationships are causal, to be sure, but it is more difficult than one might think to determine exactly how one element of a system causes another. Does the arid environment, and thus the relative scarcity of food and water, cause low population densities and consequently a flexible small-group social organization? Perhaps. But we usually think of a cause as being active, whereas the environment just sort of sits there. Besides, the relationship between society and environment is one of constant feedback; people not only adapt to their surroundings but also change their physical and social worlds to meet their own needs. In other words, when classifying social systems, it is often more productive to think in structural relationships, in the sense that one element logically implies another. A useful typology, then, would be one that delineates systems, that is, units in which the parts are so structurally interrelated that from the specification of one element we can predict other elements.

However, we cannot emphasize too strongly that interrelations of social traits (e.g., chiefdoms and unilineal kinship) represent only statistical probabilities. To return to our house analogy, we might find that ranch houses can be legitimately classed together, but we would also expect an enormous range of variation of particulars within the general style. In contrast to strictly materialist theories of culture, environment and technology do not seem so much to determine social structure and ideology as to limit the range of possibilities.

Table 1 suggests some of the social and economic characteristics we might reasonably associate with each major political type. Any such chart

Table 1
Preindustrial Political Systems: An Evolutionary Typology

	Uncentralized		Centralized	
	Band	Tribe	Chiefdom	State
Type of Subsistence	Hunting-gathering; little or no domestication	Extensive agriculture (horticulture) and pastoralism	Extensive agriculture; intensive fishing	Intensive agriculture
Type of Leadership	Informal and situational leaders; may have a headman who acts as arbiter in group decision making	Charismatic headman with no "power" but some authority in group decision making	Charismatic chief with limited power based on bestowal of benefits on followers	Sovereign leader supported by an aristocratic bureaucracy
Type and Importance of Kinship	Bilateral kinship, with kin relations used differentially in changing size and composition of bands	Unilineal kinship (patrilineal or matrilineal) may form the basic structure of society	Unilineal, with some bilateral; descent groups are ranked in status	State demands supra-kinship loyalties; access to power is based on ranked kin groups, either unilineal or bilateral
Major Means of Social Integration	Marriage alliances unite larger groups; bands united by kinship and family; economic interdependence based on reciprocity	Pantribal sodalities based on kinship, voluntary associations and/or age-grades	Integration through loyalty to chief, ranked lineages, and voluntary associations	State loyalties supercede all lower-level loyalties; integration through commerce and specialization of function
Political Succession	May be hereditary headman, but actual leadership falls to those with special knowledge or abilities	No formal means of political succession	Chief's position not directly inherited, but chief must come from a high-ranking lineage	Direct hereditary succession of sovereign; increasing appointment of bureaucratic functionaries
Major Types of Economic Exchange	Reciprocity (sharing)	Reciprocity; trade may be more developed than in bands	Redistribution through chief; reciprocity at lower levels	Redistribution based on formal tribute and/or taxation; markets and trade

24

Social Stratification	Egalitarian	Egalitarian	Rank (individual and lineage)	Classes (minimally of rulers and ruled)
Ownership of Property	Little or no sense of personal ownership	Communal (lineage or clan) ownership of agricultural lands and cattle	Land communally owned by lineage, but strong sense of personal ownership of titles, names, privileges, ritual artifacts, etc.	Private and state ownership increases at the expense of communal ownership
Law and Legitimate Control of Force	No formal laws or punishments; right to use force is communal	No formal laws or punishments; right to use force belongs to lineage, clan, or association	May be informal laws and specified punishments for breaking taboos; chief has limited access to physical coercion	Formal laws and punishments; state holds all legitimate access to use of physical force
Religion	No religious priesthood or full-time specialists; shamanistic	Shamanistic; strong emphasis on initiation rites and other rites of passage that unite lineages	Inchoate formal priesthood; hierarchical, ancestor-based religion	Full-time priesthood provides sacral legitimization of state
Recent and Contemporary Examples	!Kung Bushmen (Africa), Pygmies (Africa), Eskimo (Canada, Alaska), Shoshone (U.S.)	Kpelle (W. Africa), Yanomamo (Venezuela), Nuer (Sudan), Cheyenne (U.S.)	Precolonial Hawaii, Kwakiutl (Canada), Tikopia (Polynesia), Dagurs (Mongolia)	Ankole (Uganda), Jimma (Ethiopia), Kachari (India), Volta (Africa)
Historic and Prehistoric Examples	Virtually all paleolithic societies	Iroquois (U.S.), Oaxaca Valley (Mexico), 1500–1000 B.C.	Precolonial Ashanti, Benin, Dahomy (Africa), Scottish Highlanders	Precolonial Zulu (Africa), Aztec (Mexico), Inca (Peru), Sumeria (Iraq)

Sources: Abrahamson 1969; Carniero 1970; Eisenstadt 1959; Fried 1967; Levinson and Malone 1980; Lomax and Arensberg 1977; Service 1971.

must be approached with caution. First, no society should be expected to match all the characteristics of its type, any more than we would expect to discover some perfectly average male American who is five-foot-nine, weighs 173, is Protestant, earns $28,605 per year, and has 1.16 children. Second, what this chart really shows is cultural complexity; therefore, one should not assume that politics is the primary determinant because the major headings are "band," "tribe," "chiefdom," and "state"; if this book were about kinship the headings might just as well be "bilateral," "patrilineal," "matrilineal," and so forth. Third, keep in mind that certain characteristics are better predictors than others. Oddly enough, subsistence level is a poor predictor of social organization. Statistically, the strongest predictor of political type, kinship, religion, and the like is population density (which is not included on the chart, since increasing densities from band through state may be assumed). Fourth, a chart of this kind, by its very nature, implies that each of these types is quite distinct from the others, whereas in reality these types form points along a continuum. Fifth, do not assume that a higher level of cultural complexity leaves behind all the characteristics of lower levels (reciprocity, for example, is a significant means of exchange in all societies) nor that cultural complexity is simply additive (bilateral systems of kinship appear at both the simplest and most complex levels but are replaced by unilineal kinship at the intermediate levels). Finally, we make special mention of religion, where we find a strong relation between cultural complexity and religious organization, but little or no relation in regard to belief (which is why magic, animism, polytheism, monotheism, etc., are not mentioned on the chart). If these caveats are kept in mind, the chart provides a useful summary of the characteristics of preindustrial political systems.

UNCENTRALIZED SYSTEMS

Many of the groups studied by anthropologists possess little that could be called government, at least not in the sense of a permanent political elite. In most of these traditional systems, power is fragmentary and temporary, dispersed among families, bands, lineages, and various associations. Wider political groups may be formed temporarily to counter some threat, such as warring neighbors, but these groups break apart when the problem has been overcome. Thus these social systems can best be viewed not as permanent, centrally organized societies, but rather as fluid groups that, over short or long periods, sometimes seasonally and sometimes almost randomly, coalesce into larger tribal units then disintegrate into smaller units, which may themselves be divisible. Although politics is constant in such societies as individuals seek support for leadership positions, as public decisions are made, and as territory is defended, it is not manifested in either a monopoly of coercive force or in any form of centralized economic system based on taxes or tribute. There may be great differences in individual status, but there is little in the way of class stratification, so these systems, while only egalitarian in any real sense at their lowest level—that of hunters-gatherers—do appear more democratic in decision making and access to leadership than more centralized groups.

Bands

A major conclusion deriving from a 1965 Conference on Band Organization was that the term *band*, while still useful, was regularly applied to groups as diverse as those with an average size of 25, as well as those with 300 to 400 members, rendering the term virtually meaningless. It was also argued that the usual defining qualities of bands—seasonal scheduling, lack of centralized authority structures, and hunting-gathering economy—were not sufficiently restrictive to make these units automatically comparable (Damas 1968). However, in those few societies lacking agriculture, domesticated food animals, or dependable year-round fishing, there would seem to be only a limited number of cultural options available. Similarities in the social and political structures of such widely separated groups as the Canadian Eskimo and Australian Aborigines suggest that dependence on wild foods, the consequent nomadism, and seasonal redistributions of population fix the adaptive possibilities within relatively narrow limits. For this reason, the band may have been a normal mode of social organization in Paleolithic times.

Bands are typically small, with perhaps 25 to 150 individuals, grouped in nuclear families. While there is a division of labor along age and sex lines, there is virtually no specialization of skills, with the result that the unity of the wider group is, in Emile Durkheim's term, *mechanical*; that is, it is based on custom, tradition, and common values and symbols, rather than on an interdependence of specialized roles. A strict rule of band exogamy forces marriage alliances with other bands, and this wider group is typically united also by bilateral kinship (traced equally through both parents). Lineages—in the sense of corporate descent groups holding territorial rights—would not be sufficiently flexible for the constant fluctuations of hunting-gathering societies.

Morton Fried (1967) categorizes such groups as egalitarian in economy, social organization, and political structure. Distribution of food and other needed goods is at the simplest level of sharing; bonds are established within the band and between bands on the basis of ongoing reciprocal relations. Political organization is also egalitarian to the extent that decision making is usually a group enterprise, and access to leadership positions is equally open to all males within a certain age range. Leadership, which temporarily shifts according to the situation, is based on the personal attributes of the individual and lacks any coercive power. A headman or leader in a hunt cannot really tell anyone what to do, but must act as arbiter for the group, and perhaps as expert advisor in particular situations.

This least complex of political structures may be further subdivided into patrilocal, composite, and anomalous bands. The patrilocal type is based on band exogamy and a marriage rule that the woman live with her husband's group. This type is so widespread that Elman Service regarded it as "almost an inevitable kind of organization" (Service 1962: 97). Indeed, it has the advantage of band stability, because each group is constantly replenished over time by new members coming in from outside; but it also is capable of forming wide-ranging alliances through marriage and possesses considerable flexibility. The composite band was viewed by Service as the result of the collapse of originally patrilocal structures that were rapidly depopulated from disease and war after having come in contact with civilization. It is a group which lacks either band exogamy or a marriage residence rule, and which is thus "more of an expedient agglomeration than a structured society." In the anomalous category are the Basin Shoshone and the Eskimo, both of which have social structures so fragmented that they have been characterized as typifying the family level of sociocultural integration.

The !Kung Bushmen. The Nyae Nyae region of the Kalahari Desert in southwest Africa covers about ten thousand square miles, in which there are a number of small waterholes but no rivers or streams or other surface water except for some shallow ponds during a brief rainy season. Within this area, about 1,000 !Kung Bushmen (the "!" represents a click in their pronunciation) live in thirty-six or thirty-seven bands.* Though at the lowest level of technological development, relying on digging sticks and poison-tipped spears and carrying all of their meager possessions with

---

*All examples are given in the ethnographic present, as they were at the time of the researcher's fieldwork. Today most !Kung have been settled around missions or have been assimilated.

them during their constant treks in search of food and water, they have adapted well to the extremely hostile environment. About 80 percent of the food is supplied by the women, who daily collect nuts, fruits, tubers, roots, and various other field foods. The remainder of !Kung subsistence is supplied through hunting, which is exclusively a male occupation. Various species of large antelope provide most of the meat, though occasionally a buffalo or a giraffe may also be killed. About fifteen to eighteen such large animals are killed by a single band in a year, and the meat is shared by the entire group.

While there is no separate political sphere among the !Kung, a number of political problems must be dealt with, such as the defense of territories, the protection and allocation of water, and public goals in regard to band movements and collective hunts. Each band claims a territory that must have a permanent source of water at a reasonable distance from sufficient vegetable foods for day-to-day consumption. Within such a territory are sporadic fertile areas, such as groves of mangetti nut trees, clumps of berries, and special places where tubers grow in particular abundance; these are considered owned by a band and are jealously guarded. Incursions into another band's territory occasionally occur, especially during hunting expeditions, in which case violence may be threatened; but true wars are unknown.

Headmanship is passed on from father to son. The existence of hereditary political positions seemingly defies the principle that all adult males in a band have equal access to leadership. However, the headman's authority is largely limited to control of field food and water; he plans the utilization of these various resources and has charge of the group's movements from one area to another within the territory. Most of this is firmly established by custom, and important decisions are arrived at by group consensus, so the headman position is to some extent symbolic. Visitors must ask his permission to partake of food or water within the band's territory, but custom dictates that all reasonable requests be granted. Headmanship brings responsibility without reward, and since it is also the !Kung ideal that no individual should stand above another, such positions are seldom actively sought.

The hereditary headman may or may not be the actual leader of the band. If he is too young or lacks leadership abilities, this role may fall to someone with more of the personal qualities of leadership, so that the official position becomes nominal. Also, effective leadership shifts according to the situation; a person may be an exceptional hunt leader but have little authority over public decisions, such as when and where to move camp (Marshall 1967).

The Eskimo. Despite the vast territory inhabited by the Eskimo (from Siberia to Greenland) they have been described as remarkably alike in their political and social organization. Environmental determinist arguments are especially tempting, for the Eskimo live in possibly the most hostile humanly habitable regions on earth. Their food resources—mainly fish, caribou, and seal—are seasonal and widely scattered, which would logically lead to low population densities, nomadism, and extremely fluid social organization based on small subsistence groups. The basic unit is the extended family, which can take advantage of bilateral kinship relations to join with other families in temporary bands or even villages as food supplies wax and wane during the year. A household might comprise a family of twelve, which subsists alone part of the year but joins groups of up to 270 at other times. Leadership outside the household is elementary; even villages sometimes lack a headman, and what minimal influence might be possessed by an individual rests with the local shaman, whose authority is neither coercive nor uniting. Along the coast, the owner of a whaling boat has unrestricted authority over his crew during a voyage, and might, by the prestige of his wealth, maintain a loose chieftainship over a community; but even in this case, group unity is maintained not by government but by conventionalized reciprocal obligations among kin. As with the !Kung, maintenance of order derives from the power of custom and public opinion (Weyer 1959).

While this textbook view of the Eskimo is probably reasonably accurate for a majority of groups, recent research reveals a much greater diversity of traditional social and political forms. Bilateral kinship is in some places replaced by corporate patrilineages; men's associations sometimes override kinship relations as decision-making bodies; there are large permanent settlements in some areas; and there are vast differences in types of leadership, from virtual chiefdoms to an absence of authority beyond the head of the family. Some of this variation is undoubtedly secondary, deriving from long contact with agents of Western civilization, such as explorers, whaling crews, traders, and missionaries. However, such diversity does suggest that the hunting-gathering adaptation may permit a wider range of sociopolitical variation than is accounted for in present typologies (Damas 1968).

Tribes

"If I had to select one word in the vocabulary of anthropology as the single most egregious case of meaninglessness," wrote Morton Fried

(1967: 154), "I would have to pass over 'tribe' in favor of 'race.' " The comparison is apt; like *race*, the concept of *tribe* is used to refer to a vast range of entities that have almost nothing in common with each other.

The three basic objections to the concept of *tribe* are (1) it does not encompass a discrete group of societies that share common qualities; (2) it is not sufficiently different from other types, such as bands and chiefdoms; (3) it suggests a degree of social integration, or at least boundedness, that is often nonexistent (Helm 1968).

Why, then, is the term in use at all? There are both logical and empirical reasons. First, the term is a recognition that both in sociopolitical complexity and in evolutionary development there must be a form that bridges the gap between hunting-gathering bands and centralized systems. Second, cross-cultural studies do reveal features in common to at least many of these groups.

Tribes are uncentralized systems in which authority is distributed among a number of small groups; unity of the larger society is established from a web of individual and group relations. Because these groups rely on domesticated food sources, they are more densely populated and usually more sedentary than hunting-gathering bands. As with bands, there is little political or economic specialization, except for a division of labor along age and sex lines, and there is no religious professionalization. However, according to Elman Service (1962), the defining quality of the tribe—that which separates it from the band—is the existence of pan-tribal sodalities uniting the various self-sufficient communities into wider social groups. A sodality is simply a formal or informal association, such as a family group, a college fraternity, or the Girl Scouts. In tribal societies the two types of sodalities are those derived from kinship, and those which are not. Kinship sodalities include lineages—groups tracing descent through either the male line (patrilineage) or the female line (matrilineage)—and clans, which are groups of lineages tracing common descent to an often-mythical ancestor. Nonkin sodalities include a host of voluntary and involuntary associations.

If we look at tribes in terms of the types of sodalities that unite them, or in terms of who makes the decisions for the group, we find that a number of subtypes immediately emerge. Even where other forms of sodalities are evident, kinship almost invariably is an important element of social integration. One form of political organization based on kinship is the segmentary lineage, especially common in Africa, in which a number of autonomous village groups can join together in ever-larger units for ritual purposes or to counter some threat. Many tribal societies are integrated by associations that cross-cut kinship divisions. In age-set systems the group initiated together at puberty form a continuing sodality that takes on different functions as it passes through certain age levels. For example, if the group is male, young men form a warrior society, and elders become the governing body of the community. In other tribes, such as the American Plains Indians, voluntary societies of warriors, clowns, or police may serve important integrating and decision-making functions. While tribal societies do not have hierarchies of full-time religious professionals, religion may be extremely important, especially if it is tied to some sort of ancestor veneration, as is often the case in unilineal groups. In these societies, ritual stratification may be a key element of integration as those responsible for major rituals assume decision-making leadership even in secular matters. In some tribes, village councils of elders make public decisions, usually through a process of discussion leading to consensus. Finally, throughout Melanesia certain "big men" attain significant political authority through wealth, generosity, and courage in war. Although these leaders may exercise chieftainlike authority, their positions are inherently unstable because they depend on their ability to buy followers through gift-giving and loans. A bad crop, an inability to gather sufficient pigs for a lavish feast, or failure in battle can quickly shift authority to a contender with better luck.

It is tempting to think of such a breakdown of subtypes as fairly covering the range of possibilities, but there are tribes that include elements from more than one subtype, and others that do not fit any of these forms. Why this endless profusion of subtypes? Perhaps the basic problem is in attempting to define *tribe* in political terms at all. Unlike *band*, *chiefdom*, and *state*, the concept of *tribe* really does not—and cannot—refer to a particular type of political organization, since there seem to be few structural, or systemic, limits on the variety of forms. Ronald Cohen's characterization of this midrange group of societies as noncentralized "polities based on domesticated plants and animals" might be the best we can do and still allow for the range of variation. Even here, we are faced with certain rather glaring anomalies. The American Plains Indians, some of whom lacked domesticated plants or food animals (their subsistence was almost entirely based on the buffalo), certainly had more complex integrating institutions than those found in hunting-gathering bands.

The Kpelle. Just how complex all this can get is illustrated by the Kpelle of West Africa. Here, the larger cultural group is fragmented into a number of self-sufficient communities, each with a hereditary owner of the land but also with a council of elders that makes decisions by consensus. Complementing the political power of these groups is the men's secret society (secret in the sense that its symbols and rituals are not to be revealed to outsiders). This society, the Poro, holds a supernatural political power that cuts across lineage and small chiefdom boundaries and can thus unite the Kpelle into larger groups. Actually, the Poro extends far beyond the Kpelle, including a host of cultures in Nigeria, Côte d'Ivoire, Liberia, Sierra Leone, Ghana, and Guinea-Bissau. In the past it arbitrated in local wars and even united entire countries for common action in times of emergency. Thus we find the centralization and hierarchy we expect from chiefdoms, the segmentary organization and pantribal sodalities common to tribes, and at least three of our subtypes—associational, village council, and ritually stratified—combined in the Kpelle (Fulton 1972; Little 1965).

The Yanomamo. The Yanomamo are a horticultural group living in scattered villages in Venezuela and northern Brazil. As described by Napoleon Chagnon (1968), these people are extremely aggressive and warlike. Their self-conscious fierceness derives from a vicious circle in which a premium on male warrior qualities justifies extensive female infanticide, with a resulting severe shortage of women. As men must go to war to capture wives, they have come to place a high value on masculine warlike qualities. The constant aggression of the Yanomamo creates a number of political problems both within the village and between villages. Polygamy, mainly reserved for the older and wealthier men, exacerbates the shortage of women. Also, a marriage rule gives older brothers first right for brides, and a broad definition of incest further reduces the women available to younger men. As a result, within villages brothers are pitted against brothers, adultery and accusations of adultery are common, and hostility levels are high. The maintenance of order in such a situation would seem to demand a strong headman, but, as with bands, the headman has no coercive authority. Within the village, the men are kept from killing each other by a system of conventionalized violence: taking turns hitting each other with the fist on the side or chest, or striking each other on the head with long poles. The political leader's function in these battles is to maintain the level of violence within the rules, that is, just this side of lethal.

Intervillage politics is a matter of survival. Unlike many horticultural tribes that participate in warfare almost as a game, the Yanomamo are deadly serious; it is not unknown for entire villages to be overrun, with all the men killed or dispersed and all the women taken captive. To maintain a balance of power, a village must often form alliances with former enemies. This takes place in three stages: first, ritual exchange of goods; second, mutual feasting; and finally, exchange of women as wives. Nevertheless, alliances are tenuous and may be broken with impunity, especially in the early stages.

In many ways, the Yanomamo would seem a typical tribe: their social organization is certainly more complex than that of nomadic hunters and gatherers; their villages are permanent and relatively stable (they tend to fission, or break up into smaller groups, after reaching a certain size); yet, there is no centralized coercive leadership and there is equal access to headmanship positions among the men of the village. However, these otherwise obviously tribal people seem to lack the one thing Service held to be the defining quality of tribes, namely, pantribal sodalities. Even though lineages extend beyond village boundaries, they do not unite villages; not, at least, in the absence of military alliances. In fact, because of the hostilities created within lineages through competition over women, bonds of marriage are often stronger than patrilineal bonds. There are no pantribal associations, and military alliances unite only two or a few villages. Certainly no political structure integrates the entire Yanomamo group or even a large proportion of it.

The Nuer. The Nuer of southern Sudan, described by E. E. Evans-Pritchard in 1940, provide a classic example of the segmentary lineage solution to the problem of tribal unity. About two hundred thousand Nuer live in villages, cultivating maize and millet during the rainy season, herding cattle in almost constant nomadism during the dry season. Their social system is fluid in the extreme, and individually they have a reputation for being fiercely independent. While they completely lack centralized authority, or any formal authority at all beyond the village level, they have been able to join together in large groups to counter external threats. Evans-Pritchard characterizes the Nuer as "an acephalous state, lacking legislative, judicial, and executive organs. Nevertheless, it is far from chaotic. It has a persistent and coherent form which might be called 'ordered anarchy.' "

The smallest corporate economic unit is the household, comprised of several patrilineally related men and their families. A group of these households may be clustered as a hamlet within a village. As one of these hamlets grows through processes of birth, adoption, and immigration, it will inevitably fission, creating another group which may form a hamlet in a nearby village. These hamlets make up a minor lineage, and several of them, spread between many villages, make up larger and larger units: major lineage, maximal lineage, and finally, clan. A clan might include thousands of people and be spread throughout all Nuerland, creating a network of social ties which these highly mobile people can call on as needed. Because clans are exogamous, marriage alliances establish hundreds of small bonds with other clans.

Parallel to the segmentary lineage system, but not identical with it, is a territorial system. Each clan owns a certain territory which is, however, open to members of other clans; in fact, the owner clan does not form an aristocracy and may actually populate only a small portion of its territory. However, those moving into a village attempt to establish relations with an owner lineage through being adopted into it or through marriage.

War and feuding are almost constant. By means of a process of "complementary opposition," increasingly larger territorial groups can be united for such purposes. For example, two sections may be fighting with each other, but they ally if another group attacks both. To counter an even larger threat, all three former antagonists may join together. The political unity of the Nuer must be defined situationally as increasingly larger units are assembled according to need, and then dismantled when the threat is gone.

The complementary opposition solution to the problem of tribal integration, shown in Figure 3, is especially adaptive for a tribe that intrudes into an already occupied territory. This is the case with the Nuer, who have within historical times expanded into the land of the Dinka. Such a system, extremely flexible yet capable of forming a powerful united force, channels expansion outward and releases internal pressures in warfare against other peoples (Sahlins 1961).

CENTRALIZED SYSTEMS

As noted previously, a valid typology should designate systems, so that within any single category the determination of one or a few variables predicts others. The category "centralized political systems" encompasses societies in which power and authority inhere in one person or group of persons. This is true by definition. By extension we can predict that these societies tend to be more densely populated than bands and tribes, are stratified by rank or class, have specialized social and occupational roles, utilize more productive technology, have economies based on centralized redistribution, and are more stable in ongoing sociopolitical groupings. Morton Fried emphasizes the basic inequalities of these systems relative to uncentralized systems: recruitment into political positions is no longer equal but may be based on membership in a certain class or in an elite lineage. Though unilineal descent groups may exist, and even hold a great deal of local power, politics is no longer

Figure 3
Nuer "Complementary Opposition"

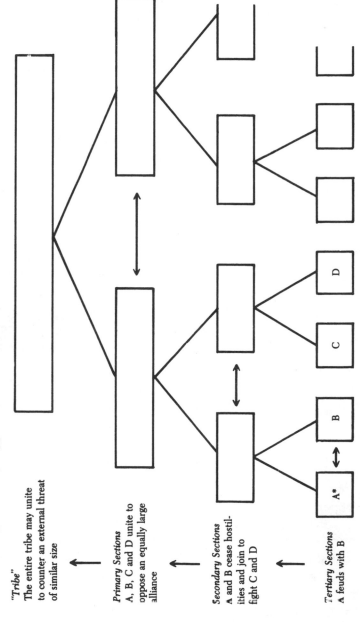

"Tribe"
The entire tribe may unite to counter an external threat of similar size

Primary Sections
A, B, C and D unite to oppose an equally large alliance

Secondary Sections
A and B cease hostilities and join to fight C and D

Tertiary Sections
A feuds with B

*Each box in the bottom row represents several allied villages.

manifested mainly through kinship; political specialization appears with full-time politicians and an attendant bureaucracy.

Chiefdoms

In respect to social integration, the chiefdom level transcends the tribal level in two major ways: (1) it has a higher population density made possible by more efficient productivity, and (2) it is more complex, with some form of centralized authority. Unlike segmentary systems, in which political units coalesce and dissolve according to the situation, chiefdoms have relatively permanent central agencies of government, typically based on collection and redistribution of an economic surplus (often including a labor surplus).

The position of chief, unlike that of headman of a band or lineage, is a position of at least minimal power—that is, the chief has access to a certain amount of coercion. The chief may be the final authority in the distribution of land, and may be able to recruit an army. Economically, he is the center and coordinator of the redistribution system: he can collect taxes of food or goods, some of which are returned to the populace, creating a new level of group solidarity in which a number of specialized parts depend on the smooth functioning of the whole. Even if the chief's position is not directly hereditary, it is only available to certain families or lineages. Although actual class stratification is absent, every individual is ranked according to membership in a descent group; those closer to the chief's lineage are higher on the scale and receive the deference of all those below. Indeed, according to Service (1971: 145), "the most distinctive characteristic of chiefdoms, as compared to tribes and bands, is . . . the pervasive inequality of persons and groups in the society."

However, the chief by no means possesses absolute power. The aristocratic ethos does not carry with it any formal, legal apparatus of forceful repression, and what obedience the chief can command may derive less from fear of physical sanctions than from his direct control of the economic redistributional system. The chief's lineage may itself become exceptionally wealthy, but ultimately loyalty is purchased by constant bestowal of goods and benefits. Though there may be the approximation of a bureaucracy, offices beneath that of chief are not clearly differentiated, and when pressures build up these lower bureaucrats can break away from the parent body and set up an opposition government. Thus a chief is in some ways comparable to a Latin American *caudillo*, in the sense that he walks a narrow tightrope between conflicting interest groups and maintains his position through a precarious balancing act.

Though definitions of tribe have often been labeled so general as to be meaningless, the previous description of the chiefdom level of political integration, derived largely from Elman Service (1962), has been accused of being too specific. According to Herbert Lewis (1968), Service has logically deduced this model according to what should exist between the tribal and state levels, then joined it with the specific model of Polynesian political structure, and proposed this hybrid as a general evolutionary type. Lewis points out many groups that appear to have chieftainships are not stable at all; they oscillate back and forth from centralized leadership to egalitarianism as strong leaders come and go. By this time, such looseness in our categories should be assumed without another long disclaimer.

Precolonial Hawaii. The eight islands of aboriginal Hawaii were under the domination of a number of rigidly stratified hereditary chiefdoms. The paramount chiefs were believed to be descendants of the gods and were so charged with mana—supernatural power—that even the ground they walked on could not be touched by lesser mortals. The chiefly personage was thus surrounded by an elaborate set of taboos, the breaking of which could mean a sentence of death. The chiefs were supreme economic, military, and ritual leaders, though most of these functions were delegated to a group of noble administrators and war leaders who formed the upper strata of society. There were two other levels below these administrators: lesser nobles and commoners. Each individual belonged to one of these strata, and the nobles were also ranked according to the order of their birth and their nearness to the high chief. The higher nobles, or lesser chiefs, were accorded a great deal of deference; for example, commoners had to throw themselves face down on the ground as they passed. To keep the chiefly line pure, the heir to the position of high chief was supposed to be the firstborn son of the chief and his firstborn sister (a form of incestuous endogamy also found in ancient Egypt and Inca Peru).

Lesser chiefs controlled allocations of land and water—the latter exceedingly important, since much of the productive land was irrigated. They also, de facto, controlled the communal labor of commoners. Tribute was paid to the high chief by the upper level nobles, who collected from the lower nobles, and so on down the line to the commoners. This tribute—or some of it—would be used in public works, mainly irrigation canals and warfare. Nobles also subsidized a group of professional craftsmen from the tribute till.

What kept these polities from attaining the status of states was partially the lack of differentiation of the political sphere; these were hereditary theocracies in which authority was still relatively undifferentiated from religion and kinship. Also, though a chief might hold life and death power over his subjects in some regards, the central governing unit by no means held a monopoly on this power, which was distributed among a number of lesser chiefs. Nor was there any legal structure to administer such force. Finally, these governments were far from stable. Warfare was constant, and chiefdoms were regularly overthrown, in which case the entire noble class would be replaced by the conquering group (Davenport 1969; Service 1975; Seaton 1978).

The Kwakiutl. Indian societies of the Northwest Coast of North America are usually categorized as chiefdoms, though these groups do not fit the ideal pattern as neatly as do the Hawaiians.

The Kwakiutl Indians of Vancouver Island were never studied in their aboriginal state; by the time Franz Boas began his fieldwork among them in 1885, they had already had almost a century of contact with white traders, missionaries, sailors, and Indian agents, and had been decimated by disease. At that time their level of living, based on hunting and fishing and virtually devoid of domesticated food supplies, was among the highest in North America as measured by material possessions—houses, canoes, utensils, tools, and such art objects as totem poles.

The Kwakiutl were divided into about twenty-five villages, each of which was comprised of from two to seven *numayma*, or tightly cohesive units made up of from one to several extended families. *Numayma* were stratified in terms of prestige within the village, and each individual was ranked within his *numayma*. Ranks, which were obtained mainly through heredity or marriage, were intricately elaborated by titles, crests, and ceremonial privileges.

Such prestige positions were by no means rare; out of a population of about 1,500 individuals, there were 650 named positions, some of which were held by more than one person at the same time. These social positions were maintained through the medium of the potlatch—an elaborate feast in which an enormous amount of goods was distributed to all present. One could also insult a rival by destroying goods in his presence, but these rivalry potlatches, though dramatic, were not as common as is often believed.

The Kwakiutl obviously suggest many elements of the classical chiefdom: a strong system of ranking, specialized leadership roles based on heredity, permanent agencies of government, and redistribution. But the fit is far from perfect. First, there was no integration beyond the village, and precious little within it, because most political integration was focused in the *numayma*. The highest ranking chief in the village would supposedly have some extra authority, but in practice the *numayma* was the day-to-day political entity, which means that politics was manifested through kinship, as in tribal society. Also, it is debatable that the potlatch really represented a system of redistribution. No one in Kwakiutl society was wealthy enough to give a potlatch without both calling in debts and borrowing. The potlatch was the center of a complex economic system based on an intricate web of loaner-debtor relationships. Though an invited *numayma* might not be directly involved in such debts, it was expected to reciprocate the potlatch, preferably with greater abundance. Also, the main article distributed at a potlatch was the Hudson Bay blanket, which could hardly be eaten and was most valuable as a form of currency used for further loaning and borrowing. The potlatch suggests a system of reciprocity, common to bands and tribes, rather than the centralized redistribution that supposedly defines the quality of chiefdoms. In other words, the Kwakiutl, and perhaps all the cultures of the Northwest Coast, would seem to represent a blending of elements of both tribes and chiefdoms (Codere 1950, 1957; Drucker and Heizer 1967).

The State

For Elman Service (1975: 163), the distinguishing quality of the state, that which separates it from the chiefdom, "is the presence of that special form of control, the consistent threat of force by a body of persons legitimately constituted to use it." Morton Fried (1967), on the other hand, emphasizes stratification: the state has special institutions, both formal and informal, to maintain a hierarchy with differential access to resources. This stratification goes beyond the individual and lineage ranking found in less complex societies; it involves the establishment of true classes. For Ronald Cohen (1978a, 1978b), the "key diagnostic feature" of the state is its permanence. Unlike lower order forms of political organization, the state does not regularly fission as part of its normal process of political activity.

States are generally large, complex societies, encompassing a variety of classes, associations, and occupational groups. Occupational specialization, including a full-time political bureaucracy, unites the entire group in a web of interrelated dependencies. Because of the vast range of individual and class interests within a state, pressures and conflicts unknown in less complex societies necessitate some sort of rule of

impersonal law, backed by physical sanctions, for the ongoing maintenance of the system.

The Precolonial Zulu. The Nguni family of Bantu-speaking peoples
included about a hundred thousand pastoralists and shifting cultivators
living in about eighty thousand square miles of southeastern Africa. The
basic residence unit was the patrilineally extended family. The largest
permanent political unit was the clan, though several clans might
temporarily form a tribe. Actually, these were classic chiefdoms, as
described earlier.

During the early years of the nineteenth century, most of these
independent chiefdoms were united through conquest into the powerful
and highly militaristic Zulu state. To a great extent, this relatively
undeveloped state owed its continuing unity to the threat of the Boers
and British who were pushing at the edges of its territory (the British
conquered the Zulu in 1887). Regiments of conscripted soldiers, belong-
ing to the king alone, were stationed in barracks concentrated in the
capital. The king had the power not only to command military and labor
service but also to collect gifts from his subjects, which made him the
wealthiest man in the kingdom. In turn, he was expected to be generous
in providing food and other goods for his people. He had a council of
advisors whose recommendations, ideally, were followed. He was also
the ultimate appeals court for cases referred from the lower chiefs' courts,
and he reserved to himself the right of passing death sentences (though
the chiefs did not always respect this reservation). Individuals and clans
were stratified according to their genealogical closeness to the king.

Thus, though inchoate and short-lived, the Zulu state displayed many
of the attributes of more complex states: it united a large number of
disparate groups under a central authority; it claimed, at least in theory,
a monopoly on the use of force; its power was allocated through a
complex bureaucracy; and it maintained government by objective law.

However, much of the old chiefdom stage remained—so much that the
people themselves seemed to think of the state as a glorified chiefdom.
The state was essentially a collection of clans that were still relatively
independent. Loyalties were inevitably divided between chief and king,
with the people often siding with the local group. Chiefs retained
day-to-day rules, including the right to use force to put down rebellions,
as long as the king was informed. The idea persisted that a bad king could
be overthrown, just as a bad chief could, as long as the individual and
not the system was changed; in fact, kingly succession was largely a
matter of assassination or rebellion. Also, while there was definite social
stratification, it was much the same as that of the Hawaiians (individuals

and clans ranked according to their genealogical closeness to the king). Nor was occupational specialization much more developed than in the prestate period. In short, while definitely a state in regard to unification of a number of formerly autonomous groups under centralized government, the precolonial Zulu encompassed many of the aspects of the chiefdoms on which it was based (Gluckman 1940; Service 1975).

The Inca. At the beginning of the fifthteenth century, a powerful chiefdom in the Cuzco Valley of Peru began the military expansion that would create the largest of the pre-Columbian New World states. At its climax, the Inca empire extended twenty-seven hundred miles from Central Chile to the present-day border of Ecuador and Colombia, an area that was united without the use of animal transportation (though llamas and alpacas were used as cargo carriers). Contemporary characterizations of the Inca as Communist, socialist, or a welfare state do little justice to this unique adaptation to the ecological, social, and historical conditions of the Andes.

The Inca empire was integrated as much by a system of economic redistributions as by military force or political centralization. Food production was greatly expanded, not through technological innovation but through the increasingly efficient organization of labor—in agricultural terracing, for example, or in constructing extensive irrigation systems—and through transferring entire communities to formerly underutilized areas. Throughout the empire, land was divided in thirds to provide for the common people, the state religion, and the secular bureaucracy. After 1475, there was increasing state ownership, especially of lands newly developed for cultivation or pasture.

Three bureaucracies were supported by this economy. At the top was the central bureaucracy, comprised of ethnic Inca nobles and others who had attained the status of Inca through their contribution to the state. This Cuzco-based bureaucracy consisted of a royal court (made up of eleven minor lineages, each with its own palace), a royal advisory council, and more or less specialized agencies to administer the judiciary, the military, education, transportation, and communications. A parallel, and to some degree separate, religious bureaucracy administered a state religion that was fairly open in the sense that it was quite capable of incorporating the gods, idols, and rituals of the conquered tribes. As much as one-third of the Inca's entire gross national product was devoted to religious ceremony. Finally, a provincial bureaucracy encompassed about eighty regional groups through a hierarchy of local chiefs called *curacas*.

The existence of such sophisticated bureaucratic structures might give the impression that the Inca state had completely overridden and replaced earlier forms of social organization. Yet over millennia, and through the risings and fallings of civilizations, the basic unit of Andean social structure remained the *ayllu,* a lineage-based community in which land was held in common and redistributed according to need. The *ayllu* was highly self-sufficient, unified by common territory and by complex interrelationships of social and economic reciprocity. Each *ayllu* had its own leader, who lacked coercive authority. The *ayllu* cared for its own infirm and aged and achieved public building and maintenance goals through cooperative labor. Many *ayllus* were united into larger tribes and confederacies for trade and defense.

Conquest by the Inca left this fundamental social structure intact, and many state governmental forms and practices were based on those of the *ayllu.* For example, the system of conscripted labor by which the Inca built their phenomenal roads (one road was almost two thousand miles long), public buildings, and agricultural terraces was a direct extension of traditional *ayllu* collective labor patterns. Even at the highest levels of government the *ayllu* form was the model: each new Inca emperor began a new royal *ayllu* consisting of all his male descendants. According to John Murra, the widespread belief that the Inca polity was divided into groups based on a decimal system is but a literal reading of a census taker's shorthand (records were kept on knotted ropes); the actual division of the empire was the traditional one of *ayllu*, tribe, and confederacy. Thus, despite its complexity, the Inca state does not represent a quantum leap in social organization, except in sheer magnitude; rather, it was a drawing together of a number of intact traditional units (Mason 1957; Murra 1958).

The *ayllu,* it might be noted, has already survived the Incas by four centuries, has survived Spanish colonialism, republicanism, and a myriad of dictatorships, and continues to exist intact in many areas of Peru and Bolivia. Today the *ayllu* finally shows signs of succumbing, not to political pressures or conquest, but to the effects of overpopulation and industrialization (Lewellen 1978).

The value of a typology depends as much on what we want to do with it as on the criteria used in forming it. The classification suggested in this chapter is quite general. However, it is necessary to have some means of developing evolutionary sequences and establishing a standardized vocabulary. Specialists—in peasant politics, for example—require more precise classification, and may develop any number of subtypes. The specialist in a single culture area, such as the Arctic, might focus on the variety of adaptive strategies and thus be fully justified in rejecting any typology at all.

Perhaps a more serious objection to classification is that the itemization of ideal types ignores the very particular processes or developmental sequences by which specific social forms emerge (Upham 1990). This argument is valid, however, only if creating typologies is viewed as an end in itself. In reality, there should be no conflict between a process approach, which attempts to explain, and a typological approach which merely tries to elucidate the units to be explained. Even the most ardent process-theorists continue to use terms such as *tribe*, *chiefdom*, and *state*.

Many of the objections to classification of political systems derive from unsuccessful attempts to directly correlate specific-level data with general-level categories. Criticism should be at the level of the typology itself, that is, at the level of broad cross-cultural statistical probabilities. The crucial question is: Which elements of these societies appear together with sufficient regularity for us to consider them integrated parts of the same system? This is an empirical question, and as it is answered with increasing precision we may expect a corresponding increase in the refinement of our classifications.

SUGGESTED READINGS

Cohen, Ronald, and John Middleton, eds. *Comparative Political Systems* (Austin: University of Texas Press, 1967). Though this anthology seems random in its selection, it does provide studies of a wide range of political types. Among those groups represented are the !Kung, Eskimo, Nambikara, Mapuche, and Inca. The list of authors of these twenty articles reads like a *Who's Who* of cultural anthropology: Claude Lévi-Strauss, Robert Lowie, John Murra, F. C. Bailey, and S. N. Eisenstadt, among others.

Fried, Morton. *The Evolution of Political Society* (New York: Random House, 1967). Fried classifies political systems in terms of an individual's access to power. This gives him the basic categories of egalitarian, rank, and stratified, each of which is described in detail.

Johnson, Allen W., and Timothy Earle. *The Evolution of Human Societies: From Foraging Group to Agrarian State* (Stanford, Calif.: Stanford University Press, 1987). A highly readable evolutionary approach that provides an alternative typology to that presented in this chapter. Each socioeconomic level (the family, the local group, the "big man" collectivity, the chiefdom, the archaic state, and the nation-state) is described in detail, with examples.

Levinson, David, and Martin J. Malone. *Toward Explaining Human Culture* (New York: HRAF Press, 1980). This is an admirable attempt to collect in a single short volume much that has been learned about cross-cultural regularities from statistical studies using the Human Relations Area Files. Many of the chapters are valuable in providing quantitative data to support or refute speculation on the classification of political systems.

Service, Elman R. *Primitive Social Organization: An Evolutionary Perspective* (New York: Random House, 1962) This book established *band*, *tribe*, *chiefdom*, and *state* as the basic "levels of sociocultural integration." Despite its subtitle, the book is largely descriptive and makes little attempt at suggesting causes of evolutionary change.

Ancient Egypt is one of the world's six primary states, that is, those that developed uninfluenced by previously existing states. Its rise may have been in response to population pressures within a narrow strip of arable land circumscribed by desert.

Chapter Three

The Evolution of the State

About fifty-five hundred years ago, on the fertile floodplains of the Tigris and Euphrates rivers in what is today Iraq, there developed a society unique to its time. After millennia during which humanity gradually turned from migratory foraging toward seasonal settlements based on a few domesticated plants and animals, and then toward year-round farming villages, there came into being the world's first true cities, and with them a novel form of political organization. Previously, society had been structured according to kinship networks; now there appeared a permanent administrative bureaucracy that demanded loyalties transcending lineage and clan. Local chiefs relinquished much of their authority to a ruling class who had the power to gather the agricultural surpluses and call forth the labor necessary to create large-scale irrigation projects and monumental architecture. Fortified cities, such as Uruk and Ur, boasted populations of upwards of forty thousand. A full-time caste of priests presided over a complex temple religion. Craft specialists manufactured the obsidian knives and gold and silver figurines that would tie vast areas together through webs of trade. The state had been born.

Today, when national populations are counted in the hundreds of millions and power is so concentrated that the word of a president or a premier could unleash a holocaust of unthinkable proportions, it may be difficult to realize the significance of the thirteen or so small city-states collectively known as Sumeria. Just as we can legitimately speak of an agriculture revolution or an industrial revolution to suggest quantum changes in human social complexity, so can we speak of a state revolution. Various authorities might argue the defining characteristics of the early state, but none would demean its importance; for here was a new kind of society—a seed bearing the genetic code for the giant nation-states of the modern world.

The Mesopotamian state developed through a long series of adjustments to a particular environment and a specific set of social problems. In retrospect, however, the process seems almost inevitable, for we find similar adaptations leading to similar sociopolitical structures in Egypt, in the Indus River Valley of India and the Yellow River Valley of northern China, in Mesoamerica, and in Peru. These primary states are illustrated in Figure 4. Though these six states appeared hundreds or even thousands of years apart (see Table 2), and though there was minimal commerce between a few of them (such as India and Mesopotamia), each seems to have originated independently of the others. This poses a problem: If the state evolved autonomously not once but six times, can we discover fundamental processes that were common to all?

Though far removed from the state, the rudiments of human social evolution can be found in man's closest animal relatives. Among higher primates characterized by marked sexual dimorphism (differences in size and musculature between sexes), such as baboons and gorillas, we find strong male dominance, specialization for defense, and various patterns of ongoing family organization. Some primate species reveal extremely complex elaborations of social structure. Cynocephalus baboons, for example, live in stable groups of forty to eighty individuals, and these bands exhibit clear hierarchies of status and considerable specialization of function among both males and females. Hamadryas baboons forage in small one-male groups but join together in troops of several hundred for sleeping. Some primates pass on significant learned skills from generation to generation and reveal remarkable cooperation in rearing the young, collective defense, grooming, and sexual behavior. However, only the genus *Homo* has extended such basic primate adaptations by cultural means. The most significant of these are symbolism, through which humans communicate and embellish both individual and group ideas, and sharing—reciprocity—which underlies the division of labor, creates the potential for increasingly elaborate social organization, and ties kinship groups together.

More than 99 percent of humanity's two- to three-million-year sojourn on earth has been spent in small bands—flexible, egalitarian, nomadic groups comprised of several extended families. Since contemporary hunting-gathering peoples occupy only the most marginal environments, we should be careful about generalizing their social organization to our

Figure 4
Primary States

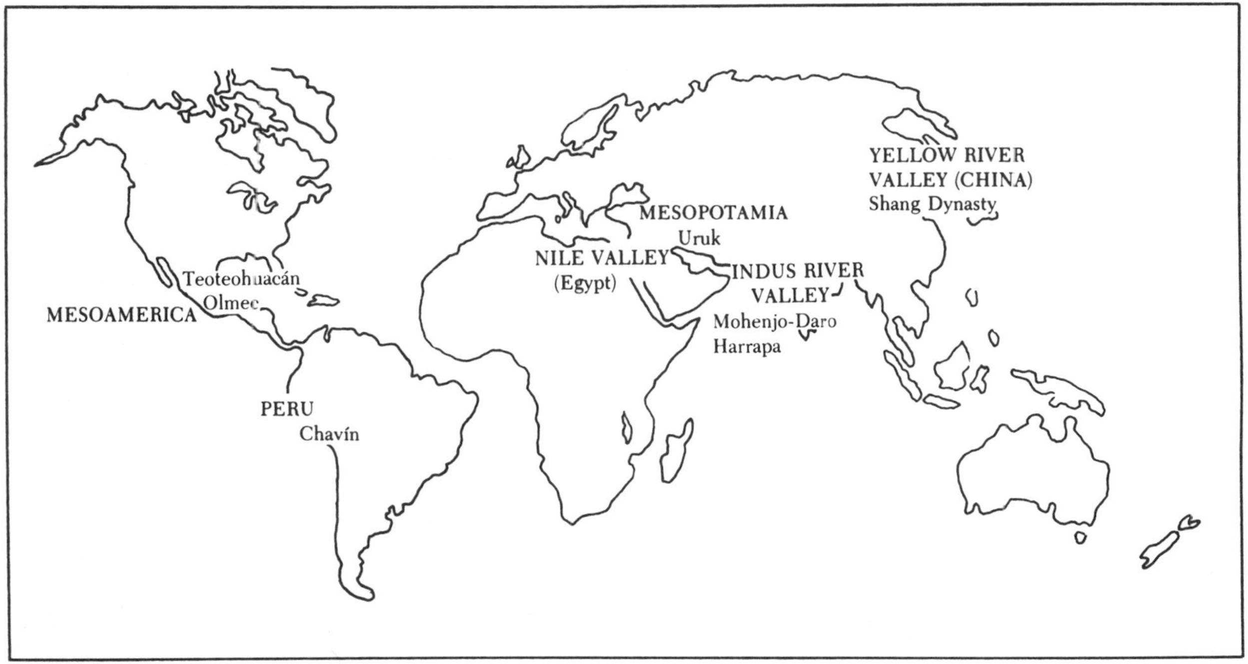

MESOAMERICA

Teotehuacán
Olmec

PERU
Chavín

MESOPOTAMIA
Uruk

NILE VALLEY
(Egypt)

INDUS RIVER
VALLEY
Mohenjo-Daro
Harrapa

YELLOW RIVER
VALLEY (CHINA)
Shang Dynasty

Table 2
Chronology of Primary State Development

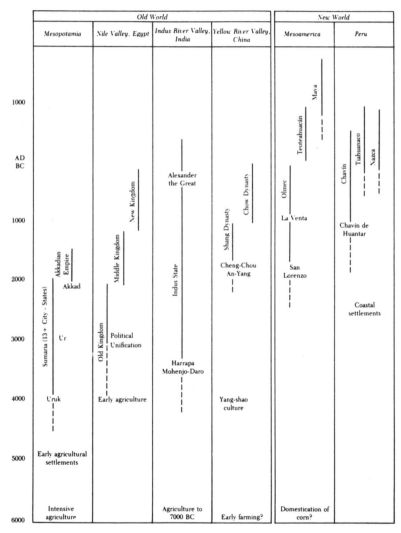

Sources: Claessen 1978; Fagan 1978; Jolly and Plog 1979; Pfeiffer 1977; Wenke 1980.

remote ancestors, who lived in more hospitable places and climes. Yet archaeological evidence from Paleolithic times suggests little elaboration on the basic band form. One reason that this structure may have persisted for so long is that it was an evolutionary dead end. The hunting-foraging adaptation (the Pygmies and traditional Eskimo are contemporary examples) requires an almost perfect ecological balance, in which populations must be maintained below the food supply; thus, there would have been little selective pressure for change. What requires explanation is not why such an excellent adaptation should have lasted so long, but rather why a few groups of people—very few, at first—abandoned it for more complex forms of subsistence and society.

Radically new types of social structure appeared only with the sedentary life-styles and greater population densities brought about by the domestication of plants and animals. It should not be supposed, however, that this "revolution" was sudden, or that it immediately led to the formation of the state. Agriculture and animal husbandry apparently developed independently in a number of areas throughout the world, but only a few of these went on to evolve states. In the Tehuacán Valley of Mexico, the period of development from hunting-gathering bands to agriculturally based states was more than seven thousand years (Flannery 1968). In other areas of primary-state development, too, centralization of government was long preceded by sedentary agriculture, permanent villages, and even extensive irrigation works.

American and Dutch anthropologists have tackled the problem of the origin of the state with enthusiasm (the British and French tend to ignore evolutionary questions). Until recently, such theorists carefully distinguished the six primary states from secondary states (those which developed out of or through contact with already existing states). Because virtually all theories focused on the former, evidence was exclusively archaeological. Today, some researchers have abandoned the primary-secondary distinction for a typology that allows the inclusion of even recent states, such as the Ankole of Uganda, as long as they remained pristine. We examine some of this important research later, but first we must look at the classical theories of state origins.

INTERNAL CONFLICT THEORIES

The doctrine that the state evolved through class struggle is implicit in many of the writings of Karl Marx. However, these ideas were not fully worked out until Frederick Engels' major work, *The Origin of the Family, Private Property and the State* (1891), which was published after his mentor's death. According to Engels, who borrowed heavily from American evolutionary anthropologist Lewis Henry Morgan, the earliest form of social organization was communistic: Resources were shared equally by all, and there was no strong concept of personal possession. Technological innovation gives rise to surplus, which allows a class of nonproducers to develop. Private ownership is simply a concomitant of commodity production. Once established, private property stimulates an inexorable chain of cause-and-effect that leads to an entrepreneurial class—owners of the means of production and buyers and sellers of human labor. This, in turn, results in differential access to resources, and thus to vast discrepancies in individual wealth. To protect its interests against the masses of active producers (who understandably want to share in their own production), the elite must erect a structure of permanent centralized force to protect its class interests.

Given its time, this analysis is sophisticated and subtle. We find in it the perception that the primary means of economic exchange in band and tribal society is reciprocity, and that more complex systems involve concentrations of wealth and redistribution through a central agency, be it chief, king, or bureaucracy. Engels artfully applies Marxian material-ism to long-term social evolution; the basic causes of change are held to be technological and economic, not ideational. Also, we find here a clear recognition that social stratification is one of the defining qualities of the state.

Unfortunately, as Elman Service (1975: 283) has observed, "there is absolutely no evidence in the early archaic civilizations themselves, nor in archaeologically or historically known chiefdoms and primitive states, of any important private dealings—i.e., evidence of capitalism." Indeed, the very concepts of *communism* and *capitalism* seem absurd when projected onto band and chiefdom societies, so different from modern industrial states.

Morton Fried (1967), who bases his evolutionary typology of political systems on the degree of individual access to resources and positions of prestige, offers a variation on the class-conflict model. Once true stratification exists, Fried notes, the state is already implicit because the maintenance of a class system requires that power be concentrated in the hands of an elite. By its very nature, this creates conflict within the society. Differential access to resources, and the exploitation of human labor, create pressures quite unknown in less complex societies. Conflict arising out of social stratification should not be thought of as the cause of state formation; rather, such conflict is merely a prior condition for the development of the state. Incipient social stratification is so unstable that a society which finds itself at such a stage must either disintegrate to a lower level of organization or continue its process of centralizing political power. In other words, once classes begin to separate themselves from hierarchies based on individual or kinship status, power must be fairly rapidly assumed by the privileged elite if the true state is to come into existence.

EXTERNAL CONFLICT THEORIES

In the Biblical version of social evolution, the development of cities is a direct result of Cain's primordial murder of his brother Abel. This idea, that states are born in blood and war, was given scientific respectability with the emergence of social Darwinism in the latter half of the nineteenth century. Herbert Spencer, chief spokesman for the more violent interpretations of evolutionary theory, applied the idea of survival of the fittest mainly to individuals, but it took little imagination to extend this concept to societies. The stronger, more militaristic organizations would inevitably prevail over weaker groups, uniting them under a powerful centralized government with a monopoly on the use of force. Militarism alone, even without warfare, would be sufficient; merely the existence of an external threat which required a large standing army could push a loosely structured society in the direction of strong centralized leadership. Implicit or explicit in such theories, of which Spencer's was one of many, is the idea that state government is modeled on military organization in its hierarchical structure and centralized control of physical force.

A nineteenth-century tendency to oversimplify and overgeneralize is evident in these theories, which are based on a gross misunderstanding of physical evolution. Darwin's rather prosaic idea that the mechanism of evolution is differential reproduction (parents with the most surviving offspring pass on more traits) was transliterated into "the law of tooth and fang," with imagery of big tigers devouring little tigers with much sound and fury. When applied to society, such a theory could—and did—provide the philosophical justification ("Law of Nature, you know!") for colonialism, imperialism, monopoly capitalism, and every other form of exploitation.

As we shall see, cross-cultural research does support the hypothesis that war and conquest are important factors in the development of some states, but there are two important objections to the theory that war is the primary cause: first, a society can marshal forces only according to available levels of population and organization, so warfare might better be viewed as a function rather than a cause of a given level of social integration; second, warfare among tribes and chiefdoms is more likely to prevent state formation than to cause it, because groups simply disperse when threatened by a power greater than themselves (Service 1975; Price 1979).

This latter point is a salient consideration in Robert Carniero's (1967, 1970, 1978) theory of environmental circumscription. Because warfare is virtually universal and usually has the effect of dispersing people rather than uniting them, conflict could only lead to centralization in particular situations. After examining primary-state development in both the Old and New Worlds, Carniero notes that a common denominator is that "they are all areas of circumscribed agricultural land"; that is, they are bounded by mountains, sea, or desert. When there is no such circumscription, population pressures on the environment can be expanded outward, and losers in a war can resettle in a new area. This is not possible where the only arable land is surrounded by unproductive land. Population pressure must then be resolved by unification and by increases in productive capacity—both characteristics of the state—and losers in a war, lacking means of escape, must submit to their conquerors. Amazonian Indians waged frequent war for revenge, the taking of women, personal prestige, and the like; but these wars never resulted in widespread conquest by a central power because new areas of forest could always be found in which to start a new village. However, the riverine valleys of coastal Peru—surrounded by sea, desert, and mountains—offer no such options. As the small, dispersed villages of the Neolithic grew and fissioned, the narrow valleys became increasingly crowded. Intensification of agriculture, through terracing, for example, would only solve the problem temporarily. Revenge warfare would turn to warfare over land, with one group trying to increase its productive capacity at the expense of others. Yet for the weaker in these conflicts, there would be no place to escape that could provide even minimal subsistence; submission to a dominant force was the only viable survival strategy. In this way, a number of independent chiefdoms would be brought under a single hierarchical military government.

Circumscription need not be strictly physical; it can also be social. The Yanomamo of the Venezuelan jungle are not physically circumscribed, but village fission and expansion into virgin territory is easier for those at the periphery of the tribal group than for those near the center. According to Carniero's theory, we would expect that central villages, surrounded by other warring villages, would tend to be larger and have more powerful headmen than peripheral villages, and this is indeed the case. While the Yanomamo are far from the state level of cultural integration, the socially circumscribed villages do exhibit greater tendencies toward centralization.

Carniero subsumes these processes under "the principle of competitive exclusion," derived from evolutionary biology. This principle states that "two species occupying and exploiting the same portion of the habitat cannot coexist indefinitely"—one must ultimately eliminate the other. In applying this idea to societies, Carniero observes that throughout history chiefdoms have been united into states and states have gone to war to create larger states, with competition and selection increasingly tending toward larger and larger units. In plotting the decreasing number of autonomous political units in the world from 1000 B.C., Carniero predicts the political unification of the entire planet by about the year 2300. (However, the breakup of the Soviet empire suggests there may be countercurrents working against sheer hugeness.)

Hydraulic Civilization

The importance of irrigation to state formation was recognized as early as the writings of Marx and Engels, who noted that a major difference between small-scale agricultural communities and state societies was that the latter required the support of extensive irrigation systems. More recently, Julian Steward (1955) has emphasized irrigation as the fundamental mechanism of state development because water control permitted sufficient agricultural intensification to create large population densities, and the construction of massive hydraulic systems required new levels of social organization, power, and coordination of labor.

Karl Wittfogel (1957) elaborated the hydraulic theory in such detail that his name is now almost exclusively associated with it. Neolithic farmers in the areas of primary-state development, such as Egypt or the riverine valleys of Peru, depended on flood irrigation; their fields were watered once a year and new soil was deposited by the annual flood. But flood irrigation is quite variable, and even in the best of times it provides only one crop per year. Slowly, farmers began to control the floods with dikes and reservoirs, preserving and taming the precious water that could then be released as needed through a network of canals. Early irrigation systems were small and primitive, involving only the labor of a few neighboring farms; but as the productive capacity of the land increased and the human population burgeoned, irrigation works grew in size and complexity. A group of specialists emerged to plan and coordinate the construction of these systems, and later to control the flow of water. This group, whose hands now quite literally held the very life of the community, developed into an administrative elite that governed despotic, centralized states.

This model has fared surprisingly well. Irrigation seems to have been important in all of the primary states. The lowland Maya of the Yucatan Peninsula in Mexico were believed to be an exception until recent aerial photographs revealed that this civilization, too, was reliant on elaborate irrigation systems. However, the hydraulic theory should not be interpreted in too rigid a cause-and-effect manner: in some areas, for example, complex irrigation systems long preceded state development, while in others (such as Mesopotamia) large-scale water control systems only developed after at least the initial stages of the state. Furthermore, in the American southwest and other areas, large hydraulic systems existed for centuries without political centralization. Finally, the theory has only the most tenuous application to secondary states, many of which possessed the most rudimentary irrigation.

These objections may be beside the point. Marvin Harris (1977) has noted that Wittfogel's theory is not really about the origin of the state per se, but rather about the development of certain managerial systems. To postulate centralization of despotic power around the management of water supplies is not to deny the importance of population density, trade, warfare, environmental circumscription, and other factors that have had key roles in the increasing integration of society.

Population Pressure

From about 23000 B.C. until A.D. 2000, world population will have grown from an estimated 3.5 million to 6.5 billion and from a density of .1 persons per square mile to 124 per square mile (Campbell 1979: 462–63). The correlation between this increase in population and the rise of the state has been noted by virtually all evolutionary cultural anthropologists. Robert Carniero (1967) plotted the relation between population density and social complexity in 46 societies and found a significant statistical correspondence between the two variables. Though the correspondence held, at least loosely, for arithmetic density (that is, the average number of people per square mile over an entire territory), we find a much stronger relationship if economic density alone is considered. Economic density is the relation between population and sources of production. For example, in Egypt the vast majority of people are concentrated in a narrow strip of arable land on either side of the Nile.

According to the early-nineteenth-century economist Thomas Malthus, population is negatively checked by disease, famine, and war as it threatens to outgrow the food supply. However, if this were the only principle operating, population growth would have stabilized at a much lower level than today's. Certainly, one possible response to population pressure on food supply is exactly the opposite of the Malthusian checks; the food supply itself may be increased through some sort of intensification of production, often involving the development of a new technology or the refinement of an existing one. Irrigation, terracing, fertilization, using animal labor, cultivating more types of crops, and exploiting previously unused lands can significantly increase the carrying capacity of a given territory. The resulting increases in population density require more complex forms of social and political organization. This correspondence between population and social evolution was most extensively elaborated by Ester Boserup (1965). In a slight variation on the theory, Michael Harner (1970) argues that population pressure is not only directly responsible for some form of intensification of food production but also leads to unequal access to resources and subsequently to increasing social stratification.

Marvin Harris, in *Cannibals and Kings* (1977), incorporates these ideas into a complicated technoenvironmental determinist argument that views social organization and ideology as the results of a society's technological adaptation to its physical environment. Harris begins by noting the main objection to population pressure theories, namely, that populations usually tend to stabilize comfortably below the carrying capacity of the land. Indeed, all societies have cultural means of supplementing Malthusian checks on population. Hunting-gathering groups maintained relative population equilibrium for tens of thousands of years, and the few such societies surviving today depend on balancing population to food supply. In all preindustrial societies, such practices as female infanticide, two- or three-year-long taboos on sexual intercourse with a woman after she has borne a child, and prolonged nursing (which delays ovulation) serve to keep population in balance with food production. It is only in modern times that population has been allowed to grow unchecked. If population equilibrium was the norm in most premodern societies, we must ask why population might increase to the point where it would force more complex forms of social organization.

Harris's explanation is that during the Pleistocene Era, which lasted until about ten to fifteen thousand years ago, hunting bands had come to rely on an abundance of large game, and populations had stabilized at levels made possible by such resources. At the end of the Pleistocene, hundreds of big game species became extinct—for reasons still not entirely understood—with the result that people had to rely increasingly on alternative sources of food. Wild plants susceptible to domestication had always been available but had been rejected for cost-benefit reasons; without population pressure, hunting and foraging was more expedient for expending a minimum of calories. Now, plant domestication raised the carrying capacity of the land, allowing populations to increase. Population would tend ultimately to stabilize, but over time—perhaps hundreds of years—a gradual and inevitable decrease in productivity occurs as agricultural land loses nutrients and game is overhunted to supply animal protein. In other words, pressure is created not only by population growth, which might be quite slow, but also by a natural decline in the productivity of the land.

In tribal societies, populations are often controlled through a male supremacist complex that develops out of constant warfare. A premium on masculine fierceness diminishes the value of women, so that female infanticide—certainly one of the most effective means of population control—becomes virtually normative (some societies have institutionalized the killing of the firstborn if it is a female). Agriculturalists have another option: instead of reducing population, they can increase their work load or add a new technology to augment production. This leads to agricultural surpluses, which are collected and redistributed by "big men" who use their role to gain and maintain status and power. These redistributive chiefs—often war chiefs as well—take on the role of a centralized coercive force. At this point, Harris brings in both Carniero's circumscription theory and Wittfogel's hydraulic theory to show the conditions under which centralization will continue until the state is formed.

Note that to Harris the initial kick for this whole process is population; but, in a reverse on the Boserup theory, he sees a relatively stable population adapting to a diminution of food supplies. A major element of the theory—one not too auspicious for the future of civilization—is that any form of productivity gradually leads to depletions of primary resources, with the result that all societies must sooner or later face the alternative of collapsing or moving to a new level of intensification. Once the domestication of plants and animals becomes the basis for subsistence, there can be no long-term stabilization.

Harris's argument, while appealing, is open to challenge because these processes do not appear to be universal. For example, population pressure on resources cannot, in every area that became politically centralized, be related to decline in productivity. Also, Boserup may be

more correct in placing her emphasis on population growth rather than
resource depletion. Even relatively minor changes in nutrition can
radically alter the size of a population. Food supplies are quite elastic
and can easily be affected either by a redefinition of usable food resources
or by slight changes in technology. As Harris and others have pointed
out, population growth may indeed need explaining, but not very much
explaining.

The Institutionalization of Leadership

Elman Service, in *Origins of the State and Civilization* (1975),
proposes an integrative theory. After an extensive review of the rise of
the six archaic primary states and a number of modern primitive states,
he rejects all conflict theories. Warfare and conquest, he points out, are
too universal in human experience to count as causes of a particular form
of social organization, and "the only instances we find of permanent
subordination from war are where government already exists" (Service
1975: 271). Arguments based on irrigation or other forms of intensification admit too many exceptions. In ancient Peru, for example, agricultural intensification was achieved through canal irrigation fifteen
hundred years before the first truly urbanized state. The idea that
population pressures create conflicts that can only be solved by centralized government is rejected partially on the grounds that such pressure
could just as well lead to increased sharing.

These negative conclusions derive from a particular reading of the
data; they would hardly be convincing to an ardent proponent of any of
the theories rejected. Indeed, while it is conflict theory that is specifically
rebutted, implicitly what is being rejected is cultural materialism. What
Service has done is to shift the argument from ecological determinants
to strategies of decision making.

Service traces a logical development from the basic inequality inherent
in human society to formalized and centralized inequality. In all societies,
even the most egalitarian bands and tribes, certain individuals stand out
by reason of their exceptional talent, intelligence, strength, or beauty.
While it is completely natural to confer status on such people, the
resulting inequalities remain individual, rather than class-based, and do
not confer privilege or wealth. Certain circumstances tend to favor
centralization of effort; for example, when a variety of local ecological
niches forces specialization of production and symbiotic trade, or when
collaborative work on public projects requires a division of labor. Such
circumstances also favor centralized redistribution, which is naturally

handled by the exceptional people of the society (such as the Melanesian "big men," who are usually war chiefs). Because such centralization offers obvious benefits, a snowball effect leads to increasing concentration of administration. This enhancement of leadership, though economic, is not based on ownership, as Engels would have it; rather, it is "the result of a form of dependence that in primitive society results from generosity, from favors given" (Service 1975: 293).

Such leadership is unstable because it depends on an individual, who may get sick, die, or simply run out of luck, and there is no normal method of succession. For a society to maintain the benefits of centralization, temporary charismatic leadership must be transformed into a permanent hierarchy. When this stage is reached, we have a chiefdom, the first true institutionalization of power, which is also an institutionalization of inequality. As this power center grows, so does the need of the newly developed ruling class to protect its privilege. One method of doing so, aside from the use of force, is to legitimize the power elite by connecting it with the supernatural, by giving it divine sanction. The use of force, then, far from creating the state, actually represents a temporary failure of the state to function responsibly by providing such benefits as protection, redistribution, and coordination of trade. Thus, "political evolution can be thought to consist, in important part, of 'waging peace' in ever wider contexts" (Service 1975: 297).

It should be evident that this is not merely a shift of emphasis from population pressure, irrigation, or environmental circumscription, but rather a shift in the kind of theory offered. The "considerable exaltation" a leader's successes could produce "in the minds of his followers" (Service 1975: 291) would be of little relevance to Robert Carniero or Marvin Harris, who view whole social systems as reacting in survival terms to material environmental determinants. Service's theory shifts the weight of argument from environment to cognition, that is, to the people's perception of accruing benefits. Service also uses models based on cooperation and integration, whereas most other theories have held conflict and instability to be the fundamental conditions out of which the state develops.

Service's point of view is refreshingly innovative. Yet conflict and integration are definitely not mutually exclusive; all societies are involved in both, alternately and simultaneously. Similarly, societies are materialist and cognitive at the same time. Each perspective offers much in the way of explanation, but to claim exclusivity for one or the other is rather like claiming that a glass of water is half full rather than half empty.

SYSTEMS THEORIES

Few anthropologists today would hold to a single-cause model of the evolution of states (it should be pointed out that those theories regularly referred to as unicausal—Carniero's, Wittfogel's, Boserup's—are really singular only in emphasis). All involve interactions between such factors as population, environment, technology, and irrigation. Synthetic models, like that of Marvin Harris, make these interactions more explicit. However, all such models are based on the idea that, given certain preconditions, particular causes lead to particular effects in a more or less sequential manner.

Unlike theories that designate specific causes, systems models are based on sets of principles, drawn mainly from physics and biology. These include negative and positive feedback, initial kick, system self-maintenance, and system self-development. Negative feedback is the process by which a stable system minimizes any deviation from equilibrium. For example, in a hunting-gathering society, an increase in birth rate is balanced by higher infant mortality rates if population threatens to overgrow the food supply. Positive feedback is just the opposite: a small deviation may set in motion a process of increasing change. If the response to population growth is intensified agriculture, the result is further population growth that in turn generates more intensification, and so on until some limit is reached. The initial kick that stimulates a negative feedback system into a positive feedback system may be very small. Kent Flannery (1968) hypothesizes that in the Tehuacán Valley of Mexico, the processes leading to the development of civilization were set in motion when nomadic foraging bands began to take care of a few edible wild plants. Over generations, this human intervention caused genetic changes that allowed increased dependence on these semidomesticated foods, and this led to more sedentary life-styles and larger populations, which in turn increased dependence on domesticates. This chain of events led eventually to the people settling into year-round farming villages. Stable societies are self-maintaining insofar as they are constantly making small adjustments to changes in the physical and social environment. Once positive feedback processes are set in motion, a society becomes self-developing as population growth, agricultural intensification, urbanization, and political centralization feed on one another in constant circular causality. Note that this is almost the exact reversal of the Newtonian principle that every action must have an equal and opposite reaction; with positive feedback, the most minute initial kick can, over the long run, lead to massive change. It is no longer necessary to explain the state as the effect of some equally momentous cause.

A number of different systems theories of political evolution have been developed. Some of these focus on environment and technology, while others employ a decision-making perspective. Common to all, however, is the idea that societies respond adaptively to many conditions. The goal of explanation, then, is not to pinpoint one or two factors that cause change in all cases, but to specify the processes by which social systems alter their internal structures in response to selective pressures. As Ronald Cohen (1978b: 142) puts it, "The formation of a state is a funnel-like progression of interactions in which a variety of prestate systems, responding to different determinants of change, are forced by otherwise unresolvable conflicts to choose additional and more complex levels of political hierarchy." The opposition between force and benefit theories, between materialist and cognitive paradigms, and between conflict and integration models becomes blurred because a systems model can incorporate these various perspectives simultaneously.

One such approach has been developed by Clifford Jolly and Fred Plog (1976). In their specific example of the Valley of Mexico, population growth was the initial stimulus, but theoretically any other stimulus which put exceptional stress on the equilibrium system would have been sufficient to cause significant change. Several options were available, given such stress: to reduce the population through infanticide or other cultural means, to disperse the larger settlements, to migrate to new areas, or to intensify agricultural production. Of these alternatives, only the latter would have led to the formation of the state. There are several conditions under which the option for intensification might be chosen: agricultural land might be circumscribed so there would be no place to disperse; farmers could drift into intensification without realizing it, perhaps through a slight new technology like small irrigation canals; or the people might be forced by a conquering group to pay tribute and thus to increase production. In any case, once the option is chosen, it leads by a series of feedback loops to nucleation, stratification, differentiation, and centralization. Nucleation (roughly synonymous with urbanization) becomes necessary for large cooperative labor projects; in turn, as people concentrate in relatively small areas, pressure on local resources is aggravated, requiring further intensification of food production. Economic stratification develops as more productive farming techniques amplify slight environmental differences, so that a person possessing even marginally better agricultural land becomes richer relative to his neighbors. These forces also promote centralization of decision making because such concentration is more effective for planning large-scale projects and organizing labor. Farming becomes more differentiated as entire fields are turned over to a single crop to increase the efficiency of plowing and irrigation. A surplus of food ensures that some do not need to work as farmers at all, and this permits the development of craft specialization. Finally, each one of these factors stimulates the others. The model developed by Jolly and Plog is shown in Figure 5. This model uses many of the same elements as the so-called unicausal and synthetic theories. However, a major difference between this model and that of, say, Marvin Harris is that Jolly and Plog are much less specific about the actual train of events. The processes with which they deal (nucleation, differentiation, etc.) are abstract and can involve stresses deriving from any number of sources. Society is viewed not as a row of dominoes falling in a predictable pattern, but as a flexible, adaptive system making constant internal adjustments to various stresses. These adjustments modify the environment, and this requires further adaptations of the social system in a self-developing process.

THE EARLY STATE: THE CROSS-CULTURAL EVIDENCE

The Early State (1978), edited by Henri J. M. Claessen and Peter Skalník, brings together cross-cultural data on nineteen formative states, ranging from Egypt in 3000 B.C. to the contemporary Kachari of India. Curiously, the distinction between primary and secondary states is ignored. This omission is both deliberate and legitimate. So much emphasis has been put on primary state development that the rich evidence of social evolution provided by other historical states, even those that developed with a great deal of autonomy, has been too often neglected. However, most of the theories discussed here were originally applied almost exclusively to primary states making it difficult to appraise Claessen and Skalník's evaluations, based as they are on evidence drawn from a different set of societies.

In any case, this massive work offers a wealth of data and conclusions from a wide range of social systems that fall within the authors' definition of the early state as

a centralized sociopolitical organization for the regulation of social relations in a complex, stratified society divided into at least two basic strata, or emergent social classes—namely, the rulers and the ruled—whose relations are charac-

Figure 5
Systems Model of State Development

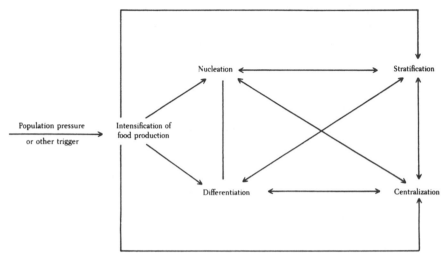

Source: Jolly and Plog 1979; 365, based partially on Logan and Sanders 1976.

terized by political dominance of the former and tributary obligations of the latter, legitimized by a common ideology (Claessen and Skalník 1978: 640).

This definition, which summarizes many of the regularities found in the sample, supports the view that class stratification is a primary quality of the state; but it is not necessarily a cause because differential access to material resources may exist long before the state comes into existence. Indeed, social stratification together with an economy capable of producing a surplus are considered predisposing factors without which the early state is impossible.

Four factors are singled out by the authors as directly causal: (1) population growth and/or population pressure; (2) war or the threat of war; (3) conquest; and (4) the influence of previously existing states. Most early states seem to have developed out of a combination of these, interacting with each other and appearing in no particular sequence. Wittfogel's hydraulic theory is not supported, since less than half the sample was clearly dependent on extensive irrigation systems. However, both Carniero's environmental circumscription model and Boserup's population pressure theory would be supported, but only if assimilated

Table 3
Typology of Twenty-One Early States

	Inchoate	Typical	Transitional
Examples (and period covered in sample)	Ankole (Uganda) 1650–1900 A.D. Hawaii 1700–1850 A.D. Norway 900–1100 A.D. Tahiti 1700–1800 A.D. Volta (Upper Volta and Ghana) 1400–1900 A.D. Zande (Sudan) 1750–1850 A.D.	Angkor (Cambodia) 1150–1300 A.D. Axum (Ethiopia) 25–625 A.D. Egypt 2950–2500 B.C. Inca (Peru) 1425–1532 A.D. Kachari (India) 1800 A.D.– Mongolia 1200–1325 A.D. Scythia (Ukrain) 400–725 A.D. Yoruba (Nigeria) 1400–1900 A.D.	Aztecs (Mexico) 1425–1521 A.D. China 250 B.C.–225 A.D. France 900–1100 A.D. Jimma (Ethiopia) 1825 A.D.– Kuba (Zaire) 1850–1900 A.D. Maurya (India) 1100–1275 A.D.
Trade and Markets	Of limited importance.	Developed at the supralocal level.	Fully developed and of great importance.
Mode of Succession to Office	Predominantly hereditary.	Hereditary and by appointment.	Mainly by appointment.
Ownership of Land	Private ownership rare. Mainly communal ownership of land and livestock.	Private ownership of land limited, but increasing ownership by the state.	Private ownership of land important for both aristocracy and common people.
Judicial System	No codification of laws and punishments. No specialized formal judges.	Incipient codification of laws and punishments. Formal judges and general (nonspecialized) functionaries who decide cases.	Codification of laws and punishments complete. Administration of justice in the hands of formal judges.
Taxation	Irregular voluntary tribute and occasional labor.	Regular tribute. Major works undertaken with aid of compulsory labor.	Well-defined taxation system with complex apparatus to insure regular flow.

Source: Claessen and Skalník (eds.) 1978.

into some sort of systems model in which these factors are viewed not as primary causes, but as elements interacting with many other elements. In Table 3, the characteristics of twenty-one early states are outlined.

Though no other book has gone so far in classifying the early state or in delineating its common elements, the conclusions regarding the genesis of this form of political organization seem anticlimactic. As the scope of theory broadens from the primary states to the scores of systems that can be classified as early states, we would expect fewer generalizations to hold for the entire sample, and the influence of preexisting states is probably powerful, subtle, and immeasurable. There has been progress, of course. The search for a single dominant cause has been abandoned in favor of theories that stress the systemic interaction of many causes. One wonders, however, if systems approaches have really added that much to our understanding because these mainly combine forces and processes that have been known for a long time. Essentially, what the systems theorists have done is raise the model of the evolution of the state to such a high level of abstraction that it is no longer easy to find exceptions to every generalization. Because of the resulting loss in specificity, one feels the need to fill in blanks in the model, to reestablish the sense that we are talking about real human beings—living, dying, warring, struggling to make it against the odds. The generalizations must be taken back to the archaeological digs, to the sad pottery shards and broken amulets and old walls of lost civilizations; back to the nascent states of Africa and India where kings and peasants contended in an eternal game of conflict and accord. Theory must hold a middle position in anthropology, for ultimately everything begins and ends in the field.

SUGGESTED READINGS

Claessen, Henry J. M., and Peter Skalník, eds. *The Early State* (The Hague, Netherlands: Mouton, 1978). This massive work (nearly 700 pages) begins with four chapters on the theory of state origins, then offers twenty chapters on individual states, and closes with four chapters synthesizing these specific studies and making cross-cultural comparisons. As a treatise on secondary state formation, the book is definitive. However, it deliberately avoids the distinction between primary and secondary states and, therefore, cannot deal with some of the most basic theories of state formation.

Cohen, Ronald, and Elman R. Service, eds. *Origins of the State: The Anthropology of Political Evolution* (Philadelphia: Institute for the Study of Human Issues, 1978). The introduction and first chapters provide brief overviews of the major theories of state formation. Two other articles strike me as especially valuable: Henry Wright's "Toward an Explanation of the Origin of the State," which puts many of the major theories in easy-to-understand flow chart form; and Robert Carniero's application of the "principal of competitive exclusion" (from evolutionary biology) to state formation.

Haas, Jonathan. *The Evolution of the Prehistoric State* (New York: Columbia University Press, 1982). A clearly written and comprehensive theoretical overview that attempts to consolidate the conflict and integrative approaches. Once the foundations of centralization have been laid, the author contends, the crucial variable becomes the increasing power of individuals and elites in controlling basic resources.

Harris, Marvin. *Cannibals and Kings: The Origins of Cultures* (New York: Vintage, 1977). Harris covers so much territory, from cannibalism among the Aztecs to the sacred cow in India, that it is easy to forget that, as a whole, this book is a theory of state formation. Harris has been accused of sometimes stretching facts to fit his materialist theory, but even when controversial he is always entertaining.

Pfeiffer, John E. *The Emergence of Society: A Prehistory of the Establishment* (New York: McGraw-Hill, 1977). This panoramic overview of cultural evolution never attained the best-seller status of the author's earlier *The Emergence of Man*, though Pfeiffer's knack for presenting hard scholarship in a popular manner is quite evident. Among other topics, the book covers the rise of domestication, state development in all six primary areas, and the diffusion of civilization.

Upham, Steadman, ed. *The Evolution of Political Systems* (New York: Cambridge University Press, 1990). This volume is not concerned with the evolution of states but with the processes of change leading to middle-range polities, such as chiefdoms. The authors challenge various models of state development, without, however, emerging with a coherent theory to replace them. The ten articles range from the broadly theoretical to specific studies of the Sausa of Peru and the Iroquois.

An early–twentieth-century king of Cambodia draws much of his political legitimacy from religion.

Chapter Four

Religion in Politics

It may not be true, as Georges Balandier (1970: 38) has contended, that the sacred is always present in politics; but it is seldom far away. As Myron Aronoff (1984b: 1) observes, "Religion and politics have been inextricably interrelated since the dawn of human culture and civilization." Viewers of Leni Riefenstahl's classic propaganda film *Triumph of the Will,* made at the 1934 Nazi Party Conference in Nuremberg, might justifiably wonder whether they are watching a political rally or a religious ceremony. An implicit sacredness underlies the Declaration of Independence and the Constitution of the United States, and offers a divine legitimacy to political succession. In modern-day Iran and Ireland, political conflict may be indistinguishable from religious conflict. However, in preindustrial societies the boundaries of the various subsystems— political, kinship, economic, religious, and so forth—are far less clearly demarcated than in more complex and specialized societies. An African candidate for headmanship who calls on ancestor spirits for support no more considers himself resorting to the supernatural than would a senatorial candidate in the United States who accepts a campaign contribution from a major corporation.

The role which religion plays in politics is difficult to correlate with evolutionary complexity. We find power directly based on the supernatural at all levels. Among some Eskimos, the shaman was the most powerful of men by virtue of his access to the spirit world; among the tribal Hopi of the American southwest, political power is articulated through ceremonies, dances, and religious sodalities; modern Israel is a highly industrialized and internationally powerful nation-state ultimately based on common religion and tradition. On the other hand, it would be equally easy to provide examples of hunting-gathering peoples (the !Kung), tribal groups (the Yanomamo), and states (Cuba) in which religion plays relatively little part.

The role of religion and the supernatural in politics is manifested mainly in three ways: (1) the government may be directly based on religion, as in a theocracy; (2) religion may be used to legitimize the ruling elite; and (3) religion may provide the underlying structures, beliefs, and traditions that are manipulated by aspirants to power.

SACRED LEGITIMACY

There is no clear-cut dividing line between a theocracy and a secular state. Because virtually all preindustrial states claim at least some degree of divine legitimacy, and even the most religiously oriented of administrations must solve a number of very secular problems—defense, trade, development of roads and irrigation networks—the amount of religious emphasis is a matter of degree, not kind. Even in most cases where religion plays an extremely important role, the secular and priestly bureaucracies are kept quite separate (as was true, for example, for the Inca and the Maya). While the priests may have enormous power, it is not power that would usually be expended on the mundane functioning of the government. Divine kings may, like the pope, express their divinity only on certain specific occasions and in very specific contexts. Jacobus Janssen (1978) argues that this was true of the Egyptian pharaohs, who guaranteed and maintained the cosmic order (*Ma'at*) while at the same time being subject to that order; their persons were taboo, but they were incapable of working miracles; they were omnipotent but subject to the gods and forced to rule through purely mundane means. People in states that are not as highly segmented as our own seem to have little problem dealing with the simultaneity of the human and the divine, the sacred and the secular.

Lucy Mair notes two requisites for kingship in Africa: the support of a loyal following, and some claim on the part of the would-be king to a special relationship with supernatural beings. In other words, a king requires both secular support and sacred legitimacy. The first derives from the individual king's personality and abilities and from his rightful claim, within traditional rules, to the throne; he must attain legitimacy through linking himself by myth to a supernatural ancestor responsible for the origin of the group or for some crucial event in the mythological history (Mair 1962).

The Shilluk of the Sudan believe in a semidivine cultural hero who, through an Exodus-like epic adventure, established them as a unique people, set up the first villages, and founded the basic divisions of their society. This deathless hero, Ny'ikang, simply disappeared, and his spirit enters into each succeeding king. The Shilluk were the only contemporary group chosen by James George Frazer, in his classic *The Golden Bough* (1890), to support his theory that the king represented the fertility of the land and cattle. According to Frazer, the king had to be killed in a ritual manner before he became old, in order that the mystic potency would always remain with a virile leader. Even though it is true that many such kings died young, in battle or through assassination, the belief that the king was ritually killed is itself part of Shilluk mythology. Yet Frazer, while overemphasizing the symbolic value of fertility, did hit on an important element of African kingship—the symbolic identification of the king's person with the welfare of the whole society (Mair 1962).

Religious ritual also has important political functions. The periodic reenactment of legitimizing myths unites the entire community in a sacred bond that transcends private interests and day-to-day conflicts, while reinfusing the society with the mystical power of the world of the ancestors. In some uncentralized societies, religious ceremony was the major source of tribal integration. For many of the Plains Indians, for example, it was only for two weeks during the summer Sun Dance that the entire tribe came together as a unit. It was at this time that the council of chiefs would meet and make group decisions, and when medicine bundles, which brought both mystical and secular power to their owners, exchanged hands.

Manipulation of Religious Symbols among the Lugbara

The supernatural is much more than a simple set of passive beliefs that form an unchanging backdrop for political action. Such beliefs are subject to the manipulation both of individuals who compete for power, and of those who are called to support (or withhold support from) the competitors. This is clearly exemplified in the political system of the Lugbara of Uganda. This group, which has a classic segmentary lineage system, lacked any formal government whatsoever prior to the colonial period. The smallest effective unit of society was the local patrilineal kinship group, consisting of a cluster of families, and in lieu of kings or chiefs, authority was vested in an age-set system. As members of the age-grades of youth and big youth grew older, they came in conflict with their elders over land and authority. Because violence was not permitted among kinsmen, generational conflicts had to be worked out by mystical means. If one of the parties in the conflict were to fall sick and the oracles showed that his opponent had conjured the ancestors to wreak sickness, the conjurer would gain power by having his authority affirmed. On the other hand, if it were believed that the dead had been invoked merely to gain or maintain status, rather than to benefit the lineage, the invoker could be accused of being a witch, and therefore lose status. These two interpretations are only narrowly different, but can have the effect of either legitimizing or destroying a person's authority. Thus, there is room here for manipulation of the belief system not only by the individuals involved but also by the public and the guardian of the oracle making the decision. Conflicts between local groups are not susceptible to this sort of resolution, because ghost-invocation and witchcraft are thought to be ineffective beyond the minimal lineage. Dueling, feuding, and outright warfare were common means of conflict resolution; but accusations of sorcery were often employed between close neighbors who wished to avoid open violence. In any case, all political authority was primarily supernatural, because it was controlled by the dead ancestors, and the power of sanctions derived from the same source (Middleton 1960, 1966).

SYMBOLISM AND RITUAL IN SECULAR SOCIETIES

It is comforting to assume that such sacred legitimacy is an anachronism of preindustrial societies. Yet even secular politics, in which religion is not immediately evident, is often replete with the emotional fervor that marks the realm of the sacred. David Kertzer (1988) observes that despite modern man's illusion of political rationality, of making decisions based on the weighing of objective evidence, symbolism pervades virtually every aspect of modern politics. Because symbolism, by its very nature, is unconscious and has a taken-for-granted quality, there is a tendency to treat symbols as though they were things. *Government*, *party*, and *state* are really symbolic constructions, not the concrete entities that most people suppose. Indeed, such organizations take their continuity only through symbols, since only the symbols remain constant, while the people making up the organization, including its leaders, are always changing.

There are three properties to true symbols, according to Kertzer. The first is condensation of meaning. The ideas of the United States as a physical entity, as "one nation under God," as a repudiation of European tyranny, as patriotism in warfare, as freedom and democracy (themselves ill-defined symbols), and so forth are all funneled into a single point in the Stars and Stripes. Second, symbols are multivocal, that is, they encompass a wide variety of different meanings. A single symbol, such as the Christian cross, may mean very different things to different people. Finally, true symbols possess ambiguity, so that they can never be fully and completely defined; they have no precise meaning.

Ritual is "action wrapped in a web of symbolism"; it is highly structured and is often enacted at emotionally charged times and places (Kertzer 1988: 9). It is through ritual, and through the individual's participation in it, that the ordinary citizen makes the crucial emotional bond with the otherwise unthinkably huge and often impersonal state. Symbols make power sacred. A Fourth of July celebration, a national political party convention, the inauguration of a president, the bicentennial of the Constitution—all provide the symbolic form through which the state can be emotionally embraced. Rituals need be neither positive nor routinized. The assassination of President John F. Kennedy, the explosion of the space shuttle *Challenger*, and the Iranian hostage crisis were all national-level events that provided a gut-level override of party loyalties and conflicting ideologies and drew people together in an emotional bond of shared tragedy. A major conflict, such as the U.S. involvement in the war with Iraq, is certainly real enough and tangible enough to the people who are fighting, but for the folks left at home it becomes a powerful symbol of national courage, unity, and pride.

This commonality of the nature of symbol and ritual makes it difficult to distinguish the sacred from the profane in politics.

REVITALIZATION MOVEMENTS

Religion may substitute for direct political action in cases where natives have been rendered politically impotent by an alien power or where they do not understand the nature of their situation. In such cases, a revitalization movement may arise as "a conscious, deliberate effort on the part of some members of society to create a more satisfying culture" (Wallace 1985: 319). Such movements are an almost predictable response to Western expansion, though they can be expected in any situation where cultures at totally different levels of technological sophistication or different levels of raw power come into contact. Incipient Christianity, arising within a situation of conquest by Rome, possessed all of the elements of a revitalization movement.

There are many types of revitalization movements. A millenarian movement looks forward to an apocalyptic transformation of the society through supernatural means. The Ghost Dance that swept through the Plains tribes during the last quarter of the nineteenth century was based on the teachings of Wovoka, a Piute living in Nevada, who prophesied that whites and Indians alike would be destroyed in a holocaust. Only those Indians who performed the Ghost Dance and led pure lives would inherit a world in which the buffalo would return to the plains and the people would live in peace and security in a halcyon society based on traditional Indian ways (Mooney 1896). (The religion ended tragically when hundreds of Sioux who had escaped their reservation to practice the Ghost Dance were rounded up and gunned down by the U.S. Cavalry at Wounded Knee, South Dakota.) In a messianic movement, a messiah brings about this transformation. In the mid-1700s a Seneca Indian named Handsome Lake had a series of revelations in which he envisioned a new faith that combined elements of both traditional religion and Christianity and which was more adaptive to the reservation context within which the Indians found themselves. Through a rigid proscription of liquor and an emphasis on family, the new religion was able to bring the Seneca and other tribes of the former Iroquois confederacy back from cultural collapse. Today, the Handsome Lake religion remains strong among the Iroquois, and its founder is considered a great prophet (Wallace 1972). In nativism, the goal is to purge the society of unwanted or alien elements, and in revivalism the aim is to reinstitute a former era of happiness. Most movements combine several of these types. The so-called Vailala madness, which swept parts of New Guinea in the early decades of this century, showed strong nativistic and revivalistic tendencies. After whites and their negative influences were totally expelled, believers would return to a golden age in which they would live with their ancestors (Wallace 1985).

The Vailala madness was a cargo cult, a type of revitalization movement that seeks to gain access to Western trade goods (*cargo* in Pidgin English) by magical means. When colonization or invasion by an industrialized power brings a massive influx of manufactured goods—cars, radios, processed food, and so forth—natives invariably seek some explanation for these wonders within their own cultural understandings. Because the whites are never seen making these goods but only receiving them, often by airplane or ship, it is assumed that foreigners must have some magic at their disposal, perhaps the secret words that they endlessly write on pieces of paper. Perhaps it is white rituals, such as walking up and down in military formation carrying rifles, or sitting around a table in suits and ties, that brings the cargo. Perhaps a rough airport, carved out of the jungle, or a mockup of an airplane will attract the cargo from the skies. Perhaps the cargo is really created by the ancestors, and the whites have only usurped the magical formula to attract goods really meant for the natives. There are infinite variations, all quite logical from the point of view of the natives, who are desperately trying to make sense out of a situation that would otherwise be chaotic and incomprehensible. Unfortunately, cargo cults can sometimes end in tragedy. In New Guinea in 1946, in response to wartime occupation of the islands, natives slaughtered their pigs, their main source of subsistence, in the belief that great pigs would appear from the sky at the millennium (which would be announced on mock radios attached to bamboo and rope antennae) (Worsley 1985).

According to Anthony F. C. Wallace (1985), the movements pass through a number of stages, though not all movements complete the cycle. The first stage is a premovement phase in which society is in a steady state without strong stresses or pressures for radical change. Gradually, as a consequence of alien invasion, famine, acculturation pressures, or whatever, individuals experience psychological stress while the culture becomes increasingly distorted as crime rises, alcohol or drug abuse becomes normative, and leaders are corrupted. A movement phase begins with the formulation of a new code of living by a prophet, often as the result of a vision. The revelation is disseminated to disciples who spread it among the masses until some sort of organization of believers becomes necessary. The new faith must adapt to its environment, either defeating vested interests or making modifications in the original doctrine to allay hostility and suspicion. When a significant number of people, or the whole population, has adopted the new doctrine, a cultural transformation is affected, bringing the culture into a more harmonious alignment with the conditions that precipitated the movement. Finally, in a postmovement phase, the movement becomes routinized as a mainstream religion or political party, and a new steady state is achieved.

Revitalization movements are basically attempts, often unsuccessful, to adapt to new conditions, despite the religious trappings they are basically political. The prophet's vision may be seen as a pivotal point in the history of the culture, at once combining external and internal factors, past and future, tradition and inevitable change. Over the past two centuries most such movements have arisen in the context of domination by Western powers. Thus, they may be seen as a first form of political protest, a cry of pain and accusation in the absence of the knowledge, organization or power to confront the occupiers on their own terms.

Vittorio Lanternari (1963: 20) quotes an African adage: "At first we had the land and you had the Bible. Now we have the Bible and you have the land." Indeed, many revitalization movements, including the Handsome Lake and peyote religions in the United States, borrowed heavily from missionization, using the apocalyptic vision of Christian fundamentalism against the usurpers of their lands, their freedoms, and their cultures. Once routinized, however, a religion may become a focal point of protest within the rules of Western political systems, as, say, African-American Christian sects took the lead in the civil rights struggles of the 1960s. Or the emergence of secular organizations, such as trade unions and native councils, may consign such religious movements to political irrelevancy.

Revitalization movements do not emerge only among tribal peoples. Modern industrial society is sufficiently stressful and chaotic for many individuals and groups that they may seek religious transformation. As analyzed by John Hall (1985), the tragedy of the People's Temple, in which 900 people died in an orchestrated mass murder and suicide in Guyana in 1978, was a revitalization movement that actually achieved its apocalypse. The following example, which has all of the stages set forth earlier, reveals the emergence and routinization of a messianic movement in modern Israel.

Gush Emunin—Revitalization in Modern Israel

According to Myron Aronoff (1984a: 63), Gush Emunin (*bloc of the faithful*) began as "a spontaneous, charismatic, loosely organized, extraparliamentary pressure group on the margins of the political system" and evolved into "a well-organized and functionally differentiated network of related institutions that were incorporated within the present national ruling establishment." This transformation from fervent religion to routinized semisecular political party was possible because Gush Emunin articulated a new sense of purpose and meaning within a situation rent with chaos and despair.

As described by Aronoff, the framework for the subculture from which Gush Emunin would arise was provided by the establishment in 1953 of a state religious school system under the control of the National Religious party. Virtually all of the leaders and supporters came out of this system of high school yeshivas, which combined both secular and religious instruction. This group created a virtual subculture within Israel, distinguished by the knitted skull caps which all wore. The founder-leaders were all graduates of the advanced Yeshivat Merkaz Harav, which they attended after fulfilling their military obligations, and all were disciples of the late Rabbi Zvi Yehuda Kook, who saw himself as interpreter of his father's teachings. Kook, who was heavily influenced by the mystical Cabala, was an unlikely candidate for charismatic leadership. He was difficult to comprehend and often barely articulate, but his ideas, especially as they were modified and elaborated in the concrete politics of Israel, provided a new faith that inflamed his young followers.

Though Gush Emunin never developed a complete ideology, it proclaimed a sort of neo-Zionism, a revivalistic return to the historic vision of Zionism that had languished with the establishment of the Israeli state. Formerly sacred creeds had been corrupted by secularism, and these creeds needed to be reinterpreted according to new realities. It was the duty of Jews to liberate all of their ancestral lands. In fulfilling this historically inevitable aspiration, Jews would reclaim all that was great, heroic, and beautiful from their past. The territories acquired in the wars of June 1967 and October 1973 thus became the focal points of the movement. There could be no withdrawal from any occupied territories, no sacrifice of any part of the Holy Land.

The event providing the political opening for Gush Emunin was the chaotic and morally ambiguous October 1973 war that led to widespread doubt and agony among the people and a crisis of confidence in the government. The liberal Labor party, which had dominated Israeli politics almost since the nation's inception, found itself under severe challenge from a conservative backlash. Within this atmosphere of confusion and general malaise, Gush Emunin commenced its active protest.

As a newcomer to the political scene, the movement was not constrained by the established rules of political order. The leaders believed it was their duty to operate outside of the legal system. Democracy was acceptable only as long as it subscribed to the proper Zionist framework. Toward its goals, Gush Emunin developed a pattern of protest against retreat from the occupied territories or accord with Israel's enemies. Demonstrations, including mass rallies and marches, opposed both the Camp David Accords and Egyptian President Anwar Sadat's historic visit to Jerusalem. A major "Movement to Stop Retreat from the Sinai" involved not only marches but also attempts to establish settlements in the occupied desert. When the government went ahead with plans to return the Sinai to Egypt, Gush Emunin followers broke into abandoned houses there and obstructed efforts to forcibly remove them. When such tactics threatened a backlash among the majority of Jews, who saw the pact with Egypt as a first step toward security and peace, Gush Emunin launched a policy of victimization, designed to ensure that future settlements on the occupied West Bank and in the Golan Heights and Gaza Strip would not be abandoned. Settlement became the primary strategy for retaining occupied territories and a central tenet in Gush Emunin ideology. In 1976 a suborganization, Amana, was established to promote the settlement of the occupied territories.

All of this was opposed by the Labor government. However, in 1977, Labor was replaced by the conservative Likud party that shared much of Gush Emunin's hawkish ideology and was allied with the National Religious Party from which Gush Emunin had originally emerged. With a like-minded government in power, the stage was set for the routinization of the formerly opposition movement, which now gained access to many government ministers and members of the Knesset. With routinization inevitably came bureaucratization: the once loosely structured group was organized into sections for promoting settlements, for lobbying, and for political party activities. Today Gush Emunin has been incorporated into the normal institutional framework of Israeli society and politics.

Noting that Gush Emunin involves aspects of millenarian and messianic movements, Aronoff (p. 81) observes that such "political-religious revitalization movements provide serious critiques of contemporary political and cultural systems. They offer dramatic alternative definitions of reality, symbolic systems of cultural meaning, and political agendas that they seek to impose in place of those that are currently dominant."

THE ADAPTIVE VALUE OF DEVIANT RELIGION IN PERU

Even normally traditional religion can have a revitalization effect when transferred to a new setting. Seventh-Day Adventism is a fundamentalist denomination of Christianity which in the United States tends to be highly conservative. Its main difference from other fundamentalist groups is that it holds Saturday, not Sunday, to be the sabbath. When transposed to the mountains of Peru, however, it became an important mechanism for adapting to new conditions.

The Aymara Indians living in the community of Soqa, in the Lake Titicaca region of Peru, were first missionized by Seventh-Day Adventists around 1915. At that time, most Aymara followed their traditional earth-mother religion. (They had adopted from Catholicism a few saints and the Virgin Mary, who had been added to the indigenous pantheon, and a fiesta system that consisted largely of dancing and getting falling-down drunk for a few days every year.) The Aymara were economically self-sufficient, monolingual, and cut off from any but the most cursory market relations with the exploitive *mestizo* class. The Seventh-Day Adventists, after many years of utter failure, established a mission in a small village and began to offer their religion as a package deal: health, education, and Jesus—in that order. Contrary to the usual theory, it was not the cultural deviants, but the more intellectually oriented, often community leaders, who were willing to try the package, which in practice meant abstinence from alcohol, some degree of modern medical aid, and sufficient education to read the Spanish-language Bible and hymnal. To the north of the lake, where literacy threatened the federal haciendas, there were many murders and burnings of Adventist churches, but the worst that happened to the freeholding Adventists near the lake was that they were once beaten and dragged off to jail. Generally, persecution consisted of Adventist baiting, such as capturing them at fiesta time and forcibly pouring liquor down their throats until they were drunk. Though persecution was relatively mild, it was constant; the small group was ostracized, their formal leaders lost all authority, and so the situation remained for almost four decades.

The political system at that time was based on the *ayllu,* discussed in Chapter 2. Over the centuries, many *ayllus* had become so loosely structured that they were held together largely by means of numerous and proliferating fiestas throughout the year. These fiestas provided both leadership, through sponsors, and an excuse to come together as a unified social and political group. However, in the early 1950s, as population began to overgrow the carrying capacity of the land for subsistence farming, the fiesta system with its enormous outlays by sponsors became too expensive to be maintained. In 1955, with a federal government engineer as guide, young progressives replaced the *ayllu* system with a community-based political structure, complete with mayor, vice-mayor, and lieutenants. This radical transformation, considered and decided by democratic means, accomplished two important things for the handful of Seventh-Day Adventists on the island: First, because the mayor was directly responsible to the provincial governor and the vice-mayor was directly responsible to the commandant of the regional army post, formal lines of communication were established between Soqa and the *mestizo* world. Second, the end of the *ayllu,* which had been held together by the Catholic fiesta system, meant the secularization of local government for the first time in centuries. The Seventh-Day Adventists, who had been persecuted and ostracized for three generations, had been educating themselves all that time. They were the only ones in the community who could read and write Spanish. And because they had fought for their right to practice their religion in the halls of government as far away as Lima, they were experienced in dealing with the national bureaucracy. Naturally, the Adventists quickly stepped into both formal and informal positions of power in the new Soqa government. Their unique abilities allowed them to act as culture brokers during this time of transition from a subsistence-agriculture economy to a money economy. At this writing, the long-despised Adventists continue to hold a monopoly of political power in numerous communities throughout the Peruvian *altiplano*. Because Adventist schools tend to be vastly superior to public schools, the power derived from education will probably be retained for many years—perhaps generations—to come (Lewellen 1978, 1979).

The Aymara study shows how a deviant religion, such as Protestantism in a traditional Catholic society, can provide the pool of variability necessary for adaptive change.

SUGGESTED READINGS

Aronoff, Myron J. *Religion and Politics: Political Anthropology,* Vol. 3 (New Brunswick, N.J.: Transaction Books, 1984). A slim volume collecting five articles on religion in modern state societies, four of which are on the Middle East. The fifth article is a historical examination of the Bible in U.S. political tradition. Unfortunately, two introductory overview essays, one by editor Aronoff and one by sociologist Irving Herskovits, are very brief and offer little that is new.

Kertzer, David. *Ritual, Politics, and Power* (New Haven, Conn.: Yale University Press, 1988). For Kertzer, Political Man responds better to gut-level symbolism than to rational arguments and objective facts. Ritual is the glue that holds states and societies together, and the author offers a detailed, and highly readable, examination of political ritual from the Aztecs to the United States. The focus is on secular ritual, but it quickly becomes evident that it is not that easy to distinguish the secular from the sacred.

Lanternari, Vittorio. *The Religions of the Oppressed* (New York: New American Library, 1963). Though written by a historian, this book deserves mention here because of its basically anthropological and political point of view. The author interprets prophetic and messianic movements, such as the Peyote Cult of the American Southwest and the many cargo cults of Melanesia, as "cries for freedom" of oppressed peoples.

Middleton, John. *Lugbara Religion* (London: Oxford University Press, 1960). The Lugbara of Uganda lack any formal political institutions, so power and authority are manipulated through oracles, divination, witchcraft, and sorcery. Middleton's analysis is minute and masterful.

Packard, Randall M. *Chiefship and Cosmology: An Historical Study of Political Competition* (Bloomington: Indiana University Press, 1981). In contrast to Middleton's synchronic analysis, this study of the interrelation between politics and religion among the Bashu of Zaire is very much of the process school. The author not only shows the ritual functions of chiefship today but also traces historical adaptations over the last century and a half.

Wallace, Anthony F. C. *The Death and Rebirth of the Seneca* (New York: Vintage, 1972). A detailed history of the Handsome Lake movement of the Iroquois, a revitalization movement based on the visions of a Seneca prophet. Wallace goes deeply into the reservation culture of the period and into the dynamics of the religion's dissemination and growth.

A cannon squad in revolutionary Mexico. True revolutions—involving structural change in the state system itself—have been rare in Latin America.

Chapter Five

Political Succession

Power must be counted among the scarcest—and the most desirable—of resources. Although it may not be useful to posit a Political Man who always maximizes power over others, in the same way that economists have created an abstract Economic Man who always maximizes profit, there always seem to be sufficient power-oriented individuals willing to fight for that tiny room at the top, a room that is almost always occupied by just one individual at a time. Though government-by-committee is often tried, it is extremely unstable, as the Founding Fathers must have known when they wrote a strong presidency into the Constitution (a presidency which, it might be noted, grows stronger as society becomes increasingly complex).

Just as there is usually a single leader, there tend to be many in the second position. If there were only one person next in line to leadership, that person would be very dangerous. Far better to keep a group of princes with relatively equal power in a constant state of rivalry. There are other advantages to not being overly specific in regard to who will succeed the leader. If the rules are too rigid—if the firstborn inherits leadership, for example—the state might end up in the hands of a child, a weakling, a psychotic, or an idiot (European history provides examples of all of these). A power struggle is an excellent way for various competitors to show their stuff in manipulating public opinion, gaining support of various factions, killing rivals, making war, and otherwise proving themselves capable of meeting the requirements of the job. As Max Gluckman (1960, 1969) pointed out, a society can actually be strengthened by rebellion and conflict because they resolve tensions and bring the strongest to prominence. For this reason, inflexible and highly formalized rules of succession—as in the United States—are rare in history.

Unless the rules of succession are carefully spelled out, however, that period between the death of the old king and the crowning of the new is extremely precarious for the group as a whole. A state recently formed out of a number of chiefdoms might revert to smaller units. Moreover, when two competitors can garner relatively equal support, there will almost certainly be civil war. Thus, too much rigidity in political succession threatens the polity because of weakness at the top; too much flexibility may rend it in pieces. This is the fundamental problem of political succession. Through history it has been answered in five different ways (or in combinations of these five): (1) diffused leadership, (2) hereditary succession, (3) republican government, (4) periodic military intervention, (5) and government by committee.

DIFFUSED LEADERSHIP

In band and tribal societies, the problem of succession to leadership positions is solved very easily: there is no succession—at least not in the sense of power being passed from one person to another. With the death of a leader, so dies the power, and any contender must build a power base from scratch. As we have seen, in hunting-gathering bands leadership may be situational, and is in any case minimal. What power exists beyond the family is confined more to arbitrating decisions than to making them, and leadership is based on personal characteristics or abilities that cannot be transferred. This is also true in horticultural or pastoral tribes, though here power may be more actively sought and there may be well-defined rules of the game.

Among the Siuai of the Solomon Islands in the South Pacific, an aspiring "big man" has to collect as many wives as possible to form alliances with other families and to provide an ongoing visible symbol of status. In addition, pigs must be accumulated, and the taro must be grown to feed them, so that they can be used in competitive feasts designed to humiliate rivals while enlisting followers. If a few hundred men can be recruited—through force of personality, generosity, and perhaps success in war—to build a large clubhouse, status is fairly assured, though it must then be constantly maintained against usurpers. The process tends to snowball: The more power one has, the more followers are attracted, and the more pigs can be rounded up for a feast that in turn attracts more followers and more glory. Some of these "big men" have garnered considerable power, complete with semi-redistribution-al economies and the ability to make war. However, loyalties remain focused solely on the individual. His lineage establishes no permanent superiority through his actions, so with his death the whole structure collapses, and loyalties are shifted to another, or several other, power seekers (Burling 1974: 14–17).

This is another demonstration of one of the defining differences between uncentralized and centralized systems; in the former, a leader—no matter how powerful—can neither pass on power nor build on that of a predecessor.

HEREDITARY SUCCESSION

Political succession in chiefdoms and early states is almost invariably hereditary, which simply reflects the emphasis on kinship, especially unilineal kinship, at this mid-level in political complexity. In fact, unilineal kinship systems can be the foundation on which centralized societies are originally constructed. As the state increases in complexity and requires that its administrators possess specialized knowledge and skills, kinship is gradually overridden as the dominant force in politics.

Table 4 shows some of the available alternatives in political succession, with a focus on hereditary systems in chiefdoms and early states. Within hereditary systems, both extremes are usually avoided: no single person (e.g., eldest son) is designated as successor, but neither are all males within the lineage eligible. Succession is circumscribed by rules restrict-ing the number of contenders, while providing a sufficiently large pool of variability (to borrow a concept from evolutionary biology) from which the fittest might emerge.

Martin Southwold's (1966) historical analysis of political succession among the Buganda of Uganda prior to the establishment of the British Protectorate in 1894, reveals the complexity of the succession process, even in a hereditary system. The Buganda bureaucracy consisted of a powerful, but not divine, king; a prime-minister who was a commoner; an aide to the king, who was also a commoner but who took the leading role in choosing the king's successor; and a series of chiefs and subchiefs who administered the various territorial divisions of the country. There were about fifty patrilineal clans, including the royal clan of the king, though the latter had no totemic animal and was less formally inclusive than the others. Clan membership, though normal, was not automatic; one had to be accepted by the clan chief to belong. This fact gave clanship a selective character and made clans important political factions.

Table 4
Succession Alternatives in Chiefdoms and Early States

	Major Strength	Major Weakness	Comments
One Ruler *vs* Collective Leadership	More efficient; stronger in competitive situations May be more responsible to group demands; no power vacuum during periods of succession	Disunity and competition during period of succession Unstable because of competition within group; cannot make decisions quickly in periods of emergency	In centralized political systems there seems to be a tendency for one person to dominate even in systems designed around collective leadership; thus, true collective leadership is rare
Heredity *vs* Nonhereditary Succession	In early states with unilineal kinship, descent forms a natural power base that is economically interdependent; this prevents free-for-all during succession Allows wider range of leadership potential, gives all equal access to power	Other kin groups may not support system because of lack of access to power Society liable to be dismembered during period of succession because of many competitors	Hereditary succession is virtually universal among early states; a lack of such legitimate succession is a major difference between "big man" tribal systems and centralized systems
General Inheritance of Power *vs* Restricted Inheritance	Provides a wider range of leadership options Reduces competition for office	Creates competition among all kinsmen of noble lineage, thus disruptive to the kinship system, which is basis of royal power May prevent natural leaders from assuming office	General inheritance would be so unstable as to be virtually nonexistent; all hereditary polities restrict succession to certain kin only
Patrilineal Succession (Restricted) *vs* Matrilineal Succession	Men hold power; succession is to sons; more direct In a matrilineal society, matrilineal succession would maintain power within a single lineage	In a matrilineal system, patrilineal descent will cross kin-group lines and confuse loyalties Succession would pass from leader to nephews, of which there might be a great many; indirect	Patrilineal succession is found in matrilineal societies because it is more direct; nowhere would we expect to find matrilineal succession in a patrilineal society

Fraternal Succession	Less likely a child will come to power if king dies young; less competition for power since younger brothers are still in line to succeed	Who succeeds to power on the death of the last brother? Creates competition among sons of all brothers	These categories are not mutually exclusive; filial succession may be temporarily replaced by fraternal succession if there is no heir or if a child inherits the throne
vs	Competition limited to a few; leadership typically younger than in fraternal succession	Possibility of a child inheriting the throne or of no heirs at all	
Filial Succession			
Designated Succession	Eliminates competition and threat of disunity during period of succession	Weak and incompetent persons can automatically attain kingship	Rules of priority usually limit succession struggles, but entirely determinant succession is rare since such a principle would ignore personal qualities of leadership
vs	Permits the "best man" (i.e., the strongest) to attain power	If too many competitors, chaos threatens; competition needs to be tempered by rules of eligibility	
Free Competition for Leadership			

Source: Burling 1974:46–52.

Southwold distinguishes five categories of rules, customs, and principles by which a successor to the king was chosen: (1) prescriptive rules, (2) preferential rules, (3) personality factors, (4) political factors, and (5) the electoral institutions. Prescriptive rules are those held consciously by the people themselves. The primary such rule was that, although all descendants of the king were counted among the royals, only the Princes of the Drum (the sons and grandsons of the king) were eligible for the highest office. In addition, the firstborn son of the king was ineligible, and grandsons could only be selected if all eligible sons were dead. It was the responsibility of the prime minister to care for the sons of the chief, and he would make recommendations, based on the personality factors of the contenders, to the aide who was most responsible for selecting a successor. One son who liked to torture mice and small birds was rejected, for example, on the entirely reasonable assumption that he might prove cruel to the people. The ideal personality type was one who was restrained and humble. Commoners held the ultimate power to choose the king, and they would be careful to make sure his power was not too centralized. Many political factors, then, were involved in the selection. Because Princes of the Drum were ineligible for any office but king, and therefore in direct and intense competition within their own lineage, they would usually turn to their mothers' lineages for support, specifically to their mothers' brothers who might hold power as chiefs or subchiefs. This meant that the power and influence of each mother's clan was a primary consideration in the king's selection. Also of prime importance were the electoral institutions themselves; though the king's aide had the greatest voice, many other commoner and royal chiefs were involved in the process, and their opinions and strengths had to be considered.

All this is somewhat ideal because it is based on the assumption that the sons really inherited the kingship, that the prescriptive rules were actually followed. However, by analyzing the actual list of kings, Southwold found that often, especially during a certain extended period, succession was fraternal rather than filial, and the mode of succession was rebellion rather than election. In other words, outside the prescriptive rules was a set of preferential rules, one of which stipulated that in periods when maturity and strength were important, brothers were preferred over inexperienced sons.

THE LATIN AMERICAN MODEL

Though the republican (or representative democracy) form of succession has been analyzed by anthropologists, as has the collective leadership of the Soviet Union and other Communist countries, such modern forms of nation-state rule continue to be more within the domain of political science than political anthropology. We look at some of the anthropological perspectives on industrial-state governments in a later chapter. However, we include here a discussion of Latin American politics, which, even at the national level, have been of perennial interest to anthropologists.

The peaceful succession which Western democratic nations consider normal, may in fact be the norm neither within the vast span of history nor in most modern-day developing countries. It is common knowledge that the turmoil of recent African history derives from the fact that these nations are new, having gained their independence from the colonial powers only after World War II, and that things will settle down as these nations mature. But a glance at Latin America reveals that such expectations may be wishful thinking. Through more than a century and a half of independence, violence has been a legitimate means for the transfer of power in many countries of Latin America, and governments have sometimes changed types—from caudillo to oligarchy rule, from military dictatorship to representative democracy, from one-person rule to junta— as often as they change leaders. Since the mid-1980s, Latin America has been engaged in a widespread process of democratization. This may be fragile, however, because Third World democracies have not proven particularly adept at solving the vast economic inequalities that underlie much violence. In some countries, death squads, usually made up of the military and police, operate with impunity even within democratic settings.

The reasons for this political volatility are legion, but certainly history accounts for a great deal of it. The conquest of North America was accomplished through settlement by vast numbers of immigrants who claimed the land and worked it themselves (or brought in slaves from Africa to work it), and virtual genocide against the native population. In Latin America, with the exception of coastal Brazil and the southernmost countries, the land was viewed as a supplier of raw materials to Spain; thus the Indians were left in place to work vast tracts of land given to conquistadores for their service to Church and crown. As a result, right from the beginning of European conquest arable land—and thus wealth— was concentrated in the hands of very few families. Much of the population remained traditionally Indian, living in closed peasant communities with their own languages and their own folk cultures. Over time, intermarriage between Indians and the Spanish conquerors produced an intermediate class of mestizos. In colonial times, all higher government offices were held by Spanish administrators, and creoles (American-born Europeans) had to make do with local councils drawn from the richer families. With the coming of independence, the only experience that the creoles had with government was within these weak and ineffective councils, which often were quickly dominated by strong men on horseback who possessed sufficient charisma to develop militant personal followings. Throughout the nineteenth and much of the twentieth centuries these caudillos have dominated Latin American politics at all levels.

National leaders of the caudillo stripe, such as Juan Peron of Argentina, play at politics in a strongly personalistic way and often draw their power from appeals to the workers, or to some working-class segment of society. A dictator is a slightly different phenomenon; men such as Anastasio Somoza in Nicaragua, Rafael Trujillo in the Dominican Republic, and Fulgencio Batista in Cuba were skilled in manipulating the richer elements of the society, in forming personal armies, and especially in using the United States' paranoia of communism to centralize enormous wealth and power. They made only nominal concessions to the masses.

Few dictators have held absolute power, at least in the early years of their rule. A basic job requirement is the ability to balance many forces within the country while simultaneously juggling rival claims and rival interests. Historically, the two key forces have been the oligarchy and the army, either of which might assume the reins of government. Oligarchies originally consisted of the landed elite. In many countries, such as Peru and Uruguay, the big money has been shifted from land to industry with the result that it is no longer possible to speak of a few families who control most of the arable land. Today, elites are formed out of agrarian-industrial complexes with close ties to multinational corporations based in the United States, Europe, and Japan. There is often a symbiotic relationship between the army and the elite in these countries. At the same time, the army usually has a high degree of autonomy, which it jealously guards. Armies have not always acted predictably—they have sometimes been willing to step aside to civilian rule, to allow total chaos to develop (as in Argentina) before assuming dictatorial power, and even to impose extensive popular reforms (as in Juan Velasco's government in Peru). In contrast to the developed Western countries, however, the army is autonomous of any government it does not itself run.

All Latin American governments have constitutions. Some have closets full of constitutions, abrogated and rewritten as often as governments change. Because some of these countries lack any real commitment to constitutional succession, have long repudiated the idea of hereditary leadership, and possess massive illiterate and semi-literate populations that often identify more with particular ethnic groups than the state, it is little wonder that the more peaceful means of political succession have not always found favor in Latin American countries. In the absence of any direct means of popular input, the primary goal of government has been to protect the wealth of the elite and the power of the military. Of course, adjustments are made as deemed necessary to suppress popular discontent; these can range from agrarian reform and minimum wage laws to brutal repression.

Eric Wolf and Edward Hansen (1972) have developed a typology of Latin American succession. *Machetismo* refers to the process, long the norm at the local rural level, by which one caudillo is able to garner enough bald power to impose his absolute will through a following of armed men (in the nineteenth century, often cane workers armed with machetes). When raised to the national level, this type of succession may involve scores of regional strong men, each with his own private army, fighting to attain the status of *jefe maximo*; one such conflict in Colombia between 1899 and 1903 cost one hundred thousand lives. *Cuartelezco* refers to a barracks rebellion (*cuartel* = barracks). The classic pattern is for one group of military officers to coordinate simultaneous attacks on communication centers, military supplies, and the seat of government, immediately followed by the announcement of a new junta and of reforms. If carried out smoothly, at a time when the standing government is sufficiently unpopular and is alienated from the military, such a change of power may be relatively bloodless. A *golpe de estado* (the Spanish phrasing of coup d'etat) may bypass the military; it strikes directly at the seat of power, through either the assassination or the detention of the president.

The obvious problem with such violent means of succession is that the new government may possess little in the way of legitimacy in the eyes of the people. One method of gaining such legitimacy is to sponsor an election; this has the added advantage of providing the elected government (assuming it is allowed to come to power) with a friendly pat on the back from the United States. However, the legitimacy of an election can be contrived to some degree through *imposición*, a process by which the ruling forces handpick a candidate and rig the election to make sure he wins; or by *candidato unico*, in which the ruler holds an election with himself as the sole candidate. A more subtle approach to prolonging power is *continuismo*, by which a president's term of office is extended through manipulation of the existing constitution, by writing a new constitution, by new legislation, or by a favorable judicial ruling. Even where there exist all of the formal trappings of democracy, an autonomous military probably maintains enormous control over the levers of power, and the constant threat of a *golpe* may have to be considered in government decisions. Also, democracy may in some cases offer no more than the opportunity to vote for one or another faction of the elite, while elite rule is legitimized by the illusion that the masses have the ability to affect substantive change. In reality, little structural change—toward a more equitable wealth distribution, for example—has been effected in Latin American democracies.

All of the more violent forms of political succession are what Max Gluckman (1960) would have called rebellion: the head of state changes, but the system remains intact. True revolution—actual structural change in the system itself—has occurred only in Mexico, Cuba, and Nicaragua. This is not to say that massive changes have not taken place in virtually all Latin American countries; but in the majority (and this may be true, to a great degree, of Mexico also) these changes are more in the line of adaptive adjustments that have permitted the old economic structures to remain intact through making some, often minimal, concessions to popular unrest, or which have brought new elites into the political process.

SUGGESTED READINGS

Burling, Robbins. *The Passage of Power: Studies in Political Succession* (New York: Academic Press, 1974). The introduction and conclusions provide a theoretical framework for the specific studies of political succession that make up the body of the book. Included are the Marathas of India, Manchu China, Latin America, and contemporary Eastern Europe and the Soviet Union. The depth and range of Burling's research is impressive.

Goody, Jack, ed. *Succession to High Office* (Cambridge: Cambridge University Press, 1966). In contrast to Burling, who uses only state-level examples, Goody focuses on more conventionally anthropological subjects, namely, chiefdoms and incipient states in Africa. The four articles are written for a professional audience, but make for worthwhile reading if one is willing to wade through some complex kinship diagrams.

Early structural-functionalists often ignored the colonial context of the societies they studied. Here a native king is flogged by British colonial soldiers.

Chapter Six

Structure and Process

"Structure may go to the wall," wrote F. G. Bailey in 1968, "but people survive." This could have been the rallying cry for an entire generation of political anthropologists who, during the 1950s and 1960s, guided the transition from the study of norms, values, and atemporal social structures to an emphasis on competition, conflict, history, and change. The paradigm so self-consciously and often vehemently repudiated was the structural-functionalism of A. R. Radcliffe-Brown, which had dominated British anthropology for more than twenty years. Because the new political anthropology is to a great degree a reaction to this theoretical orientation, it is worthwhile to take a critical look at it.

STRUCTURAL-FUNCTIONALISM

If one were to reduce the structural-functionalist position to only four words or phrases, they might be *synchronic, teleological, Africa*, and *closed system*. Synchronic is defined by Webster as "concerned with the complex of events existing in a limited time period and ignoring historical antecedent." This definition would be favored by the critics of structural-functionalism, who constantly complained that societies were ripped out of their historical contexts and treated as though they were static over long periods. Yet in reality the early political anthropologists did not so much portray their societies as excessively stable or unchanging (though this might be implied from their method of analysis), but rather as *outside of time*, in the same way that a still photograph captures an instant without denying temporal processes. And just as a still photograph may suggest a great deal of movement, as well as a past and a future, the structural-functionalists allowed for all sorts of tensions and conflicts within their frame of reference.

In a sense, then, we might think of these researchers as comparable to intelligence personnel who analyze aerial photographs. They tried to look at society from above, as a whole, and to map the interconnections between the various subsystems of the society—kinship, marriage, religion, politics, and so forth. The society itself was considered not only outside of time but also isolated in space. Though a tribe or chiefdom might be contained within a nation-state, it was viewed as a thing unto itself, relatively independent of its wider social environment, that is, as a closed system with its own culture, its own values, its own mechanisms of adjustment.

The question immediately arises: Adjustment to what purpose? The structural-functionalists had a ready answer: adjustment to the equilibrium of the whole. Far from being static, institutions within the society were constantly changing shape as smaller groups formed and reformed, as alliances were made, as feuds and wars were fought—but all of these were interpreted as contributions to the integrity of the whole. Thus, any particular institution was analyzed in regard to the way that it functioned to aid the survival of the larger system. In this sense, structural-functionalist causality was the reverse of Aristotelian causality; effects were not pushed from behind, so to speak, but pulled from in front. One would not explain a religious ritual in terms of its historical development but rather in terms of its purpose or function, which was ultimately the maintenance of societal equilibrium. In short, institutions and activities were analyzed teleologically (i.e., in terms of a goal toward which they were directed). It was recognized, of course, that the people themselves would offer completely different reasons for their behavior; but these manifest functions, while certainly important and often recorded in great detail, were not analytically significant. The anthropologist was much more interested in the latent functions, of which individuals were unaware, and these could only be determined by looking at the whole system (just as, for example, the liver can only be understood in relation to the survival of the body).

One reason that this paradigm could be sustained for so long was that virtually all fieldwork was done in the part of Africa that was under British colonial rule, where cultures remained separated by language barriers, distinctive cultural patterns, and the paternalistic prejudices of the ruling class of British administrators. Also, there was a tendency to seek out for fieldwork the more typical villages—those which were most traditional—and to use these to represent the entire language group. This naturally had the effect of minimizing culture contact.

All of these elements are either implicit or explicit in E. E. Evans-Pritchard's classic *The Nuer* (1940a). The basic goal of the book, including a chapter on the political system, was to show how a society of two hundred thousand people could maintain equilibrium despite almost constant feuding and an utter lack of any kind of centralized government. Evans-Pritchard's explanation, based on the concept of complementary opposition (which we discussed in Chapter 3), demonstrates how the equilibrium of the whole can be maintained, not just in spite of conflicting parts, but actually as a result of them.

It is no accident that the demise of structural-functionalism coincided almost exactly with the demise of British colonialism after World War II. The synchronic approach required a fairly clear still photograph, and the image tended to blur when the action got too chaotic or when too many different groups crowded into the frame. The repudiation of structural-functionalism began blandly enough, but quickly turned to revolution, with all of the vehemence radical change seems to require. Most of the criticisms now seem rather obvious: Societies are not in equilibrium; teleological arguments are not scientific; no society is isolated from its social surroundings; societies are not homogenous; colonial Africa is not the world. Structural-functionalism, and British anthropology as a whole, were accused of having been servants of colonialism. Perhaps the most telling criticism was simply that the theory had become routinized and was threatening to degenerate into a simplistic game in which one could point out, with a semblance of great profundity, that a religious ritual brought lots of people together and thus maintained social equilibrium.

All these objections are justified. Process does indeed stand triumphant over "equilibrium." But it is possible to look back from the vantage of victory and discern in the defeated enemy certain admirable qualities that were not visible through the smoke of battle. In retrospect, a book such as *The Nuer* seems an enduringly brilliant and perceptive piece of analysis. The idealized portraits painted by the structural-functionalists of entire societies are very close to pictures of what is now being called political culture—that set of values and interactions common to a traditional society. In this respect, structural-functionalism seems close to the symbolist school of political anthropology, which views culture, including politics, as involving powerful sets of unconscious symbols. These symbols form a setting in which political action takes place; what has been added is the emphasis on the ways in which symbols are used and manipulated by individual actors. Even in the midst of the repudiation of structural-functionalism, one of the pioneers of the new process school, F. G. Bailey (1960: 240), felt it necessary to caution his colleagues, "I cannot emphasize too strongly that without the fixed points which are provided by a static structural analysis, we have no means of describing the change that is taking place."

The idea of latent functions has been taken over, virtually intact, by ecological anthropologists, who view societies as unconsciously adjusting to maintain ecological balance. *Teleology,* once considered one of the most taboo words in science, has been incorporated into both biology and physics and has now moved, via general systems theory, into the social sciences, where goal-direction is legitimately viewed as a prime force for both individuals and groups. Also from general systems theory comes the concept of *boundaries*, the defining qualities of a social system blocking or filtering input from outside the system. Within these boundaries, constant adjustments are taking place to maintain the system, but the boundaries themselves may be stable for long periods of time. It should be obvious that, *for a relatively closed system*, the picture one gets from applying the concepts of general systems theory are not especially different from that of the structural-functionalists. Although the superiority of a process approach cannot be denied—if only because its scope is so much wider and its analytical tools so much more diverse—there is indeed in society something that is continuous, something that forms the backdrop for change. This is what the structural-functionalists were able to describe with such perception.

THE PROCESS APPROACH

It is easy, in retrospect, to impose too much coherence on the reaction against structural-functionalism, to suppose that these writers had some philosophical view in common and were all moving in the same direction. Actually, their explorations could hardly have been more varied. Victor Turner's *Schism and Continuity in an African Society* (1957) and Edmund Leach's *Political Systems of Highland Burma* (1954) represent opposite poles, one focusing on a few individuals in one small village, the other on ethnic populations interacting within a modern nation-state. Perhaps the only thing these two seminal works have in common is that both seem to cling to the old paradigm with one hand while feeling their way toward a new paradigm with the other. In fact, the field situation itself—whether uniform in population or of great ethnic diversity, whether tribal or state, in conflict or at peace—was much more significant in determining the line of analysis than any common theoretical point of view.

It is a curious fact of political anthropology that its major position papers are often contained in relatively brief introductions to anthologies. In 1940, the introduction to *African Political Systems* provided the stimulus and theoretical basis for the first generation of political anthropologists. In 1966, three writers who were in the forefront of the reaction against structural-functionalism—Marc Swartz, Victor Turner, and Arthur Tuden—modified the foundation concepts for a generation of process theorists in their introduction to *Political Anthropology*.

For these authors, the study of politics "is the study of the *processes* involved in determining and implementing public goals and in the differential achievement and use of power by the members of the group concerned with these goals" (Swartz, Turner, and Tuden 1966: 7). There are several key words in this tight definition. The emphasis on process is obvious, but the political anthropologist is only concerned with public processes. This provides an escape from overgeneralized views of politics or power that seem to include almost any relation of power, even at the level of the family; but still it leaves enough flexibility to include neighborhood or nation. The concept of *goals* has taken a marked shift from the orientation of the synchronic analysts, who were interested mainly in the latent functions that led to the goal of equilibrium or survival. The process theorists were much more interested in the consciously held goals of the group, whether they be lower taxes, better roads, or leadership in war. The ability to make and enforce such decisions constitutes power. Political anthropology thus consists mainly in the study of the competition for power, and the way that group goals are implemented by those possessing power.

Three broad trends emerged. First, *process* became the key word of political anthropology as societies were studied in their historical, or at least temporal, context; thus, the emphasis shifted from equilibrium to change. Second, a significant group of researchers narrowed their focus to a sharp concentration on the activities of individuals vying for power within very limited political settings. Third, another group of researchers broadened the perspective to include the national system, with a strong emphasis on the adaptive changes traditional cultures must make as they are incorporated politically into the modern industrial state; sometimes the state government itself is the subject of analysis. The three theoretical perspectives are summarized in Table 5. Though these three trends are intertwined, each is distinctive enough to deserve its own chapter. The remainder of this chapter focuses on the general elements of what has

Table 5
Three Theoretical Perspectives in Political Anthropology

	Structural-Functionalism	The Process Approach	
		Process Theory	Action Theory
Goals	To show how particular institutions serve to maintain the equilibrium of the whole society	To define the processes involved in political competitions and in implementing public goals	To describe individual strategies for gaining and maintaining power
Unit of Analysis	A society, tribe, social group, etc., usually treated as an ideal whole; this group was considered for analytical purposes as a closed system insofar as little regard was paid to the wider environment	The "political field," a flexible and relative concept referring to any area in which political interaction takes place; may involve a part of society or extend beyond social or ethnic boundaries	The "political arena," an area in which individual actors or small groups vie for political power. Political arenas may be, or be comprised all or in part of, factions, patron-client relations, parties, elites, and other informal parapolitical groups
Analytic Approach to Time	Synchronic: society is viewed as though outside of time, in ideal present	Diachronic, or "in time": analysis may focus on actual history or on ideal processes of change through time	Diachronic, but often focused on the actions of individuals within the duration of the anthropologist's fieldwork
Attitude toward Change	In some writings, there was simply no interest expressed in change; society was treated in a purely structural fashion; in other writings, change (in the sense of adaptive adjustments of the parts) was emphasized, but the whole was seen to be in equilibrium	Conflict, tension, and change are viewed as the normal condition of society	Change within a political arena is virtually constant, though there may be a relative stability of the wider system
Key Terms	Structure, function, equilibrium, integration	Process, competition, conflict, power, legitimacy, support	Strategy, manipulation, decision making, roles, goals, games, rules
Examples	African Political Systems, ed. Fortes and Evans-Pritchard	Political Systems of Highland Burma, by Leach (transitional)	Schism and Continuity in an African Society, by Turner
	The Nuer, by Evans-Pritchard	Political Anthropology, ed. Swartz, Turner, and Tuden	Lugbara Religion, by Middleton
			"Political Anthropology: Manipulative Strategies," by Vincent, in Annual Review of Anthropology 1978

come to be known as process theory, but is better referred to as the process approach.

Field and Arena

The unit of study was formerly a specifiable group, even if that group was not always well defined. Anthropologists examined political structures within a village, a lineage, a clan, a tribe—even sometimes a culture (usually meaning a particular language group). Unfortunately, politics does not confine itself so neatly to such social units, and even if we were able to discover the locus of political behavior within a society, it may not stay put. For example, if we were to examine a medium-size American town over time, we would find that most people were both apathetic and ignorant about the day-to-day running of the government. Local elections would create factions, but these might encompass only a minority of the citizens. Hot issues, such as busing to attain racial balance in the schools, or a threatened police strike, might involve almost the entire community. Periodically, the people would be drawn into statewide elections and statewide political problems, and every four years many of the people would become involved in national politics along with local politicians trying to get a grip on the encumbered coattails of one or another presidential candidate.

This recognition—that political structures overlap but do not coincide with other social structures, and that they tend to wax and wane over time—led to the concept of the *political field*. The structural-functionalists seemed to conceptualize politics as a one-set stage play; there might be hints of a wider world, but the action was confined within a coherent and specifiable environment. Process theorists tend to view politics more in the sense of a passion play: there is an ongoing coherence of plot, and the same actors and groups may participate continuously, but the action shifts from area to area over time. This would be the political field, a fluid area of dynamic tension in which political decision making and competition takes place. To return to our passion-play analogy, much of the action would involve broad scope and grandeur, but periodically the drama would narrow to a sharp focus on two or a few actors. Even though these actors might be essential to the story line, their behavior could only be understood in relation to the wider setting. In this case, out of the whole field we would have chosen to concentrate our attention on one small arena.

Actually, the concepts of *political field* and *political arena* remain ill-defined. Some writers use the terms interchangeably; others have very specific meanings in mind. F. G. Bailey (1969), for example, considers a political field as one in which the rival groups do not share agreed-on rules for regulating their conflict; he sees an arena as an area in which the same rules are accepted by the various competitors. Pragmatically, the very relativism of the two concepts is their primary virtue. A political field is nothing less, or more, than the wider area of political activity defined by a particular researcher, while an arena is an area within the field on which the researcher wants to concentrate at a particular moment. While these concepts are quite relative, they need not be arbitrary; different field-workers in the same society might choose to concentrate on different levels of political interaction, but they would probably have little trouble agreeing (to the extent that anthropologists agree on anything) on the boundaries of the various levels. With the concepts of field and arena, we both allow and insist that the researcher precisely define that aspect of the social system which has been separated out as the unit of analysis.

Power

A Maori shaman cures meningitis through an infusion of an invisible force—*mana*—into the body of his patient. A Cree Indian chief plans a wedding. A United States president unleashes a bombing of unprecedented scope on a Middle Eastern country. A Lugbara sorcerer invokes ghosts to inflict sickness on a neighbor. An Aztec priest tears the living heart from a human sacrifice.

What these disparate actions have in common is that they all exemplify the use of power. In the first case, the shaman's power is impersonal and supernatural. The United States' war with Iraq was a case of the direct application of massive force by an advanced technological society. Among the egalitarian Cree Indians, planning a wedding is one of the few areas in which the chief is permitted to exercise authority and demonstrate his leadership. For the Lugbara, actual sorcery, as well as making accusations of sorcery and witchcraft, is a common means of manipulating public opinion to gain political support. Finally, for the Aztec, the priest became the servant of the enormous power of religious tradition.

Any concept that must encompass such a range of situations can hardly be defined in too narrow a fashion. Power does not come from physical force alone. During the Iranian revolution, Shah Mohammad Reva Pahlavi had direct access to the best modern weaponry that state's enormous oil riches could buy, as well as to an efficient police apparatus skilled in murder and torture. Yet the real power, it emerged, belonged to the Ayatollah Khomeini, a fundamentalist Islamic holy man with neither weapons nor troops. Even in the United States, the president, who as commander and chief of the armed forces commands great world power, may lose that power simply because his right to hold office has come into question, as the Watergate incident so aptly illustrated. This is not to say that power cannot exist independently of public support. The right to rule of many governments has been based on control of armies, secret police, and death squads. Any definition of power must include both that which relies on force and that which does not, that which derives from the individual and that which derives from a system or an office.

Ronald Cohen (1970: 31) defines power as "an ability to influence the behavior of others and/or gain influence over the control of valued actions." This is broad enough to include the gamut of our examples, but requires that we further distinguish between private power (e.g., power exercised by a domineering father over his family) and public power exercised in the political arena. It is the latter that is of interest to the political anthropologist.

Power may be independent or dependent (Adams 1975). Independent power is a relation of dominance based on the direct capabilities of an individual, such as special knowledge, skills, or personal charisma. Many North American and Oceanic societies conceive of power as an objective force inherent in individuals. Everyone possesses some of this force, but real power relationships come into being when one individual is recognized to have more of the kind that is needed for group decision making. At the band and tribal levels of political development, such personal qualities are the primary means by which one person gains influence over the group, an influence that is usually limited to arbitrating disputes or setting an example. In more centralized societies, independent power may become objectified and formalized, attaching to a particular office, no matter who holds that office; also, it may give rise to extremes of political domination, as we see in the elaborate ritual and taboos surrounding the divine Inca, the ancient Hawaiian chiefs, or even the emperor of Japan. Although these extreme examples may be foreign to American democratic values, in reality everyone is constantly assessing the power of those with whom they come into contact and adjusting their behavior accordingly, either through simple deference or through obedience to elaborate social rituals. Dependent power comes into existence when an individual with independent power, either by nature of personality or office or both, lends another person the right to make decisions. This can be done in three ways: (1) an individual can grant decision-making powers to another; (2) a group holding power can allocate such rights to individuals; or (3) a group or individual can delegate such rights to a number of other people.

Another way to look at the concept of power is to separate that which is based solely or largely on force and coercion from that which is based on group consensus. Force alone is certainly effective as a short-run means of political control, but when it is the only basis for the people's assent to be governed, the society is extremely rigid. Talcott Parsons once compared force in a political system to gold in a monetary system: it is effective as long as it forms a basis for other systems, but day-to-day transactions require a lesser coin if the system is not to become so rigid that it cannot adapt to new conditions (Swartz, Turner, and Tuden 1966). The Cuban revolution is a case in point. Fulgencio Batista's regime was so corrupt and brutal that it alienated the majority of people, including many from the upper and middle classes who would later oppose Fidel Castro as well. Because wealth was centered in a small elite and there were few methods for redressing popular grievances without threatening the system as a whole, Batista's main basis of support came from the army. It is doubtful that Castro won the revolution in any military sense because his own army never consisted of more than two thousand men and he never succeeded in controlling a single province. But the Batista regime had become so ingrown, so self-serving, and so alienated from the populace that it virtually collapsed under the weight of its own corruption. When Batista took his money and ran, the old system lacked resilience enough to form a new government; Castro, with the only major organized force in the country, simply stepped into the power vacuum.

A government may maintain itself through force: Joseph Stalin, Idi Amin, Rafael Trujillo, Papa Doc Duvalier, Pol Pot, the British in India and Africa—twentieth century examples are, unfortunately, legion. But if such a government is to have the flexibility to adapt to entirely new conditions, it must also possess consensual power which derives from the assent of the people. In state societies, such assent is not given to the wise and just alone; children, idiots, sadists, and lunatics may well be the beneficiaries of popular assent as long as they take office through established means of succession, such as being born into a kingship. Consensual power may, in fact, derive more from a grudging acquiescence to tradition than from respect—much less love—for those in positions of domination.

In states, consensual power is always, by definition, conjoined to centralized control of the use of physical force, so it may be difficult to tell whether one is consenting out of respect for the system or out of fear of being thrown in jail. Would I pay my full income tax if the government did not impose physical or economic sanctions? Perhaps not. Would I voluntarily pay some part of my salary to support roads, schools, welfare, police and fire protection, and other benefits of government even in the absence of sanctions? I like to think that I would. But I would be hard-pressed to specify just how many of my tax dollars are calculated to keep me out of jail each year and how many go for support of a system which seems to provide me with certain benefits. In other words, within a state society consensual power and power by force are so intertwined that there may be something artificial in separating them for analysis. However, the distinction provides a useful basis for evaluating governments both objectively and morally. Objectively, a government that possesses very little in the way of consensual power is too rigid to make the necessary adjustments to serve all its people; morally, such a government would have little justification for continued existence.

In uncentralized, egalitarian societies, leaders do not usually have access to physical coercion, but must depend entirely on consensual power. This may mean little more than setting an example. In *The Feast*, one of Napoleon Chagnon's many films on the Yanomamo Indians of Venezuela, a village headman is shown alone on his knees scraping the ground with a machete to shame his neighbors into helping him clean up the village compound. Similarly, during my fieldwork among the Aymara of Peru, the community mayor had to work for three days, virtually alone, on roofing a public building before others slowly began to join the labor; by the fifth day almost the entire community was involved.

In these examples the benefits of following the leader were immediately obvious, but in many cases a leader must get people to do something they do not want to do in the absence of foreseeable benefits. This may be especially true of a community leader working with a national government. The Aymara community mayor just mentioned was, on another occasion, faced with the problem of implementing a census and questionnaire for the Peruvian Ministry of Education. The people were fearful that this information would be used to tax them or to cooperativize their privately held lands, and they knew the federal government could do nothing to punish them if they refused. The fact that they finally did assent to the questionnaire (and provided surprisingly accurate responses) suggests that they believed their mayor would use this cooperation in a long-term strategy to gain benefits—such as roads, schools, food aid, and a clinic from the government. This lack of specificity about the reasons for performing an action sharply differentiates consensual power from power based on threat, and differentiates legitimacy from coercion.

Legitimacy

Consensual power has the advantage of being free from specific sanctions and specific rewards; it can, therefore, be employed in a wide variety of situations. People perform public duties because they trust either their leaders or the system the leaders represent to bring about general benefits over the long run. In the United States it is probably true that no individual likes every president, and many may vehemently disagree with the policies of one president or another; but few would object to a president's right to hold office. In other words, a president's legitimacy depends not on the continuing support of the people (indeed, polls show that at some point a majority of the people might despise a given president) but on the legal process by which that person came into office. The president draws power from the Constitution, two hundred years of history, and the belief of the American people (a belief into which they have been socialized since birth) that this particular form of government is better than the alternatives.

We might compare the situation in the United States with that of Bolivia, which at last count had undergone over 150 coups in as many years. A major reason for the instability of Bolivian governments, and for their periodic dependence on the most brutal repression to maintain power, is that there is very little basis in Bolivian society for the legitimacy of any government. In the absence of kingly succession, or any evident divine guidance, one government is about as good as another, and none can claim much right to rule. In such situations, if there is economic collapse or social unrest under democratic rule, it might be democracy itself that is called into question, not a particular leader or political party, and there might be widespread calls for a return to military dictatorship.

The legitimacy of power derives from the group's political culture, the people's expectations about the nature of power and how it should be attained. For a Polynesian "big man," legitimacy may be obtained by giving the largest pig feasts; for a British king, by being born to the proper lineage; for a prime minister, by having the controlling votes of the parliament; for a nineteenth-century Cheyenne chief, by being brave in battle when young and wise in age. There are cases in which legitimacy does not derive from tradition at all, but is earned in a novel manner. A dictator who comes to power through rebellion or a coup might gain legitimacy by providing benefits to the people.

Legitimacy may, moreover, have very little to do with how power is actually used. Adolph Hitler was a legitimate ruler (he became dictator through a legal loophole in the enlightened Weimar constitution); so was Joseph Stalin. Masses of people may be sustained in subjection and poverty for literally hundreds of years under legitimate governments—witness ancient Egypt and Rome, or the despotic dynasties of China. As we learn again and again from European history, a king's arbitrariness and incompetence may not deter a devoted following if his claim to the throne is legitimate. On the other hand, dictators who have no legal or traditional claim to power almost invariably try to legitimize their positions through orchestrating demonstrations of support, staging fraudulent elections, rewriting the constitution, or creating a parliament of sycophants.

Support

Legitimacy and coercion are opposite kinds of *support*, a term defined by Swartz, Turner, and Tuden (1966: 10) as "anything that contributes to the formulation and/or implementation of political ends." If we consider that warring, police arrests and intimidation, striking, public speaking, voting, and simple persuasion are all encompassed in this definition, we can see that there is a continuum of supports that run the gamut from legitimacy to forceful coercion. Because support can be lost as well as gained, a government would be well advised to seek out and employ as many forms of support as possible. In analyzing a political group, we find different supports operating in different areas and various political competitors trying to manipulate the various sources of support in their favor.

Support may be either direct or indirect. Even considering the anachronistic complexities of the electoral college, when I vote for a president in the United States, I am providing direct support. In England, however, one votes not for a prime minister but only for a representative of a certain party, so support for a given person as prime minister is once removed, or indirect. Similarly, an African village headman may try to sway his people directly by speaking out against an opponent, or he may do so indirectly by initiating a rumor that his opponent has been indulging in witchcraft.

Process, political field, power, legitimacy, coercion, and *support* are some of the primary conceptual tools found useful by the post-structural-functionalists to analyze political systems. Although these tools do not comprise a coherent philosophical school of thought, they do provide the means for analyzing a wide range of political systems.

SUGGESTED READINGS

Eisenstadt, S. N. "Functional Analysis in Anthropology and Sociology: An Interpretive Essay," *Annual Review of Anthropology, 1990,* 19:243–60. The author, an important figure in political sociology, outlines the major arguments against classical functionalism, then offers a reevaluation to bring functionalism into the 1990s. The article, which includes an extensive bibliography, reveals that functional analysis is still alive.

Evans-Pritchard, E. E. *The Nuer* (Oxford: Oxford University Press, 1940). The author sets out to discover how an African pastoral group totally lacking in government cannot only maintain continuity and cohesion but also rapidly form a united military force when necessary. His analysis is hotly argued even to this day—perhaps the highest form of compliment for one of the foundation works of political anthropology.

Fortes, M., and E. E. Evans-Pritchard, eds. *African Political Systems* (Oxford: Oxford University Press, 1940). This is the book that started it all. The eight ethnographic studies, all by big men of British anthropology, represent the high standards of fieldwork already attained during the 1930s. Special mention might be made of Max Gluckman's contribution on the Zulu (which already reveals the seeds of his later rebellion against structural-functionalism) and Evans-Pritchard's highly compressed summary of Nuer political organization.

Gluckman, Max. *Custom and Conflict in Africa* (New York: Barnes and Noble, 1956). The titles of the chapters—"The Peace in the Feud," "The Frailty in Authority," "The License in Ritual," for example—give a good idea of the author's fondness for paradox. Gluckman, founder of the Manchester School of social anthropology, believed that constant tension and conflict created a rough equilibrium. Although some writings from this period might now be relegated to the status of historical curiosities, Gluckman remains a jolly good read.

Swartz, Marc J., Victor Turner, and Arthur Tuden, eds. *Political Anthropology* (Chicago: Aldine, 1966). The introduction to this book provides an incipient philosophy and model for the process approach, and the book as a whole is a virtual manifesto against structural-functionalism. The articles are too diverse to fit neatly into the categories provided by the editors, but many of them are of high quality. Of special mention: Ralph Nicholas's "Segmentary Factional Political Systems," Ronald Cohen's "Power, Authority, and Personal Success in Islam and Bornu," and John Middleton's "The Resolution of Conflict among the Lugbara of Uganda."

Chiefs among the Kwakiutl of the Northwest Coast of America maintained their power through hereditary titles, crests, and ceremonial privileges. Purchase of an expensive copper shield brought great prestige.

Chapter Seven

The Individual in the Political Arena

Two quite different lines of inquiry are implicit in the process approach. On the one hand, the breakdown of the domination of structural-functionalism freed anthropologists to widen the scope of their study of relatively uniform tribal societies to include complex nation-states. On the other hand, researchers could also shift their focus from the broad structural view of whole systems to the actions of individuals or small groups operating within those systems. The latter orientation came to be called *action theory,* a term derived from German sociologist Max Weber and applied to political anthropology by Abner Cohen (1974: 40–43).

As is true with so many theories, action theory was developed ex post facto by seeking out the common denominator of a wide variety of studies by authors who probably had little conception that they were part of a coherent new orientation. That common denominator was the focus on individuals and their manipulative strategies to gain and maintain power. The individual involved in this process might be a named person, described with as much depth of characterization as one would find in a good novel, or an abstraction: Political Man. In contrast to a close cousin Economic Man, Political Man does not maximize wealth or profit, but rather power. Place two or more of these beings in the same arena (which is redundant, because their presence in fact creates a political arena) and we have the personae for a social drama or, if one prefers, for a game in which various moves are restricted by rules and in which there can be but one winner at a time.

In this microcosmic setting the crucial concepts include goal orientation, manipulative strategies, maneuvering, and decision making. But
individuals can never act alone in politics; they must seek followers,
make alliances, and interact with other individuals in positions of either
dominance or subordination. It is therefore impossible for anyone who
studies politics to ignore groups. But action theorists tend to look at
groups from the point of view of individuals and to emphasize groups—
such as factions, cliques, and elites—which can best be understood in
face-to-face interactions.

THE SOCIAL DRAMA

One of the earliest studies to develop this orientation is Victor Turner's
Schism and Continuity in an African Society (1957). Though in the line
of Max Gluckman's Manchester School of anthropological theory, this
work had several aspects that were unique. Instead of examining the
whole group of the Ndembu of northern Rhodesia, Turner focuses on
individuals as they pass through a series of crises (in Turner's words,
social dramas). Each of these dramas is analyzed as the culmination of
a long period of building tensions in which new power alignments and
shifts of allegiance have been taking place.

For Turner, "the widest community of Ndembu is . . . a community
of suffering"; and indeed his central antagonist, Sandombu, is a true
tragic hero. In the first of a complex series of social dramas involving
this man, who has ambitions to be headman of Mukanza village,
Sandombu twice insults the village headman, Kahali, as a challenge to
his authority. This results in a fierce dispute between them, each
threatening the other with sorcery. Sandombu leaves for another village
where a notorious sorcerer is supposed to live. A short time later, the
insulted headman falls sick and dies. Sandombu is allowed to return to
Mukanza, but there is sufficient suspicion to prevent him from replacing
the headman, and a man from another lineage is chosen.

This train of events is deceptively simple. Sandombu's insult to Kahali
was a breach of one of the deepest principles of Ndembu social
organization—the authority of the elder generation over the younger.
Furthermore, Sandombu was Kahali's sister's son, and succession from
older to younger within the same lineage was looked on with disfavor.
There were other reasons to put a check on Sandombu's ambitions. He
was sterile and his sister was barren. This, in itself a sign of sorcery, had
important implications; because the Ndembu are matrilineal and a leader
must draw his strength from his kinsmen through the female line, the

sister's lack of children would narrow Sandombu's basis of support. Also, his indiscriminate generosity—a function of his ambition—had brought in strangers who were threatening to the conservative villagers. Finally, rivals for headmanship had an obvious vested interest in accusing Sandombu of sorcery. The result was that the village's three most powerful lineages united in opposition to Sandombu.

For Turner, the norms and structures which had so interested the generation of the 1940s have become the social field, the background before which the real action takes place. Lineage systems, marriage rules, values, and behavioral norms are not unalterable realities but social idealizations subject to constant manipulation. For example, the norm regarding succession within the lineage was applied to Sandombu but not to Kosanda, who later succeeded his mother's brother as headman. Accusations of sorcery were used to justify public consensus that Sandombu should not be headman; they were only secondarily the basis for such consensus. Thus norms and rules were not abjectly followed but were emphasized or de-emphasized according to a complex set of criteria.

Such an approach rests on certain underlying assumptions about the nature of society. Society is viewed as a field of forces in dynamic tension in which centrifugal and centripetal tendencies constantly pull against each other. When the tension between fission and cohesiveness becomes acute, a crisis develops, climaxing in the reestablishment of a temporary and unstable equilibrium. There is seldom a complete resolution of tensions; rather, the result is a readjustment of forces that lends more strength to one side and depletes the strength of the other. Turner, along with Marc Swartz and Arthur Tuden (1966) has elaborated this process into a diachronic model of political phase development in which a period of mobilization of political capital is followed by an encounter or showdown. The latter involves some sort of breach of the peace in which one party in the conflict attempts to openly challenge the other. This leads to a crisis—"a momentous juncture or turning point in the relations between components of a political field"—that in turn brings about counteracting tendencies as the social group marshals peacemaking forces to avoid complete cleavage of the two sides. Deployment of adjustive or redressive mechanisms may involve informal arbitration, legal machinery, or public ritual. Finally, there is restoration of the peace as the two parties either readjust to a new set of asymmetric power relations, or schism entirely.

Though Turner's book was transitional and still grounded in the structural-functionalism of the 1940s (his stated goal was "to isolate the cardinal factors underlying Ndembu residential structure"), many of the ideas that would later coalesce as action theory were already evident. In Sandombu we see Political Man as a real-life individual, manipulating cultural rules, making choices, developing strategies—in short, making goal-oriented decisions.

A major reason for focusing on individuals rather than on groups is that in the individual a number of different systems meet. A group may act out a single role at a particular time, but the individual always embodies conflicting roles, at once father and son, leader and follower, warrior and peacemaker. The individual thus expresses the contradictions that may be invisible in studies of groups.

GAME THEORY

An interesting and influential variation of action theory is the non-mathematical game theory developed by F. G. Bailey in *Strategems and Spoils* (1969). Because this is one of the more comprehensive anthropological political analyses, it is worth reviewing in some detail. Bailey started this book after he became fascinated by the revelations emerging from the television interrogations of Mafia informer Joseph Valachi. These exposed not only a rational structure underlying organized crime but also a set of rules of the game by which mobsters fought and murdered one another in ongoing power struggles. Processes of leadership succession seemed to be nearly identical to those described by Frederick Barth (1959) in his game-theory analysis of the Swat Pathans of Pakistan. It seemed that "the edge of anarchy is fenced off with rules," that no matter how amorphous a political system may be, political combat is regulated by a code of which the participants may or may not be consciously aware.

Each culture develops its own set of these rules of political manipulation. It is therefore possible to view politics as a competitive game with agreed-on rules and, equally important, an agreed-on goal. In a real sense, politics is this set of rules, for a struggle in which each party could make up rules along the way would be simply a fight. There are two types of political game rules: Normative rules are publicly professed and usually vague (honesty, ideals of fair play, etc.); they are yardsticks against which actions may be judged ethically right or wrong. Pragmatic rules have to do with the actual winning of the game, as opposed to public display. Bailey focuses on the latter, because the real question, as he sees it, is not whether an action is publicly approved, but whether it is effective. Competition takes place within a political field that may be defined as a society or segment of society in which two or more rival political structures exist, but in which there is an absence of an agreed on set of rules between these structures. Within the political field are arenas where teams that accept such rules attempt to build support for themselves and to undermine their opponents through subversion. Competition may not be confined to an arena but may move from one arena to another within the wider political field, and sometimes competitive groups within an arena might unite temporarily against an outside threat.

There are five major elements of political structure when it is viewed as a game. First, there must be prizes or goals, that are culturally defined and must be sufficiently valued by the participants to make competition meaningful. Second are the personnel involved in the conflict: this includes the entire concerned political community, the political elite (those entitled to compete), and the political teams involved in competition. The third element is leadership, which includes the individuals supported by a group of followers, on the one hand, and those individuals who actually make decisions and settle disputes, and who may be quite different from the overt leadership, on the other. Fourth is the competition itself, that is of two types: Confrontation, or a move within the political arena that announces to an opponent one's strength in resources and one's possible intentions; and encounter, in which both contestants publicly agree to test their strength against each other. Finally, there are judges, who define the rules to be followed when one or another of the opponents breaks the rules.

Even though Bailey emphasizes rules as essential to the game of politics, he notes that outright cheating or playing one set of rules against another are also part of the game. In the Watergate scandal (an example Bailey could not have foreseen in 1969), pragmatic and normative rules came into conflict. Spying on opponents has long been part of American party politics, and might even be considered legitimate within the pragmatic rules. But such behavior must be kept out of sight. When the attempted bugging of the Democratic headquarters surfaced, a Pandora's box of purely pragmatic actions emerged with it—an enemies list, dirty tricks played on Democratic candidates, tampering with evidence, a cover-up conspiracy, and the like. None of this should have been particularly surprising to American voters, who as a group are fairly well imbued with a healthy cynicism toward politics. Perhaps even more damaging than the actual crimes was the revelation in the Watergate tapes of the appallingly petty and downright sleazy manner in which the most powerful men on earth were conducting business. With Nixon's resignation and the criminal conviction of his aides, normative values temporarily triumphed over pragmatic politics, even creating the temporary illusion that a government could be conducted by normative rules. Jimmy Carter ran for election on the basis of his high morality; he even promised that he would never lie to the public. He lasted only four years.

Political Teams

Broadly speaking, the two types of political teams are: contract and moral. A contract team is one that is united, not by conscience, but by the profit or potential profit to be derived from following a certain leader. A relatively loose form of contract team is the transactional team, which is based largely on interchanges of a material nature—money, food, clothing, contracts, licenses—so that the bond between leaders and followers is based strictly on perceived material benefit. In "big man" systems, such as those found in Polynesia, the leader must buy loyalty through loans and feasting. In a labor union, the leader's power may depend on subordinates' perception that he or she can gain them more pay and benefits than competitors within the movement. Since a leader's position may be based on face-to-face transactions with individual followers, and since a leader would be well advised to avoid sharing power for fear of creating a rival, such teams are extremely limited in size. The bureaucratic team, another form of contract team, avoids some of these difficulties. Here, leadership is allocated to a number of different functionaries, each with a specialized place in the hierarchy of power, so the core leader can avoid any direct challenge. Such a group also has the advantage of being able to expand indefinitely, because it does not depend on personal interactions with one individual.

In contrast to teams in which loyalties depend on personal benefits, a moral team is united by a shared ethic—religious belief, nationalism, or a utopian political ideology. A leader in such a team pays the price of being rigidly confined within the normative values of the group, but a certain sense of security may also be derived from the knowledge that followers will not shift to one who can offer better material benefits. The leader of a moral team may claim a monopoly on certain mystical attributes, such as access to the gods, which effectively cuts off opposition. For example, among the Lugbara of Uganda only the elders can use the power of the ancestor spirits—a fact that prevents the younger generation from ever seriously challenging the elders' authority.

Whatever the type of team, a leader must fulfill certain functions: decision making, recruitment and maintenance of the group, and interaction with the world outside the team. Day-to-day decision making follows the lines of normative or pragmatic rules, or a combination of both, so that real leadership is called for only in conditions of uncertainty.

In making decisions, the leader must always calculate the political expense, especially when normative rules cannot be routinely applied. The safest strategy in such cases is for the leader to make the decision that requires the smallest social adjustment possible. The least expensive decision is consensual; that is, the leader gains prior consent and simply announces the decision of the group. But attaining such consensus can be a long, difficult, and divisive process and might even suggest weakness in the leader. The most politically expensive form of decision making is simple command. The leader who knows the game would, of course, seek that middle ground to assert power while maintaining maximum support.

Political Encapsulation

Over the long run, teams that regularly compete for power must be more or less equal in strength. Periodically, however, politics in one arena spill over into another, larger arena in which one team finds itself encapsulated by a much larger political structure; neither the normative nor the pragmatic rules of either group apply to the other. Three types of relations are possible in such cases: First, the larger structure may maintain only the most nominal relations with the smaller, especially if the cultures of the two groups are markedly different and the smaller group maintains a significant degree of power within its limited domain. During the colonial period in India, for example, large areas on the borders of China and Burma were ignored by the British overlords except for paramilitary tours of inspection to maintain an illusion of control. (However, British normative values were so offended by the practices of human sacrifice and infanticide among these people that they ultimately fought a twenty-year war to subdue them.) A second alternative is predatory encapsulation. At its most primitive, this is simply a national form of the gangster protection racket: As long as the weaker group pays its tribute, it is left alone. A more sophisticated version is the indirect rule elevated to an art by the British in Africa. Finally, the smaller group may be incorporated into the larger, through either radical change or abolition of the indigenous political, economic, and social structures. This has been tried periodically with the American Indians through processes of forced detribalization; but it has failed because the values of the dominant and the subordinate groups have differed too radically for such incorporation to take place. (Chapter 10 discusses how indigenious peoples carve out niches of power for themselves within situations of encapsulation.)

Whatever the process of encapsulation, *middlemen* will assume an important political role in mediating between the two structures. The success of a middleman depends on an ability to deceive, because a compromise is usually possible only if each side is misrepresented to the other. As a result, these middlemen are despised by both sides. This is evident, for example, in the use of the term *cholo*, which has a derogatory connotation, for an intermediary class of Indians who are between the peasants and the mestizos in highland Peru and Bolivia. *Cholos* are Indians who have left the land for jobs in trucking, contraband, and small-market sales, and who prefer to speak Spanish and dress in mestizo-style clothes. Though distrusted by the peasants—who consider them exploitive—and despised by the mestizos, *cholos* fulfill an important function in bridging two radically different cultures during a period of rapid acculturation.

The problem facing any encapsulated political structure is one of survival—how to maintain itself with a minimum of change within its changed environment. A moral team, especially one based on a religious ideology, might assume the fanatic's stance and vow to fight to the last man, woman, and child. Unfortunately, the more powerful group may be thoroughly unimpressed, in which case the encapsulated group finds itself forced to change. Bailey isolates three types of political change: Repetitive change, so well described by Max Gluckman (1960, 1969), is quite radical change that can take place within a wider equilibrium. All groups, for example, must face the problems of losing a leader and finding a replacement, of periodic war, of famine, and so forth. In such cases, normative rules and pragmatic rules, such as rules of succession, are sufficient to bring the society back to normal. Although repetitive change has no cumulative element—small changes do not necessarily add up to a fundamental change of structure—in adaptive change there can be no return to the original equilibrium. In this case, normative rules can be maintained, but the pragmatic rules have to change to account for new conditions. When Plains Indian tribes were forced onto reservations, they were able to maintain most of their original culture and political values, even though their political situation had shifted from one of autonomy to one of abject dependence. In cases of radical change, both normative and pragmatic rules are irrevocably altered—the independence of the British colonies after World War II, for example, or the collapse of the Soviet empire in the 1990s.

FACTIONS

One of the direct outgrowths of the process approach in the late 1950s was an increasing focus on the role of temporary political conflict groups or factions. As long as equilibrium was considered the goal of social organization, factions were viewed as maladaptive. From the point of view of process theory, however, it was evident that in certain circumstances factions could be more adaptive than conventional politics in organizing and channeling political conflict, especially during periods of rapid social change. Factionalism could even comprise the permanent politics of a group. Edwin Winkler (1970: 333) proclaimed the concept of faction to be "perhaps the most distinctively anthropological approach to the study of inputs to a political system." It was factionalism, in Winkler's view, that had refocused anthropology from its structural obsessions to a concern with how structural principles are manipulated. Naturally such enthusiasm required dampening. Janet Bujra (1973: 132) protested that factions and factionalism "are fashionable concepts enjoying a vogue which outstrips their present clarity of usage." In any case, faction seems firmly established in the anthropologist's lexicon and so must ultimately face the same barrage of criticism as terms such as *tribe* or *segmentary lineage*.

In contrast to ongoing corporate groups with fixed structural properties—such as political parties, lineages, clans, or secret societies—factions tend to be informal, spontaneous, leader-follower groups organized for a particular purpose and disbanding when that purpose is accomplished or defeated. They are primarily conflict groups organized in opposition to one or more other groups; thus, by definition, there can never be only one faction in a specific political arena. Because a faction leader draws support from any and all available sources, partisans may cross normal party, class, or caste lines, with the result that there is often a lack of ideological focus.

Within this broad definition, a number of different factions may be delineated. Common-parlance *factionalism* refers to temporary conflicts within formal political groups, for instance, within the Republican party before a national convention. By contrast, pervasive factionalism develops when external pressures cause the breakdown of normal political mechanisms. In such circumstances, unorganized and temporary factions may arise with little provocation (Siegal and Beals 1960). The phrase *segmentary factional political system* has been applied to groups in which factions constitute the dominant mode of political organization. Though cohesive, the potter caste in Govindapur village, India, is not large enough to act as an effective political unit. It therefore serves its own interests by regularly aligning with one or another of the factions of the dominant caste. As with pervasive factionalism, this type is usually found in systems undergoing rapid change, where rules of political conflict have become ambiguous (Nicholas 1965, 1966). On the other hand, relatively stable political systems may have factionalism as a virtually institutionalized form of decision making. This would be true, for example, of the Ndembu or of modern Japanese government with its myriad fluctuating political parties.

Because factions are born and nourished in conflict, they cannot reach a point of even relative equilibrium and still maintain their status as factions. There are four possibilities: First, a faction may so decisively defeat its rival that it becomes legitimized and begins to organize itself as a formal group, while the defeated faction disappears altogether. Second, in states where there is only one legitimate political party, as in Communist China, factionalism may simply serve the functions of party politics. A third possibility is that factions within an arena may continue over time with neither side winning a victory, so that conflict itself becomes increasingly ritualized and gamelike. Finally, factions may be institutionalized as political parties (Bujra 1973).

POLITICAL SYMBOLISM

For Abner Cohen (1974) people are fundamentally two-dimensional—both symbolists and political beings—and these two functions are in constant and inseparable interaction. Power is no less than what is expressed in any relation of domination and subordination, and is therefore an aspect of all social relationships. To think of power as physical force or coercion is to miss entirely the subtlety with which it is usually manifested, for in day-to-day transactions power is "objecti-fied, developed, maintained, expressed, or camouflaged" by means of symbolism. All symbolism—or virtually all—has a political component.

Directly political communication, no matter how eloquent, may not be particularly effective. A blatantly political speech is incapable of further elaboration or manipulation and may actually be divisive; the funeral of a statesperson, on the other hand, resonates with unimpeach-able and deeply felt meaning—a reaffirmation of cultural values, ideas of continuity and rebirth, and much more. Politics is thus most powerfully manifested in overtly nonpolitical institutions such as kinship, marriage and other rites of passage, ethnicity, elitism, and various group ceremo-nies.

If symbolism is virtually synonymous with culture, and if all symbolism is political, one might suspect that Cohen has postulated that "political anthropology is nothing other than social anthropology brought up to a high degree of abstraction." This is, in fact, a direct quote from Cohen (1974: 81), one for which he admits to having been widely criticized. Symbolism and politics would seem to be such wide-ranging concepts that they lose meaning, almost as though one were to resort to God as a primary element in scientific explanation. If this were truly so, Cohen would rate no more attention from his colleagues than so-called scientific creationists rate from evolutionary biologists. Fortunately, however, Cohen is quite capable of bringing these abstractions down to earth, defining them precisely, and demonstrating their application in specific incidents, as he has done in some insightful political ethnographies.

All symbolism is bivocal: It serves both existential and political ends. It is existential in the sense that it integrates the individual personality while relating that individual to a group. A painful puberty initiation ritual involving circumcision, for example, is a powerful personal experience in which the child feels that he is in some way transformed, that his old self has been obliterated and a new, more adaptive self reborn in its place. At the same time, the ritual is an opportunity for a lineage to come together to reaffirm its unity, for the mythology of origin to be reiterated, for decisions to be made, for leaders to present themselves, and for males to reaffirm their moral and physical domination over females, elders over young, and wise over merely strong. Though symbolism is largely unconscious, and is virtually constant in every person's life, its political component is most clearly manifested in the compressed dramas of ritual and ceremony. A study of these within any particular group reveals the location of power as well as how it is manipulated. In this sense, Cohen is elaborating on the ideas of Max Gluckman and Victor Turner, as well as the symbolic transactionalist school of political sociology.

In *The Politics of Elite Culture* (1981), Cohen applies these general concepts to politics in a small African nation. Sierra Leone is a nation-state of about 2.5 million people, of which something less than 2 percent—nearly all of whom live in the capital, Freetown—are Creoles who view themselves as the descendants of slaves emancipated by the British. They are not an ethnic group, a tribal group, or a class (many non-Creoles share the same economic status). Their relation to slave-ancestors is partly mythical, because their kinship system is sufficiently open that many have been incorporated who can make no claims to special ancestry. They possess virtually no executive power in the state, lack any access to physical force, and have only the most negligible role as businessmen or producers of tangible goods.

Yet the Creoles are not only a closely knit, on-going group, they also control enormous political power within Sierra Leone. To understand how they have accomplished this, Cohen examines the manner in which symbolism is used to create the mystique of eliteness and to legitimize that mystique outside their own ranks so that others accept their claim to power.

Elitism is a way of life. People outside the group can be trained, through schooling or apprenticeship, in the technical and administrative skills necessary for government, but one can join the elite only through undergoing a long period of socialization. Elitism derives not from wealth or specific social functions, but from a vast and complex body of symbols including manners, styles of dress, accent, recreational activities, rituals, ceremonies, and a host of other traits. Skills and abilities that can be taught are conscious, while that great body of symbols that form true elitism are, by and large, unconscious.

Such symbols must serve a dual purpose: They must be at once particularistic, serving to unite the group and maintain its unique identity, and universalistic, legitimizing it as an agency of power to the great majority of outsiders.

The continuing existence of the Creoles as a separate group is constantly threatened. Most Creole wealth rests on property ownership in Freetown and vicinity, and rising property values have created a strong temptation to sell to outsiders. In addition, a former power base in the civil service has been eroded as educated provincials compete for these positions. While Creoles comprise 64 percent of all professionals—dominating the judiciary, medicine, teaching, and the clergy—they have already lost the niche they once held in business. To counter these challenges, the once loosely knit Creole elite has had to create more formalized institutions and more intensive means of communication, and to increasingly emphasize ceremony and ritual.

Women have always played a primary role in maintaining Creole separateness, mainly through the socialization of children in group symbols and values, and through the socialization of men in proper decorum. Equally important, women are the center of both family and kin networks (as men are more preoccupied with careers and male clubs) and are thus the pillars of a Grand Cousinhood which forms the underlying structure for the Creoles as a corporate group. This cousinhood involves dense networks of overlapping families, uniting each individual to many different families through participation in various ceremonials.

For men, Freemasonry provides an important means of group maintenance and a system of interpersonal communication. While Freemasonry is not limited to Creoles, they comprise the majority of the seventeen Masonic Lodges in Freetown, and hold most of the upper positions. Frequent ceremonies, often of a costly nature, formalize and cement group relations, while an enforced system of brotherhood encourages the amicable settlement of misunderstandings among individuals. Freemasonry thus provides the setting for a group identity among men, and for individual face-to-face interaction.

All of these institutions serve not only the particularistic ends of group maintenance but also universalistic ends oriented toward the wider public. Women are involved in running a variety of associations, societies, clubs, and activities that are either partially or wholly devoted to public welfare. The Freemasons are also involved in public works projects; but more importantly, the Masonic brotherhood provides a setting for wheeling and dealing and for exchange of information among men who are responsible, either directly or indirectly, for national policy decisions. Thus the same sets of institutions and symbols that unite the Creoles into a closed group legitimize them as spokespersons for the public good.

This is true also of the various ceremonies and rituals that emerge from the five cults of the Creoles: the cults of the dead and of the Church, of Freemasonry, family, and decorum. Funerals, thanksgiving rituals, Masonic initiations, balls, marriages, and other social events are carefully orchestrated dramas, tightly defined and intensely meaningful actions set apart from the aimless meandering of the normal flow of daily life. Through such drama, private experience is elevated to collective experience. For all participants, dramas are intensely tangible and immediate, but at the same time they connect the individual and group with the timeless motifs of male and female union, victory and defeat, life and death. At every point, then, the acted symbol unites the immediate and the timeless, the individual and the collective, the parochial and the national, the selfish and the giving, the private and the public.

Although Cohen was most responsible for introducing the term *action theory* into political anthropology, it is debatable whether his symbolic approach should be so classified. He does not analyze individual or even small group action, except to provide examples for more general processes, and he is emphatic that individual decision making must not be unduly snatched from its cultural context to give an illusion of more freedom than really exists. On the other hand, Cohen, perhaps more than any other, has broadened the scope of action theory by clarifying the symbolic field within which individuals act and which provides both the constraints and the raw materials for those striving for power.

SUGGESTED READINGS

Bailey, F. G. *Strategems and Spoils* (New York: Schocken Books, 1969). Bailey's theory (summarized in the foregoing chapter) provides one of the few systematic models in anthropology for analyzing political systems. One important aspect of the theory is the explicit differentiation between the ideal political system and the real political system.

Barth, Frederick. *Political Leadership Among the Swat Pathans* (London: Athalone Press, 1959). "In Swat, persons find their place in the political order through a series of choices." This simple observation and his supporting analysis placed Barth in the forefront of the reaction against purely structural studies that ignored individual decision making. As a result, this book and several journal articles on the Pathans of the Swat Valley in Afghanistan became the basis for Bailey's political game theory.

Cohen, Abner. *Two-Dimensional Man* (Berkeley: University of California Press, 1976). For Cohen, Man-the-Symbolist and Man-the-Politician are complementary and mutually reinforcing. In this work Cohen presents his theory of the dialectical relationship between power and symbolism. The argument tends to become abstract, so it helps to read it in concert with one of Cohen's excellent ethnographic studies, such as *The Politics of Elite Culture* or *Custom and Politics in Urban Africa*.

Cohen, Abner. *The Politics of Elite Culture* (Berkeley: University of California Press, 1981). Cohen is at his best when applying his concepts of power and symbolism in the analysis of a specific group. This book is one of very few studies of a power elite based on participant observation fieldwork. Though the subjects are the Creoles of Sierra Leone, one feels that this could just as well be a study of a United States elite.

Fogelson, Raymond D., and Richard N. Adams, eds. *The Anthropology of Power* (New York: Academic Press, 1977). Power is defined in an extremely broad (and not always political) sense to provide a common thread to tie together these 26 ethnographic studies and four theoretical articles. Of the latter, Richard Adams's evolutionary model of power is a significant contribution. One also finds excellent analyses of the concepts of *mana* in the South Pacific, *Wakan* among the Sioux, and shamanism among the Northwest Coast Indians.

Turner, Victor W. *Schism and Continuity in an African Society* (Manchester: Manchester University Press, 1957). Few books in political anthropology deserve the status of classic; this is one of them. In many ways, this minute examination of power struggles within a single village of the Ndembu of northern Rhodesia is reminiscent of Chinua Achebe's famous novel *Things Fall Apart*; here also we find the tragic over-reacher, barred from the status and power he so desperately desires. In spite of Turner's scholarly presentation, Sandombu comes to life. The methodology is the case study or social drama, in which a few specific events are examined in detail.

Indira Gandhi was prime minister of India from 1966 to 1977. Women have often attained such positions of power, but this does not necessarily translate into an increase in the status or power of women in general.

Chapter Eight

Women and Power

Until recently the universal political subordination of women has been one of the accepted fundamentals of cultural anthropology. E. E. Evans-Pritchard (1965: 54) observed that "in almost every conceivable variety of social institutions, in all of them, regardless of social structure, men are in the ascendancy." Robin Fox (1967: 31) includes male domination as one of only four basic principles of kinship (along with female gestation, male impregnation, and incest avoidance). In a recent overview of cultural universals, Donald Brown (1991: 91n) categorically asserts the "universal dominance of men in the public-political arena."

To be sure, there remains in the popular mind, as well as in the humanities and some social sciences (excluding anthropology), a myth of primeval matriarchy. This view is a survival of a nineteenth-century belief, most exhaustively articulated by J. J. Bachofen in 1861 in *Das Mutterrecht*, that women's invention of agriculture gave rise to a cult of the Mother Goddess and a long period of female domination. Drawing on classical studies, rather than cross-cultural investigation, Bachofen set women's rule as the very cornerstone of civilization, the first emergence from savage anarchy. Unfortunately, no evidence for a period of matriarchy—or even for *a* matriarchy—has emerged from the ethnographic or archeological records (Webster 1975).

The myth of primitive matriarchy has often gone hand in hand with the doctrine of the biological basis of male domination. (This is curious, since the two beliefs are mutually contradictory.) From the biological or, more recently, sociobiological perspective, female subordination is an inevitable result of 2 million years of evolution that focused on—who else?—Man the Hunter. Women were too busy birthin' babies and keeping the home fires burning in the old cave to have much to do with anything as momentous as the survival of the fittest. The end result of all that evolving has been a demure and passive female forever barred from politics by her physical inferiority and lack of testosterone. At best, women could gain authority in the domestic sphere, while the public sphere remained off limits.

According to many feminists, the male domination bias has been more a result of male domination of anthropology than of any inherent character of gender itself—despite the fact that many of the influential researchers of the first generation of professional anthropologists in the United States were women. Margaret Mead and Ruth Benedict, among others, were successful in turning the question of gender from biology to socialization and in establishing cultural relativism as a major tenet of anthropology. However, women soon virtually disappeared from both ethnographies and from theory, where they were usually treated, if they were treated at all, as adjuncts to males. Despite its aspirations to be culture-free, anthropology, it turned out, was as subject to the pervasive sexism of Western culture as any other academic discipline. A major problem that revisionist researchers have encountered in searching the ethnographic record is the relative paucity of detailed information on women. The same omission is found in textbooks. As Sandra Morgen (1989: 10) observes, "Dominant anthropological understandings of gender are revealed not only by where anthropology textbooks and theory do discuss women and/or gender, but also by where those discussions are significantly absent. Two of the most striking examples of this absence are in our teaching of human evolution and of stratification, power and political economy." (The first edition of this book, for example, barely mentioned women.)

The emergence of feminist scholarship over the last twenty years has challenged many of anthropology's fundamental assumptions while helping fill out the record with new ethnographic data. Little of this material is overtly political, that is, having to do specifically with group decision making and leadership. However, in a wider sense, the vast majority of it is political, because the dominant thrust of feminist scholarship to date has been on power, especially the relative power of the sexes. Is male domination really universal? If so, what are its causes? If not, how did it evolve? What are the specific contexts that encourage or discourage gender differences in status and power? Is male domination really a meaningful concept?

As in any revolution in thinking, the questioning of anthropological assumptions about gender have intermixed both scholarship and ideology. Whether one believes that gender inequality is a universal or not, or what one believes to be the causes of male domination, both have profound implications in how one perceives the world and for how one recommends changing society. So far there is hardly any point on which feminist anthropologists would agree. But already one important implication is clear: Gender can no longer be ignored; it must be considered "an analytical category—which, like race, ethnicity, class or caste, tends to be crucial in the construction of both group identity and structures of power in society" (Morgen 1989: 8).

Several themes have emerged. First, the Man-the-Hunter perspective on human evolution has been severely challenged. Second, the biological underpinnings of sexual inequality have been questioned. Third, concepts such as status and male dominance have been brought under intense scrutiny, revealing far more complexity than has previously been recognized. Fourth, causes of gender differentials in power have been sought in cross-cultural studies of subsistence, property ownership, distribution, and the like. Fifth, the historical development of male dominance has been intensely studied by a group of Marxist anthropologists. Finally, a group of researchers, influenced by Clifford Geertz, has focused on the cultural construction of gender—that is, on male and female as symbols that fit within the entire symbol structure of the society.

MAN THE HUNTER VERSUS WOMAN THE GATHERER

The standard theory for the evolution of *homo sapiens* places the emphasis on cooperative hunting of big game. The advantages of freeing the hands to use tools in killing and butchering resulted in bipedalism, which led to greater efficiency in hunting and an increased dependence on animal protein. In a complex feedback process, selection for new skills generated larger brains; this in turn brought about more cooperatively and complexly organized hunts. Larger brains meant longer periods of immaturity for children; women were saddled with protracted child care that effectively prevented them from hunting or traveling extensive distances. Thus dependent, women were required to remain at home base, foraging a bit and taking care of children, while men elaborated their tool kits and evolved incipient civilization out of hunting strategy.

Frances Dahlberg (1981: 1) refers to this traditional Man-the-Hunter schema as a "just-so story," not that different from other myths that explain the origins of language, tool use, civilization, and so forth. Women are represented as utterly passive. The selective pressure of evolution is almost entirely on the male.

Offering an alternative perspective, Sally Slocum (1975) points out that hominid evolution is based on a relatively small amount of data, leaving gaping holes in the evidence to be filled in with hidden, and often unconscious, assumptions that cannot help but be influenced by the male-dominated culture from which such ideas emerge. For example, the earliest tools, no more than barely worked rocks, have been assumed to be hand axes when they could just as well have been used as aids in women's gathering and in preparation of plant foods. Cooperative hunting of large game, which is claimed as the initial kick in human evolution, could only have occurred after brain size had begun to increase. On the other hand, the postulated pair-bonding of one man taking care of one woman could only have taken place after the hunting adaption was already well established. Initially an increase in child dependency would have led to a pair bond between mother and offspring, not man and woman.

An alternative schema would give Woman the Gatherer at least equal weight in evolution with Man the Hunter. Natural selection obviously operated on both sexes. The lengthening of infant dependency would have placed a premium on a mother's skills in finding food for herself and her young. Far from being dependent on their male consorts, women may have supplied the bulk of the food for their families, as they do in many hunting-gathering societies today. Gathering is hardly a simple process; it involves finding and identifying edible plants, a knowledge of seasonal variation, a good sense of geography and weather, the development of containers for carrying food and babies at the same time, and the invention of tools and techniques for food preparation. Longer gestation and more difficult births would also require greater social skills and communication among women which would select for larger brains. Women, far from being the passive recipients of evolution, were certainly as active as men.

Another version of the Man-the-Hunter concept comes from sociobiology, where it is acknowledged that both women and men were instrumental in evolution, but that natural selection led to different evolutionary strategies for each sex, resulting in male dominance. The selfish gene school theorizes that from an evolutionary point of view all organisms, including humans, are basically containers for genes, and that there is an innate drive to spread one's own genetic program as widely as possible. The best male strategy is to have as many partners as possible, leading to aggression and competition. Women, on the other hand, have a larger genetic investment in their own offspring, so there would be a greater tendency toward long-term relationships and cooperation (Draper 1985). This argument is buttressed by studies of higher primates. Some species of baboons show marked sex role differentiation and strong dominance hierarchies, and many others, such as gorillas and orangutans, also reveal significant sexual dimorphism.

Feminists, however, point out that, once again, male biases are evident. In chimpanzees, humans' closest evolutionary relatives, there is little sexual dimorphism, and males compete for females not by aggression and dominance but through sociability—through mutual grooming and sharing food. Even among baboons, the most notoriously hierarchical of primate species, environment may have more to do with behavior than instinct. Among some forest-living baboons, the political decisions on troop movements are made by older females, and, though males posture and threaten when confronted by a predator, they are also the first to find safety in the trees if the threat persists, leaving females encumbered with infants to fend for themselves (Dahlberg 1981; Leibowitz 1975). In other words, the sociobiological argument often rests on which species one chooses to compare to humans.

Theorists have not yet settled on any particular evolutionary model, but it is already evident that the role of women must be considered equally to that of men, and that this consideration devastates traditional notions of Man the Hunter as the primary force in human evolution. Similarly, the consideration of the female role in evolution makes theories of male dominance based on Darwinian concepts questionable at best.

BIOLOGICAL DIFFERENCES IN GENDER

Differences in gender are indisputable, though the existence of innate behavioral differences remains hotly controversial. There are two basic perspectives: First, the culturalogical school would see the entire explanation in the socialization of children into role behavior proper to their cultures. Second, the prepared learning school would assume a biologically based propensity to learn and to perpetuate role behaviors peculiar to each sex (Draper 1985).

Psychobiological evidence comes from four sources: studies of cross-cultural uniformities, observations of infant behavior, comparisons with higher primates, and descriptions of physiological characteristics. A cross-cultural study revealed that young boys are consistently more aggressive than young girls, although in only 20 percent of the sample were boys actually socialized for aggressiveness. Also, observations of children raised together in Israeli kibbutzim, where, supposedly, socialization was the same for both sexes, revealed that boys were more aggressive and competitive and girls more integrative (affectionate, willing to share, cooperative, etc.). Research on infant behavior, ostensibly prior to socialization (including in orphanages where little socialization took place), revealed a similar pattern. Throughout mammalia, including the primates, males are normally more aggressive, though there are exceptions, as noted earlier. The muscular strength of women is 55 to 65 percent that of men. Males seem to have higher energy potentials and females lower metabolic rates. Early brain differentiation suggests diverse behavioral potentials by sex. Androgyny in girls (prenatal exposure to male hormones) leads to tomboy behavior. Finally, the association of the male hormone testosterone with aggressiveness is well-known (Parker and Parker 1979).

Each of these lines of evidence is disputable. It has been pointed out, for example, that sexual socialization of infants really begins at birth, often in very subtle ways. Intersex children, lacking an enzyme for converting testosterone and therefore growing up with ambiguous genitalia, after puberty easily assumed the male identities for which they were socialized. The study that found that prenatal androgyny led to tomboy behavior in girls has been challenged, and there are biologists who strongly contest evidence of prenatal brain differentiation between the sexes. Even muscular strength and endurance are affected by environment; differences in performance levels in sports are narrowing rapidly as women receive training and encouragement similar to male athletes (Lott 1987).

The jury is still out on the subject. However, even if there are prepatterned behavioral differences between the sexes—males being more agonistic (aggressive, exploratory, hierarchical, and competitive) and females being more socially integrative and nurturent (Parker and Parker 1979)—all behavior in humans is filtered through culture. Even if such propensities do exist, the degree to which they are manifested is determined by culture and individual psychology. The wide variety of sex role behaviors among societies and within any particular society testifies to the extent of human malleability, no matter what innate predispositions there may be.

The problem comes not from admitting possible behavioral differences derived from biologically based propensities, but rather from the logical (or illogical) jump to male domination. There is nothing whatsoever in these hypothesized innate differences to suggest gender stratification or the superiority of one sex over another (in fact, males respond worse to stress than females, are more vulnerable to physical and psychological illness throughout their lives, and have a lower life expectancy than females). The assumption that physical strength alone or higher testosterone leads to dominance is ridiculous; almost nowhere does strength or raw aggression imply leadership. In fact, leaders in many societies are selected for sociability, for sharing, and for their intuitive understanding of others, all traits that are supposedly feminine.

Also, if stratification or male dominance were biologically based, we would expect it to be universal, and it is not. As we will see, there are many examples of egalitarian societies at both the foraging and horticultural levels.

The debate over the biological bases of sexual stratification was ardently fought throughout the 1970s; presently it is pretty much a dead issue outside of sociobiology. Feminist anthropologists have gone on to more complex, and more fruitful, questions.

WOMEN AND POWER: THE CROSS-CULTURAL EVIDENCE

Although no matriarchies exist, the range of female statuses among prestate cultures is extensive. The three societies described next are more representative of the extremes than of any norm, but they do reveal how variable sexual stratification can be.

The Iroquois

Among the Iroquois, a confederacy of five culturally related tribes in the northeastern United States, women had higher status and more power than in just about any group known. This might seem odd, because the Iroquois were extremely warlike, exactly the type of group we might associate with a male supremacist complex. However, a number of factors contributed to the power of women.

The Iroquois were mainly observed in the eighteenth and nineteenth centuries, so their society had already undergone considerable change due to contact with Europeans. Individual men or groups of men were away much of the time, often for a year or more, on extensive hunting or trapping trips, trading, or involved in warfare. Thus, in the local village units the women maintained continuity. Women provided most of the subsistence, through shifting cultivation of corn, beans, and squashes, in addition to many wild foods. The society was both matrilineal and matrilocal. Matrons arranged marriages. When a man married, he moved into his wife's longhouse, a large structure of bark and wood with many compartments connected by a central aisle. Each family in the lineage occupied a compartment, sharing a fire with several other families. Matrons presided over the lineage longhouses, so that a man had no power in the house in which he lived, and had to tread lightly lest he offend his wife's female kin, who could expel him if they were so inclined. Hereditary transmission of titles, rights, and property were all in the female line. The women had the power of life and death over prisoners.

However, according to Judith Brown (1975), neither women's contribution to subsistence nor matrilineality gave women their power; rather it was women's command of the economic organization of the tribe. Women not only controlled distribution of plant foods, both domestic and wild, but they also handled the distribution of animal foods from the men's hunts. The women preserved the meat and the matrons distributed it. Women thus had the power to provision hunts, councils, and war parties. Apparently, they could in some cases hinder or prevent a war by withholding supplies.

As a result, women, while lacking official political offices, had great informal political power. The highest ruling body of the League was a Council of Elders. Hereditary eligibility for office passed through the women. Iroquois matrons could raise or depose the ruling elders, could attend the high council, and could influence council decisions. They had occasional power over the conduct of warfare and the negotiation of treaties. When a chief died, the women held a meeting to select a new candidate; if the clan chiefs vetoed the selection, the women would meet again. Women also sent representatives to the public councils.

Even though the Iroquois can by no means be considered a matriarchy because men held all formal offices, the power of women was firmly institutionalized. Also note that such power was not confined to the domestic sphere but was equally evident in the public arena.

The Chipewyan

Almost at the opposite pole from the Iroquois were the Chipewyan of north central Canada. According to Henry S. Sharp (1981), women were, and are, devalued in this society. Reputedly, women were treated worse than in any other North American tribe.

Historically, about 90 percent of the Chipewyan diet was from flesh, mainly caribou, but also moose, musk-ox, small game, and fish. After contact with Europeans in 1715, they became increasingly involved in the fur trade, and by the end of the nineteenth century had adopted repeating rifles.

The low status of women would seem to be related to a strong division of labor and to the insignificant contribution of women to the food supply. Virtually all of the food was obtained by men. Women, however, did contribute significantly to subsistence; they had the job of processing the food, mainly the long, arduous task of drying meat and fish. As in most foraging societies, some sort of sharing was necessary for survival, but this was not automatic. In difficult times, preserved meat and fish had to be borrowed, but such borrowing was antithetical to the masculine ethic. Thus women were relegated this job, though borrowing bestowed no status.

Though women had low status and were treated accordingly, they were at the same time perceived to be possessors of great power, though of a negative sort. The roles of male and female were surrounded with complex symbolism. Men gained power through hunting. Women were potentially polluting, capable of destroying the efficacy of men's magical materials. A menstruating woman, for example, could destroy the magic of a sled dog harness by stepping over it. "To be female is to be power," observes Sharp (p. 227), "to be male is to acquire power. Men *may* have power but women *are* power just by being women." This symbolic power did not, however, translate into the ability to make group decisions or to lead.

The Agta

The mountain Agta of northeastern Luzon in the Philippines is the only known culture in which women routinely hunt large game.

Centuries ago all Agta may have been dependent on hunting, fishing, and gathering, though today the language group includes a great variety of life-styles, including horticulture, farming, trading, and wage labor. The mountain Agta, who have been least in contact with outsiders, eat animal protein almost daily. Wild pig, deer (both considered large game) and monkeys are commonly hunted with bow and arrow and machetes. Some forest plant food is also gathered, though they prefer to trade for corn, cassava, and sweet potatoes.

The sexual division of labor is modest; both women and men participate in virtually all subsistence activities. In at least two Agta groups, women are active hunters who hunt frequently, sometimes with other men or women but often alone. Women make their own arrows (though blacksmithing points is an exclusively male activity). Girls start hunting shortly after puberty and continue as long as they wish.

The anthropological belief that women never hunt is based on an ostensible incompatibility with childbearing and with nurturing infants. How is this solved among the Agta? Young children may be cared for by older siblings, grandparents, or other relatives. Sometimes the father takes care of the children. Women do not hunt in late pregnancy and the first few months of nursing; despite the small size of the settlements, there are sufficient women available to hunt. Women are also more frequently, and more aggressively, involved in trade, mainly of dried meat.

No formal or institutional authority exists, and group decisions are based on consensus, which includes, of course, the women. The Agta would appear to be a truly egalitarian culture (Estioko-Griffin and Griffin 1981).

The Agta challenge a number of assumptions about women's roles, not only the old truism about Man the Hunter but also the new emphasis on Woman the Gatherer. It is true that Agta women may be unique, but then, they may not be. It is quite possible that male-dominated anthropology has missed many other cases where women regularly hunt big game. Agta women certainly prove that the childbirth and child care limitation on hunting is a cultural constraint, not a biological one.

WHAT DOES THE STATUS OF WOMEN MEAN?

Universal male dominance and the lowly status of women have been assumed with little regard for what is meant by dominance or status. These concepts have many dimensions. Status may, among other things, mean either deferential treatment or actual power over resources and decision making (Brown 1975). Thus upper-class women in the romantic traditions of feudal Europe and Victorian England were given the highest status—idealized and placed on pedestals—but they had no real power. Status can refer to the rewards society offers certain people, to prestige, to power over others, to authority without coercive power, to official office, to control of resources, or to one's freedom or autonomy, and each of these has many permutations. Also, status is not isolated but is embedded in the many subsystems of a society, so there may be separate statuses for the spheres of kinship, subsistence, politics, economics, religion, ideology, and so forth. Status in religion may not carry over into the economic sphere. Status may be fluid, changing throughout one's life and often changing from one situation to another. Indeed, the attempt by anthropologists to assess status—especially some universal concept of status—may be ethnocentric, devoid of meaning within the society to which it is applied.

This multivariate approach was validated by an extensive cross-cultural study by Martin King Whyte (1978), who examined ninety-three pre-industrial cultures, using fifty-two variables associated with gender status, such as sex of political leaders, division of domestic work, and physical punishment of the spouse. He concludes that

One can no longer assume that there is such a thing as *the* status of women cross-culturally. Nor can one search for *the best* indicator of the status of women, or for *the key* variable that affects the status of women. Instead, one has to start with a very different assumption: that there is no coherent concept of the status of women that can be identified cross-culturally (p. 170).

In other words, status is not a universal, but can only be understood within specific contexts, not merely particular societies but particular subsystems within those societies.

Whyte's findings on male dominance were similar. There was considerable variation in dominance both between and within societies, ranging from absolute male supremacy to broad equality between sexes. Though no matriarchies were found, there were spheres of activity within which women had power over men.

Women's Power and the Distribution of Resources

Such studies have added to the complexity of the issue, but they have not stopped researchers from defining particular types of status, such as social prestige or power in group decision making, and seeking key variables that would explain cross-cultural differences.

Male dominance is often related to the division of labor by sex. Cross-cultural studies reveal that women are commonly assigned such tasks as the gathering of food and fuel, grinding grain, water carrying, food preservation, cooking, pottery making, weaving, basket manufacture, dairy production, and laundering—in other words, activities performed near the home involving monotonous operations that can be interrupted and resumed. Men are more likely to engage in activities that require travel, danger, and sometimes sudden bursts of energy, such as hunting large game, warfare, lumbering, trapping, mining, herding, fishing, and long-distance trade. Such division of labor seems to be more closely related to the demands of motherhood than to size, strength, or innate propensities. Tasks that are dangerous or remove women for long periods from home may be perceived as incommensurate with the demands of childbearing and child care (Coontz and Henderson 1986: 115; Dahlberg 1981: 13; Schlegel 1977: 35).

These are only statistical probabilities, however, not universals. There is virtually no job that is not performed by women somewhere. Foragers such as the !Kung and Mbuti pygmies seem little restricted by childbearing in their extensive travels. As we have seen, Agta women regularly hunt big game. Among the nineteenth-century Plains Ojibway and in the African kingdom of Dahomey (now Benin), women were warriors. Often women are assigned the heaviest jobs, such as clearing the jungle or carrying water and firewood. In northern California, most of the shamans were women.

In any case, there is no intrinsic reason to value one set of jobs over another, and as Karen Sacks (1979: 89) points out, there is something ethnocentric about the assumption that all cultures rank economic activities; this is most common in capitalist inegalitarian societies. The division of labor by sex may become a basis of sexual stratification, but it cannot be the sole explanation.

It is sometimes suggested that the division of labor does not determine the status of women but rather women's contribution to the subsistence of the group. Cross-cultural studies, including different levels of social complexity, reveal that women contribute on the average about 30 to 45 percent of the food (Dahlberg 1981: 14–15). However, this can vary from women providing virtually none of the food (as among some Eskimos) to upward of 70 percent (the !Kung). Thus, the commonsense view that degree of contribution to subsistence determines status is wrong; cross-cultural comparison reveals no such pattern (Whyte 1978: 169).

Ernestine Friedl (1975, 1990) hypothesizes that power does not rest on the contribution to subsistence per se, but rather on the exchange of goods outside the family. Control of public exchange, not control of domestic production, is the key because such exchange creates the obligations and alliances that are at the center of political relations. The greater men's monopoly on the distribution of scarce resources, the greater their dominance over women.

This is most evident in less complex societies. In hunting-gathering groups, plant foods are distributed only within the family, while animal protein is shared with the entire band. Because, virtually always, only men hunt big game, the range should extend from egalitarianism among groups where there is little hunting to extreme male dominance where hunting is the primary means of subsistence. Among those groups in which women and men both hunt and gather communally, such as the Washo Indians of North America, women and men are roughly equal. In groups in which women and men each collect their own plant food, but men supply some meat, such as the Hazda of Tanzania, there is a slightly greater tendency to male dominance. The subordination of women is even more pronounced if there is a sharp division of labor by sex, with females gathering and men hunting, as among the Tiwi of Australia. Finally, in societies such as the Eskimo where men supply virtually the entire food supply through hunting, women have a very low status.

When this theory is applied to industrial society, jobs that do not give women control over productive resources obviously do not garner power (though, this is true of men's jobs, too).

Friedl has probably put her finger on one of many influences on male domination. However, as a universal theory, it doesn't work. Whyte did not find any single variable determining gender status in his cross-cultural study (though, his sample of hunting-gathering societies was relatively small, and he may have slighted African examples where the correlation between status, economic contribution, and control of property is more clear [Duley and Sinclair 1986]). There are also some rather blatant exceptions to her theory. As we have seen, among the Chipewyan the women distributed the meat, yet male domination was very pronounced. There also may be considerable variation within particular groups; the Eskimo women described by Jean Briggs (1970) do not seem nearly as subservient as Friedl claims for Eskimos in general.

Domestic/Public, Nature/Culture

The belated recognition that male dominance is neither a universal nor a singular characteristic, the same for all societies where it is manifested, has led to a search for the structural and cultural factors that give rise to gender differences. Michelle Rosaldo (1974) noted that men often control the public domain where the broader political issues of society are decided, while women are confined to a domestic domain largely concerned with the interests of their own families.

It is true that in preindustrial societies women's activities were most often confined within the context of the family or the lineage. This can imply considerable power, however, especially in matrilineal systems

where inheritance of property takes place through the women and where
women run local lineage affairs. If matrilocality is combined with
matrilineality, the man may have little power in the home where he lives
with his wife and inlaws, as we have seen among the Iroquois. Among
the Hopi of the American Southwest, women control the lineage pueblos,
so that men must exercise their authority through religion and through
community councils. From this point of view, politics, which deals with
public decision making and the public allocation of resources and
authority, would belong to the men's sphere. This perspective does not
deny women power, but suggests that each gender has its own sphere of
power.

This is certainly true in many societies, but the domestic/public
dichotomy is by no means universal. Women often do exercise power in
the public sphere, for example, queens and female prime ministers. The
existence of a women in an official position of power does not necessarily
raise the status of all women in that society; more often, formal power
by women serves only an elite group or maintains a patriarchy. Also, in
societies oriented around kinship, it may be very difficult to distinguish
the domestic from the public. Often the family and the lineage are the
mechanisms through which public decisions are manifested. In peasant
villages, distinctions between public and private may be all but irrelevant,
because the real locus of power—where decisions are made about land
tenure, taxes, war, and education—is outside the peasant community
altogether (Hammond and Jablow 1976). The private/public distinction
would seem to be most clear-cut in state societies, but even in patrilineal
states such as China, women moving from their natal homes at marriage
may maintain lineage ties that bind them into a wider political world
(Moore 1988). Note the paucity of information on women's participation
in public politics, partially because few researchers have been looking
for it and partially because such influence may be less formal, less overt,
than that of men.

Another dichotomy that has been suggested as useful for explaining
male dominance is nature/culture (Ortner 1974). This emerged from an
approach, influenced by the works of Claude Lévi-Strauss and Clifford
Geertz, that views gender as basically a symbolic construction that
closely intermeshes with the other symbol systems of a society. From
this perspective, females are associated with nature mainly because of
their procreativity and, in many societies, their occupation of tilling the
earth. They are bound up within such symbol sets as earth, moon,
planting, and fecundity. Men, on the other hand, are enmeshed in the
symbol sets of culture: sun, language, law, architecture, and so forth.

Such symbolic definitions tend to place women in the domestic sphere and men in the public sphere.

There are problems here, too, of course. Many societies do relate women symbolically to nature and men to culture, but many do not; some societies relate men to nature and women to culture (in the United States it is much more common to refer to men as beasts or animals, and to believe that their warfare, hunting, and football emerge from feral instincts). And, despite Lévi-Strauss's contention that the culture/nature dichotomy is embedded in the very structure of the human mind, many peoples do not make the distinction at all.

These insights may be valuable in the analysis of some particular cultures, and certainly the idea of the cultural construction of gender is a sophisticated approach, replete with possibilities. However, as anthropology has found time and time again, the reduction to simple dichotomies, no matter how extensively they may be elaborated, tends to obscure the enormous intricacy and complexity of human behavior.

Residence Rules, Socialization, and Violence

General explanations of gender stratification that rely on a single variable, whether nature of subsistence, distribution of public goods, or motherhood, have not been particularly successful; there are too many exceptions. Marc Howard Ross (1986) offers a multivariate explanation based on a cross-cultural survey of 90 preindustrial societies. The inevitable problems with any such survey are, of course, compounded by the lack of material specifically concerned with female participation and with women's ownership or allocation of resources. It was necessary not merely to code for titled offices, attendance at meetings, but also for private conversations, indirect influence, and control over information.

Female power could not be measured along a single dimension but had to be, at the least, broken into two independent categories: the first is female involvement in group decision making; the second, politically important positions or organizations controlled by women. There was no significant overlap between these two categories; each emerged in different societies.

Women's control of organizations and positions of power was most closely correlated with socioeconomic complexity, and seemed to be part of a more general social and economic differentiation. However, such organizations did not necessarily proffer higher status or more power on women.

Women's involvement in group decision making corresponded strongly with the organization of men; patrilineal kinship and other strong fraternal organizations had a negative effect on female status. Postmarital residence was also significant; women who remained within their own communities after marriage had greater power. When early socialization of the male was warm and affectionate there was little conflict between genders, with a resultant relative equality. Finally, in situations of high internal conflict, women were encouraged to be politically active in negotiations and as peacemakers; where internal violence was low, there was little stimulus for them to act outside the domestic sphere (in situations of high external violence, women were relatively excluded from politics).

Such cross-cultural studies, while incipient, suggest that differential female status and power can be explained not by a single universal cause, but by a number of factors working together.

THE HISTORICAL DEVELOPMENT OF GENDER STRATIFICATION

Many researchers have noted that cross-cultural surveys and structural explanations suffer from a common defect: Such studies are synchronic. They do not consider the crucial variable of time. A group of mainly Marxist-influenced scholars has attempted to correct that deficiency by providing the historical context of gender stratification.

It was not Karl Marx but Frederick Engels who provided the most detailed schema for the cultural evolution of the exploitation of women. According to Engels, matrilineality (or "mother right") emerged out of a period of primitive anarchy and promiscuity. Engels saw this early matrilineality as egalitarian. Property, the basis of all power, was owned communally, so that no one had control over others. With the emergence of private property, men overthrew matrilineality and installed the patriarchal family, introducing differences of wealth both within and between families. Excluded from control of property, women found themselves in a subordinate position. Women produced only for domestic use, freeing men to produce for consumption by the group or for trade. Technology, which was controlled by men, exacerbated these inequalities. Thus male control of private property resulted in female subordination.

Eleanor Leacock (1981) develops Engels' ideas. She postulates an egalitarian stage among foraging (hunter-gatherer) societies. Present-day foragers that are not egalitarian, according to Leacock, have been contaminated by centuries of contact with Western stratified society. In early foraging bands, which were highly flexible to take advantage of variations in food supply, there was a direct relation between production and consumption, with no market system to intervene. No one had the power to control or withhold resources. Each individual enjoyed autonomy; each person was responsible for his or her own activities. Group decisions were arrived at by consensus. Domestic/public dichotomies had not yet emerged. There was no necessity for women to be especially responsive to the needs of men, or vice versa.

As long as the public and private spheres were not differentiated, societies remained egalitarian. Thus, some precolonial horticultural societies, as well as foragers, were egalitarian. However, when goods began to be produced for exchange as well as for consumption, new economic ties undermined the ties of the collective household. Control of production was removed from the hands of the producer, leading to exploitation. Women lost control of their own production, which was taken over by men. Because of the constraints imposed by childbearing, a sexual division of labor developed in which women became the small-scale producers and dispensers of services within male-dominated households. Women were effectively pushed out of the public arena altogether. With the rise of capitalism, sexual stratification became even more entrenched because men, almost exclusively, control the means of production and thus can further exploit women as wage laborers.

The Bari

The Bari, tropical horticulturalists of Colombia and Venezuela, illustrate this process. Despite 400 years of successfully fighting off settlers and missionaries, they retained an internal social organization that was egalitarian; their language even lacks a term for chief. Nobody, men or women, could give orders to anyone else and expect to be obeyed. Lacking a concept of private property, they shared equal access to resources. Group decisions were made by consensus by all those men and women affected by the decision. There was a minimal division of labor—cooking, child care, housebuilding, fishing, and planting were done by both sexes—and the work of no individual or group was considered more important than that of others.

All of this has changed rapidly since 1964 when the combined pressures of oil explorers, settlers, and missionaries forced a truce that enmeshed the Bari in the processes of Western capitalism. To better deal with the people, the Colombian government officially recognized a group of chiefs or *caciques*—all men, of course. Though traditional Bari had no concept of surplus production, they were brought into the market economy and encouraged to produce manioc and plantains for sale; males came in to control the cash produced by these sales, creating a basis for male exploitation of female labor. Wage labor, available only to men, provided the cash for manufactured goods, such as machetes and clothes, thus making women dependent on the men for the new necessities. Collective fishing, a task shared in the past by both men and women, was disrupted because men were away much of the time on wage labor jobs. Fishing thus became the province of a few men with weighted nets and motorboats, excluding women from a primary subsistence activity. Women's forest-collecting has been diminished by the availability of manufactured foodstuffs, purchased with men's earnings. These, plus many other changes, are rapidly moving the culture from egalitarianism to male domination (Buenaventura-Posso and Brown 1980).

*   *   *

Leacock's theory is extremely important in providing a diachronic model for the development of gender inequality. This adds a new, and crucial, dimension to the debates. The theory is also valuable in showing how sexual stratification may be related to class stratification in general, and the important role of colonial contact in introducing inequality among foragers and horticulturalists. However, there are some real problems. Even though there is no evidence of a general matrilineal stage of human cultural evolution, as Engels claimed, neither is there such evidence for a general egalitarian stage, as Leacock claims. Many contemporary or recent-past hunter-gatherers are not sexually egalitarian, and relatively few horticultural societies might make claim to equal status among the sexes. Leacock's claim that all nonegalitarian foragers were contaminated by contact or that they were misdescribed by biased males is not convincing. Also, male dominance clearly exists in societies lacking private property. Whyte (1978: 165n) cross-culturally tested the relation between private property and female status and found only a weak correlation; relationships between status and other aspects of society were stronger. Ownership, or nonownership, of private property was not a critical factor in the status of women.

Karen Sacks (1979) offers a similar, but somewhat more complex schema, based on kinship. Foraging societies with a communal mode of production make little distinction between the roles of spouse and sibling in terms of production and ownership. Because property is owned by everyone equally, there is no claim of one person or group on another, and women live their lives among their close kinfolk as well as their own families. However, when the communal mode gives way to the kin corporate mode of production—in which ownership is claimed by lineages or clans—sisters and wives are separated into two distinct productive roles. In patrilineal and patrilocal societies, sisters share in the ownership of their lineage's resources but are removed from the exploitation of those resources. Wives, on the other hand, working within the confines of their husband's lineage, are producers but not owners. The separation of women from ownership of their own production gives husbands in particular, and males in general, power over them. Class societies, growing out of these kin "patricorporations," put the ownership of production in the hands of male-dominated elites, thus even further demeaning the role of women.

Sacks' model is subject to some of the same criticisms applicable to Leacock's, mainly that there is no evidence for a universal phase of egalitarianism in the evolution of cultures. However, Sacks' emphasis on kinship and on residence after marriage fits well with cross-cultural studies that show a correlation between patrilineality, patrilocality, and the subordination of women. Also, Sacks has pointed out the importance of women's culturally assigned roles—wife, sister, daughter—in gender stratification.

Christine Gailey (1987) applies these ideas to a complex historical analysis of the Tongan Islands of Polynesia, arguing that sexual stratification and class stratification parallel one another, but derive from different dynamics. For Gailey, state formation is an ongoing process, one which leads to an increasing decline in women's status and authority. Gailey emphasizes that in Tonga the communal mode of production that preceded the state did not produce egalitarianism. However, the woman's position as sister was traditionally more valued than that of wife, with the result that women remained in a protected position and maintained their importance in production and in the control of resources. Women were also the only creators of wealth, such as carefully crafted mats, bark cloth, and baskets. Two processes of capitalist penetration shifted the society toward increased stratification. First, commodity production and exchange transferred control to men and turned women's labor into a commodity. Second, Christian missionaries aggressively pushed for male domination while providing the moral and supernatural legitimization for such domination.

Such studies reveal that structural analysis alone is not sufficient to account for female subordination. Stratification—whether of status, rank, class, or gender—takes place within history. Feminist writers such as

Leacock, Sacks, and Gailey have provided a major first step in delineating the particular factors involved in the evolution of male dominance.

SUMMING UP

The feminist challenge in anthropology commenced only about two decades ago, so it should be no surprise that it has come up with few solid answers. However, its contribution in refuting accepted dogmas and in offering promising new directions is already evident. Among these contributions:

- The Man the Hunter myth of evolution can no longer be supported. Women had as much influence on the processes of physical evolution as men.

- It remains controversial whether or not there are significant biological bases for male and female differences in behavior. However, even if there are innate predispositions—men being more agonistic and women more integrative—these are filtered through culture and, in any case, they are an unlikely explanation for gender stratification.

- Neither status nor male dominance can be clearly defined cross-culturally. These concepts mean different things in different societies, and often there may be considerable variation among the subsystems of a single society.

- Even if, for analytic purposes, we hypothesize universal male political dominance, this is empirically false. There are many societies that are sexually egalitarian, such as the mountain Agta, the Mbuti pygmies, and, until recently, the Bari and the !Kung.

- Women's power must be measured along two divergent lines: (1) control of organizations and positions of power; and (2) involvement in group decision making. Each of these correlates with different factors in the society.

- Gender stratification cannot be predicted either from division of labor or from women's contribution to subsistence. However, in many cases (but not all), there is a correlation between women's political power and the degree to which women control resources distributed outside the family.

- Postulated dichotomies that place women in the domestic domain and men in the public domain, or which associate women with nature and men with culture, may have some value in analyzing particular societies but are not valid cross-culturally.

- As we would expect, matrilineality is more closely associated with female equality than is patrilineality. However, the marriage residence rule may be even more important; women who move into their husband's lineage after marriage may have to abandon their protected status as sisters to assume, almost entirely, a male-dominated status of wife.

- Although there is no evidence for egalitarianism as a universal primary stage of political evolution, it does appear that the development of gender stratification is closely related to the emergence of corporate kin groups and the state. In each case, the removal of women from control of their own production appears to be a crucial factor.

Many other trends are already visible. Attention is turning from concern for women's oppression to methods of resistance. Such resistance may be confrontational or even violent—in Nicaragua, women made up 30 percent of the revolutionary forces against the Somoza dictatorship— or it may be of the everyday sort (discussed in Chapter 10). Gossip, censure, ridicule, and ostracism may be important political tools controlled by women in other contexts. In addition, women may control networks of information and possess the ability to mold public opinion (Moore 1988; Hammond and Jablow 1976). Anthropological studies of women in industrialized cultures should reveal more about the relation between capitalism and gender stratification. It is possible, for example, that an initial trend toward increasing male dominance is later countered by a trend toward egalitarianism. Most important, perhaps, ethnographers, both men and women, are now looking seriously at gender in a way they never did before.

SUGGESTED READINGS

Dahlberg, Frances, ed. *Woman the Gatherer* (New Haven: Yale University Press, 1981). A very accessible collection of readings focusing on women in hunting-gathering societies. The first two articles challenge the Man the Hunter version of human evolution, followed by women-focused ethnographies on the Agta, Australian aborigines, the Mbuti pygmies, and the Chipewyan.

Gailey, Christine Ward. *Kinship to Kingship: Gender Hierarchy and State Formation in the Tongan Islands* (Austin: University of Texas Press, 1987). The most detailed ethnographic analysis to date of the subordination of women during the processes of state formation. Gailey shows how, over a 300-year period, gender stratification and class stratification developed together, though from different internal dynamics.

Leacock, Eleanor Burke. *Myths of Male Dominance* (New York: Monthly Review Press, 1981). This collection of essays, from over thirty years, is a good introduction to one of the foremost feminist scholars in anthropology. Leacock's theory of the evolution of male dominance is clearly articulated.

Schlegel, Alice, ed. *Sexual Stratification: A Cross-Cultural View* (New York: Columbia University Press, 1977). A systematic attempt to bring together the various threads of feminist anthropological theory as it existed in the mid-1970s, this anthology includes a variety of studies, ranging from the Sudan to Yugoslavia.

Whyte, Martin King. *The Status of Women in Preindustrial Societies* (Princeton, N.J.: Princeton University Press, 1978). This is the most extensive cross-cultural statistical analysis of women's status to date. Using a sample of ninety-three cultures, Whyte concludes that male dominance and status are highly variable concepts.

An American naval vessel in a Japanese Harbor in the nineteenth century. The
capitalist world economy was spread through trade and military might.

Chapter Nine

Anthropology in the World System

Within political anthropology's first three decades, field-workers were able to generate their own categories, their own vocabularies, and their own theories without much reference to what was going on outside the discipline. The functionalist studying the Nuer or the action theorist observing the political manipulations of an individual had little need for the megatheories even then emerging in the fields of economics and political science. During the 1970s and 1980s, however, it became impossible to ignore the fact that virtually all the societies that anthropologists researched were embedded in larger systems. Because the societies that anthropologists normally studied were within so-called developing countries, theories of development needed to be taken into account. Two dominant perspectives had evolved under the rubrics of *modernization theory* and *dependency theory*. (Theory is a misnomer, for these are really very broad paradigms within which exist a number of competing theories.)

MODERNIZATION THEORY

Until after World War II there was little concept of what is today commonly known as the developing (or underdeveloped) world because most of the countries now placed in that category were colonies. They were not supposed to develop. Their goals were, quite overtly, to supply raw materials, cheap labor, and status to the mother countries of which they were extensions. As these countries gained their autonomy through the 1960s, the idea that they should develop, at least in the sense of reducing poverty, became an article of faith in the First World. Aiding this process was partially altruistic, but, like the Marshall Plan that helped rebuild Europe, it was also a matter of practicality; development would undercut the appeal of communism among the poor nations, as well as provide resources and markets for the United States.

The group that came to be known as modernization theorists used what at first appears to be a commonsense approach. Underdevelopment was perceived as a sort of primal condition; it was, virtually by definition, the normal situation of a society before it began to industrialize. As countries began to develop a modern sector they would become dual societies, one modernizing and one traditional. The modern sector would take off, leaving the traditional sector behind. Simon Kuznets (1955), with his Kuznets's Curve—a mathematical graph—demonstrated that income inequality would increase as the two sectors drew apart. However, based on historical data from the West, once per capita income reached about $700 (1960 dollars), there would be a decrease in inequality, that is, income would become more evenly distributed as the poor began to participate in the modern sector. According to this perspective, the challenge was simply to expand the modern sector until it engulfed the traditional sector, then the country would be developed.

So how was this to occur? To seek an answer, some scholars examined how the Western industrial democracies did it. Supposedly, if we could figure out the steps that we went through over two hundred years, the process in developing countries could be deliberately speeded up. As articulated by W. W. Rostow (1960) development could be divided into five stages. First was traditional society, characterized by a low level of technology, a high concentration of resources in agriculture, and a low ceiling on productivity. In the second stage the basic preconditions for development are set: An effective centralized national state and the spread of the belief in economic progress. During this transition period, capital is mobilized, trade increases, technology develops, and the government begins to support economic growth. At a certain threshold, stage three, take-off, occurs, and the society kicks into high gear. From there it will drive to maturity (stage four) of its own momentum until stage five, an age of high mass-consumption (maturity?), is attained. (All this might sound uncomfortably familiar to anthropologists who recall nineteenth-century theories that postulated unilineal evolution leading from savagery to barbarism to civilization.)

While the causes of underdevelopment are seen as internal, the solutions would take place in the international marketplace. A country no longer had to wait for Rostow's stages to proceed of their own accord; the process could be helped along. After all, the developed countries had to invent all that machinery, amass all that capital, and create an entrepreneurial class out of nothing. If the First World could transfer those things to the Third World, the process of development would be enormously accelerated. Underdevelopment, from this point of view, is a matter of lacking something: the emphasis might be put on technology, capital, education, entrepreneurial spirit, or administrative ability. Much theorizing became the search for the missing factor; what was it that developing countries most lacked? Whatever, if these deficiencies could be provided through foreign aid and the investments of multinational corporations, then the countries would develop. The theory relied heavily on comparative advantage, the idea that each nation should do what it does best, whether that is producing coffee or automobiles, and share in the expertise of other nations through trade. Because the economic elite—the owners and managers—would belong to the modern sector, they would be the engines of development. Their profits would be put to work to create new production and new jobs, thus bringing the masses into the modern sector and raising their standard of living. Such modernization theory postulated a trickle-down process in which an increase in the wealth of the rich would raise those at the bottom. Objections were countered with the analogy that a rising tide—that is, a growing gross national product—raises all boats.

Logically, it should have worked, and, indeed, it seemed to be working. Between 1950 and 1975, hundred of billions of dollars and a great deal of expertise and technology were transferred to the Third World where, accordingly, per capita gross national product grew at an average rate of 3.4 percent per year, far faster than the First World had developed (Morawetz 1977).

Gradually it became evident that something was seriously wrong. The rising tide was lifting the expensive yachts a lot faster and a lot higher than the fishing trawlers—and the rowboats were sinking. A number of studies of income distribution revealed that the gap between the rich and the poor was widening, and in some cases the poor seemed to be getting poorer. This effect was seldom alleviated when the gross national product (GNP) reached some postulated level, as Kuznets had predicted (Brazil, with a per capita GNP of $1,640 by 1985, had achieved one of the worst income distributions in the world). In a hypothetical country, a GNP growth of 5 percent in a given year might mean that the very rich increased their wealth by 15 percent while the income of the masses declined. Also, one goal of the modernization theorists was to close the gap between the First World and the Third World; in reality, that gap has been widening at an extremely rapid rate.

Still, U.S. policy has been consistently based on one form or another of modernization theory, with conservatives arguing for transfers of capital, technology, and so on via multinational investment and liberals emphasizing such transfers via foreign aid. (Actually, U.S. foreign aid is not focused on development; 70 percent is either direct military aid or Economic Support Funds, designed to shore up five or six governments the United States considers essential to its national security.) The official U.S. version of modernization theory—emphasizing multinational investment, free trade, export agriculture, and an absolute minimum of government interference in the economy—was clearly articulated at an international economic meeting in Cancún, Mexico, in the early 1980s and has been embodied in such programs as the Caribbean Basin Initiative.

Social Differentiation and Social Mobilization

Much early modernization theory, insofar as it was derived from histories of the industrialized countries, seems crude by contemporary standards. However, some modernization theorists turned their attention to an empirical examination of the processes of change already visible within the Third World itself. In a series of books and articles, political sociologist S. N. Eisenstadt developed an alternative model of modernization. Far from unilineal development, Third World countries reveal a remarkable variety of development patterns, some absolutely contradictory to the stages theory. For example, there is often a negative correlation between the degree of industrial development and literacy, mass media, education, and the like; in many countries development is so concentrated that only a handful of the population share its benefits. Similarly, Rostow's school of modernization theory held that development required the breakdown of traditional inherited institutions, such as tribalism or kinship groups, whereas in many countries the maintenance of such groups is integral to economic progress. Disruption of such institutions is as likely to lead to disorganization and chaos as to modernization. Indeed, modernization may be analyzed as an unfolding of inherent traditional structures—tribes, lineages, ethnic groups, and secret societies— which may change functions and goals while actually increasing their cultural cohesiveness. (We have already seen an example of this in Cohen's analysis of the Creole elite of Sierra Leone.) The final objection to Rostow's theory is that very few Third World countries have attained takeoff, in the sense of industrial growth involving the majority of the population; Taiwan and South Korea may be the only exceptions.

According to Eisenstadt, the common core of modernization is social differentiation and social mobilization. The political sphere must be sufficiently differentiated from the religious sphere if the society is to be flexible enough to make the adjustments necessary to the constant change that is integral to the modernization process. In the Islamic countries modernization has been severely retarded because of the identity of conservative religious tradition with politics. Social mobilization refers to the process by which traditional social and psychological loyalties are broken down so that new rearrangements of society and economy may become possible. This does not mean that traditional structures cease to exist or that anomie is a necessary concomitant to modernization; rather, traditional groups may simply restructure themselves or reorient old structures toward new goals.

In relation to politics specifically, administrative centralization and political elites are crucial elements of the modernization process. Centralization requires, first of all, an ideological transformation in which at least some local loyalties are shifted to a national government, or, more likely, one in which traditional groups begin to perceive the benefits accruing to them through support of a national government. This requires establishment symbols—flags, national heroes, national origin myths, national enemies—which are flexible enough to relate many diverse groups to the center. Centralized government, which requires some sort of bureaucratic framework, calls forth new organs of political competition (such as factions, special interest groups, and political parties) which must develop new rules of the political game. These rules can range from democratic voting to the Bolivian-style coup. Modernization invariably begins with some sort of elite center—rich landowners, an entrepreneurial class, or the military. All too often, both economic and political modernization is restricted to this core group, resulting in a situation of internal colonialism in which a few small elites centered in one city exploit the rest of the country. In such patrimonial states, common to Southeast Asia and Latin America, the elitist monopoly on modernization and political process is established as a permanent condition. If modernization is to expand beyond these elites, it must proceed through ever-widening political socialization, as new groups and new strata of society are brought into the political process.

DEPENDENCY THEORY

Was the Mayan civilization of Mexico underdeveloped? How about the precontact Eskimo? Or the Bushmen of the Kalahari Desert of Africa who were hunter-gatherers until only a decade ago?

Such questions do not seem so much difficult to answer as simply absurd. Of course people who are culturally intact, economically self-sufficient, and well-adapted in their native environments are not underdeveloped. But this very absurdity reveals a fundamental problem with some modernization theory, which views underdevelopment as a primary condition characterized by a lack of technology, the entrepreneurial ethic, and capital. The Mayans, the Eskimo, and the Bushmen may indeed be considered underdeveloped today, but only because they have all been invaded by Europeans. Underdevelopment, then, is not a thing, not some sort of natural state. It is a relationship, specifically a relationship with the developed countries. Or, as L. R. Stavrianos puts it in his massive history of the Third World, *Global Rift* (1981):

[T]he underdevelopment of the Third World and the development of the First World are not isolated and discrete phenomena. Rather they are organically and functionally interrelated. Underdevelopment is not a primal or original condition, to be outgrown by following the industrialization course pioneered by Western nations. The latter are overdeveloped today to the same degree that the peripheral lands are underdeveloped. The states of developedness and underdevelopedness are but two sides of the same coin. (pp. 34–35)

This, in a nutshell, is dependency theory. The capitalist development of the First World caused the underdevelopment of the Third World. (That aspect of the modernization paradigm that emphasizes the positive effects of international capitalism is often called diffusion theory, because it postulates that it is through the spread of capitalism to the hinterlands that development takes place. Theories that emphasize the negative effects of international capitalism are grouped within the dependency paradigm.)

Dependency theory is usually dated to the early 1970s and viewed as a reaction to modernization theory. To a great extent, this is accurate. However, much of the initial formulation of dependency theory appeared as early as the 1940s when Raúl Prebisch and a group of economists from the United Nations Economic Commission for Latin America (ECLA) perceived a world system based on a center of industrialized countries and a periphery of underdeveloped countries. The Third World remained in poverty because of unequal exchange; the terms of trade in the international marketplace favored the developed countries. Far from there being a comparative advantage to world capitalism, poor countries had to sell raw materials at a low price to the rich countries which then returned manufactured goods at a high price. Not only was this situation unfair, but it was getting steadily worse. Whereas it might take 25 tons of raw sugar to purchase a tractor in 1960, twenty years later it might require 110 tons to buy an equivalent tractor. Also, most productive resources were taken up by the export sector so that little was left to raise the standard of living of the poor. The effects of export dependency are most notable in agriculture, where domestic food production declines as more and more food lands are put into production of cotton or coffee for export and more and more peasants are pushed off their land. At this point the problem was not seen to be capitalism per se but rather a conflict between international and domestic capitalism. Third World countries were prevented from developing domestic industrial and manufacturing capabilities because their products could not compete with similar goods coming from the First World, which were invariably cheaper and of higher quality.

Throughout the 1960s these studies would have a practical effect in influencing the economies of Latin American countries. Virtually all these countries, and many others throughout the Third World, turned to *import substitution* as a means to control the international market. Import substitution is a policy by which goods manufactured inside the country cannot be imported or can only be imported with the payment of prohibitively high tariffs; the idea is to encourage domestic investment, to develop indigenous entrepreneurs and skilled workers, and to reclaim the economy from foreign owners. Common markets, based on the European Common Market, were established in the various regions of Latin America to try to control trade. In retrospect, these policies were failures, though there is considerable disagreement over *why* they failed. From the modernization perspective, they failed because they interfered in the underlying logic of capitalism—the free flow of goods based on supply and demand. From a dependency perspective, they failed because they did not go far enough. Taiwan and South Korea, the two countries that have successfully developed to the point that they will soon enter the First World, both used import substitution and extensive government planning in the early stages, but they also employed a number of other changes such as massive land reform, universal access to education, government ownership of key industries, and redistribution of wealth before industrialization (not to mention hefty foreign aid from the United States because they were threatened by communism).

From the point of view of the later dependency theorists, the experiments failed because of the continuing faith that widespread development could take place within an international system dominated by capitalism. The new breed of dependency theorists were almost uniformly socialist (Chilcote 1984: 113), at least to the extent of believing that only through public ownership of major resources or through a degree of "de-linking" from the capitalist system could real development take place. Among these theorists, Immanuel Wallerstein has emerged as the most influential (or at least the most cited).

The World Capitalist System

There is a lack of time-depth, reminiscent of the structural-functionalists, in the writings of many of the early dependency theorists. Everyone, of course, recognized the economic distortions caused by colonialism, but few traced the system farther back, except in the general terms of Marxist theory. It was Immanuel Wallerstein (1974, 1980, 1989) who provided a minutely detailed account of the historical evolution of the world capitalist system and popularized the vocabulary for its structure.

In describing the past, Wallerstein uses the term *world* in a peculiar way. He speaks of early world empires based on conquest and exploitation through taxes and tribute, such as that of Rome and China. But these were fundamentally different from the world economy, based on structures of trade, dependence, and an international division of labor that emerged throughout the sixteenth century, centered in Europe. Unlike the world-empires of old, the new capitalist world economy placed economic power not in the hands of the rulers, but in the hands of the owners of the means of production. Though the modern nation-state evolved at the same time as modern capitalism and competed with the capitalists for economic power for a while under mercantilism, ultimately the state assumed a secondary position, serving the capitalist owners in three fundamental ways: The state controlled worker's demands and protected property rights, safeguarded markets and the flow of resources internationally, and brought new geographical areas into the system through conquest and intimidation.

The world system that emerged, through complex cycles of expansion and contraction, is divided into economic zones based on an international division of labor. The core countries are the economic and political centers of the system, and its main benefactors. At first, these were a handful of European countries but after the Industrial Revolution the core became associated with the fully industrialized countries, including Europe, the United States, Canada, and Japan. These countries are relatively rich, capital-intensive (reliant on machine labor), and focused on high-tech production.

The periphery includes those countries that historically have supplied unprocessed mining and agricultural products to the core. Production is labor-intensive, and manufactured exports tend to be low tech. The earliest periphery countries, that is, those first exploited for raw materials and cheap labor, were the countries of Eastern Europe, which happened to be closest to the core. Relatively quickly, the Americas were brought into the periphery, and by the early twentieth century the system encompassed the entire world.

A third economic zone, the semiperiphery partakes of characteristics of both the core and the periphery and mediates between the two. These countries, such as Argentina, South Africa, and Taiwan, have more independence than the peripheral countries, and often act as regional powers. Most are politically closely allied with the core.

Another element might be added to this structure, one widely recognized but lacking a commonly accepted name. George Shepherd (1987) calls them tributary elites. These are the owners and managers within peripheral and semiperipheral countries, often educated in Europe or the United States, who through their ties and allegiances to transnational enterprises really represent the core, as shown in Figure 6.

The system itself is relatively stable, but there is considerable movement within it. Core countries can become peripheral and visa versa, and semi periphery countries can move into the core.

The important thing about this perspective is that the world economy is seen as a single integrated system. (The role of the socialist states is ambiguous. However, to the extent that they trade in the international marketplace, they, too, must be considered capitalist, no matter what their internal economic policies.) Yet, there is no world political system. Political power is highly differentiated, consisting of numerous nation-states, of varying degrees of autonomy and power, in competition with each other. The absence of a central political authority prevents the artificial restraints that would curtail capitalism.

Dependency theory in general, and world system theory in particular, has been hotly criticized as overly simplistic in its neat division of the world and as economically deterministic, ignoring or slighting social, cultural, and political influences. One criticism is that dependency theory is unable to recognize peculiarly internal conditions that promote underdevelopment. For example, Hernando de Soto's *The Other Path* (1989)

Figure 6
The Capitalist World System

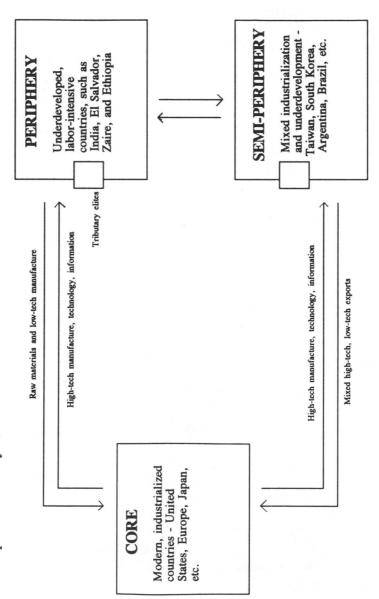

Source: Wallerstein 1974; Shepherd 1987 (on "tributary elites").

clearly documents how in Peru a Kafka-esque labyrinth of laws has created a virtually impenetrable bureaucracy that makes it extremely difficult and prohibitively expensive to participate in the legal economy. For this reason, the large majority of people live in the informal economy of squatter housing, black market exchange, and gypsy transportation. Because their economy is officially illegal, their contracts are not valid, and they can be arrested or their businesses shut down at any time. In addition, such businesses are not taxed, shifting the entire tax burden to the relatively small legal sector, that could not hope to supply sufficient funds for social programs and development. Although not really antithetical to a world system perspective (as the author claims), de Soto's data and analyses reveal a very significant internal component to ongoing poverty—and a component as political and legalistic as it is economic. This suggests that some of the more sophisticated analyses of the modernization theorists, who did look at internal factors retarding development, might have considerable value even within a dependency framework.

THE PEOPLE WITHOUT HISTORY

In many ways dependency theory and the world systems perspective, while undoubtedly influential, are at odds with anthropological tradition that has focused on more or less clearly demarcated tribes, cultures, peoples, or at least culture areas, either synchronically or within quite limited spans of time. The most contemporary of researchers might have difficulty relating their subjects to anything larger than a region or a state, and the process approach has seldom looked at periods lasting more than a few decades at most.

An important attempt to integrate anthropology and the global system perspective is Eric R. Wolf's ambitious *Europe and the People Without History* (1982). Wolf points out that a negative effect of participant observation fieldwork was to treat microcosms as wholes and thus to ignore the wider social and historical environment. There were, to be sure, attempts to reach beyond the particulars of time and place—notably diffusionism, neo-evolutionism, and statistical cross-cultural comparisons—but none quite filled the bill in exposing the crucial influences of European expansion.

Wolf categorically repudiates "the concept of the autonomous, self-regulating and self-justifying society and culture that has trapped anthropology inside the bounds of its own definitions" (p. 18). He offers nothing less than "a new theory of cultural forms" (p. 19) that includes a historically based world perspective. Even the most remote of societies, he seems to be saying, can only be truly understood by reference to the global system.

The basis for Wolf's analysis is Marx's concept of "modes of production." Marx distinguishes between work, the activity of individuals, and labor, which is always social. Production is not simply a matter of people using nature to create goods; more importantly, production—which includes labor, technology, ownership, and transportation—determines the ways that people relate to each other, that is, the ways societies are organized. A mode of production is, then, a way of deploying labor that has enormous consequences for the whole of society. Wolf delineates three fundamental modes of production:

- *The kin-ordered mode.* This mode, typical of bands, tribes, and chiefdoms, is based on an opposition between those who belong to the group, say, a lineage or a clan, and those who do not. In addition, the division of labor considers gender, rank, and relations by marriage as well as blood relations. In other words, the kin group determines the ways that labor is parceled out. This mode depends heavily on symbolism, to the extent that kinship itself is a symbolic ordering of nature and to the extent that kinship systems are often legitimized by reference to the supernatural (e.g., the ancestor spirits).

- *The tributary mode.* While production in the kin-ordered mode is mainly a social and symbolic process, in the tributary mode it is a political process, that is, it is manifested through the exercise of power and domination. The tributary mode assumes two classes, a ruling elite of surplus takers and an underclass of surplus producers. The elite gains its ability to demand tribute either by controlling a strategic part of the production process (such as the land or irrigation works) and/or by possessing a means of coercion, such as a standing army. This mode encompasses a broad continuum, ranging from the tight centralized control of monarchs to the relatively weak control of local overlords (Here Wolf combines two of Marx's modes of production, the Asiatic and the feudal.)

- *The capitalist mode.* Unlike Wallerstein, who views capitalism as a matter of exchange for profit, Wolf bases his definition on the buying and selling of human labor (in the tributary mode, the elites do not buy and sell labor, but only demand the products of labor). Marx's concept of surplus value explains how this works: That which workers produce above the value of their wages is a surplus transferred to the owners. Part of this surplus is sold back to the workers at a profit in the form of goods, and part is reinvested in new or expanded production. The two classes created by this system are the owners of the means of production at one pole and the producers at the other. Competition among capitalists requires that they constantly reduce the costs of production, by cutting wages or some other means, while increasing output through technological change and greater efficiency. The process, then, involves three intertwined aspects: (1) capitalists control the means of production; (2) laborers must sell their labor to survive because they lack access to the means of production; and (3) constant changes must increase production and cut costs. In contrast to kin-based systems, both the tributary and capitalist modes require an apparatus of coercion to protect the surplus-taking elites; this mechanism is the state.

In the year 1400, which Wolf employs as a convenient baseline, the kin-based mode was the most common in the area we now call the Third World. Outward expansion from Portugal, Spain, the Netherlands, France, and England spread European mercantilism to the far reaches of the world. Mercantilism, which superceded feudalism as the state gained control of local monarchies, was a system of state-encouraged and state-protected trade devoted to the enrichment of the state. The important thing about mercantilism for Wolf is that it is a tributary system. The spread of mercantilism thus shifted the kin-based mode of production to the tributary mode in native populations throughout the world, revolutionizing their social systems.

Tributary Transformation Among the Plains Indians

The fur trade in North America reveals this process, as one culture after another was brought into the beaver trade, the buffalo trade, or the sea otter and seal trade. Few societies were altered as rapidly and as totally as the Plains Indians—the Dakota, Cheyenne, Arapaho, Mandan, and Pawnee, among many others. In prehorse days, these woodland hunters and full-time horticulturalists lived around the periphery of the Great Plains. Two influences combined to change their societies: the horse and commerce with Europeans.

The horse was introduced into the Americas in 1519 by Hernando Cortés during his conquest of Mexico and traded northward through a complex network. The Apache got horses around 1630; the Ute and Comanche around 1700, and the Blackfoot not until 1730. With the horse, the Plains tribes became full-time buffalo hunters. Even by the early 1800s, some tribes were not only hunting for their own benefit but also for that of the Europeans by supplying pemmican to explorers and traders. For instance, the Northwest Coast Company needed almost 60,000 pounds of the preserved buffalo meat in a single year. Indians also supplied the frontier towns, such as St. Louis, with buffalo tongues and tallow. Then, the virtual extermination of the beaver in the Northeast created a new market for buffalo pelts on a massive scale. From the early nineteenth century, Indians supplied tens of thousands of skins per year to European traders (not mentioned by Wolf is the fact that female hides were preferred both for personal use and for trade, so females were killed at a ratio of ten to one, thus making the Indians major participants in the ultimate extinction of their own food supply).

These European influences touched every level of culture. With the adoption of the horse, group size, formerly small and relatively stable, became increasingly flexible. Buffalo dispersed into the mountains in the winter, requiring hunting by small bands or families, but came together in huge herds in the summer, permitting tribal size groups to coalesce. One result of the summer hunt was the expansion of the Sun Dance to the major yearly ritual, and its emphasis on the individual through a self-torture rite in which warriors skewered their chests and danced against rawhide thongs tied to a sacred pole. This new emphasis on individualism—a result of a requirement for personal prowess in hunting, trading, and warfare, challenged the old lines of authority. Ownership of the means of production, such as horses and weapons, was individualized, and this altered the old matrilineal and patrilineal kinship systems that depended on a collective ethic and collective ownership. A new bilateral emphasis arose, with kinship traced through the lines of both parents. New types of warfare emerged, mainly devoted to redistributing horses through theft. All of these changes were reinforced as the people became increasingly dependent on European trade goods—guns and ammunition, tools, cloth, and liquor. The most successful entrepreneurs, those with links to the trading posts, sometimes became the important political and war leaders.

Capitalist Transformation in Mundurucú

Though the transformations implicit in the change from the kinship mode of production to the tributary mode were far reaching, the transformations required by the capitalist mode were much greater. Because of his focus on wage labor as the defining quality of capitalism, Wolf rejects Wallerstein's contention that capitalism emerged in the fifteenth century and was contemporaneous with mercantilism. For Wolf, capitalism emerges only with the mechanization of the textile industries in England at the end of the eighteenth century, and rapidly replaced mercantilism as it spread throughout the globe. Unlike the other modes of production, the capitalist mode is expansive by its own internal logic; continuous capital accumulation combined with increases in productivity propel the owners of the means of production to constantly seek new sources of investment, new markets, and ever more resources. A fundamental difference between capitalism and mercantilism is that in the latter "merchants used money and goods bought with money to gain a lien on production, but they remained outside the process of production itself" (305). The capitalist, in contrast, takes complete control of the entire productive process, including, of course, the labor of the producers.

One major result of the spread of capitalism into the periphery was the emergence of the plantation, individual- or family-owned and employing a large labor force under strict supervision to produce a single cash crop for sale. Even though this system had long been in use under the tributary system of slavery, now labor was purchased with wages. The system was rapidly extended to include industrial crops. After the invention of vulcanization in 1839, rubber came to be used for raincoats, shoes, tires, condoms, and many other articles. Rubber tapping in Brazil reveals the effects of this capitalist mode on the Indians of the Amazonian Basin.

The Mundurucú Indians underwent a series of transformations because of their encounter with Europeans. In the late eighteenth century, white settlers became allies with these horticultural people; a radical and previously unknown division of labor was effected as the women began to produce manioc for the settlers while the men became mercenaries against other Indians. This situation, in which the men were mobile and the women sedentary, brought about a curious change in kinship, one that many anthropologists had believed impossible. The group remained patrilineal, but a matrilocal marriage rule emerged, in which the men moved in with their wives' families after marriage. The development of capitalist rubber tapping caused even greater changes. Entire highland villages disintegrated as people moved in household units to the riverside where the rubber trees were. The rubber trader replaced the chief as the locus of production and exchange. Receiving wages in goods, the men became caught up in a system of debt bondage, in which they always owed more to the company store than they could ever pay off. Their labor was now so little their own that they could not even move to another trader unless the new boss would agree to pay their debts.

Everywhere capitalism created a system in which labor was bought and sold as a commodity. Classes emerged where none had existed before, and in many places the processes of cultural collapse, detribalization, and immigration were set into effect. Machines now set the pace of work, and wages determined the amount of time that an individual would have to work to provide subsistence for himself and his family. Supply and demand, often decided thousands of miles away, determined the availability of employment, and created massive waves of migration from country to country.

For Wolf, the typical ethnography that ignores these influences is anachronistic. In the transformations of social labor, cultures everywhere are "forever assembled, dismantled, and reassembled" (p. 391).

Whatever one thinks of Wolf's Marxist perspective or his analytical focus on modes of production, his main point is well taken. The world system perspective must be considered if we are to truly understand virtually any society holistically. However, this ideal is not always easily managed. An ethnographer among the Yanomamo, up to his ears in the immediacy of mud, conflict, and kinship, might be forgiven for failing to discern the effects of eighteenth-century Portuguese mercantilism on his subjects. Even the most dedicated anthropological apostle of Wallerstein or Wolf might have trouble placing the Kwakiutl or the Trobriand Islanders within a truly world framework. However, Wolf, Wallerstein, and company have issued a challenge to political anthropology that cannot be easily ignored.

SUGGESTED READINGS

Chilcote, Ronald H. *Theories of Underdevelopment* (Boulder, Colo.: Westview Press, 1984). This short book is especially valuable for distinguishing reformist and revolutionary theories. Each major theorist is summarized individually. In his first chapter Chilcote sets the general conceptual framework, and in the final chapter he provides a critical summary.

de Soto, Hernando. *The Other Path: The Invisible Revolution in the Third World* (New York: Harper and Row, 1989). An international best seller, this book argues against dependency theory by showing how Peru's underdevelopment can be attributed to an unwieldy bureaucracy and an impenetrable maze of laws that forces most people into the informal, and illegal, economy.

Hopkins, Terence, and Immanuel Wallerstein, eds. *World System Analysis: Theory and Methodology* (Beverly Hills: Sage, 1982). Despite a formidable reputation and a tendency to half-page footnotes, Wallerstein is a remarkably clear and jargon-free writer. However, his key three-volume work on *The Modern World-System* can be overwhelming. This edited volume, which contains an article by Wallerstein, is a good start. The first chapter, by Terence Hopkins, provides a succinct overview of the theory.

Shannon, Thomas Richard. *An Introduction to the World-System Perspective* (Boulder, Colo.: Westview, 1989). This book includes details of Wallerstein's historical sequence in the evolution of the capitalist world economy, including useful maps showing the extent of capitalism's spread at different times. Also, there are clear chapters on the structure of the contemporary world system and on the dynamics of change within the system. The strongest point of the book, however, may not be its description but a long chapter on criticisms of the theory.

Wolf, Eric R. *Europe and the People Without History* (Berkeley: University of California Press, 1982). Taking a Marxist orientation to the world-system, at odds in many ways with Wallerstein, Wolf interprets mercantilist and capitalist expansion in modes of production. This is a fundamentally anthropological view-from-the bottom perspective that is more interested in the effects of such expansion on indigenous peoples than on the policies of governments. All anthropologists should be aware of Wolf's point of view, even if they have difficulty applying it in particular ethnographic settings.

Cutting sugar cane in the West Indies, from *The Graphic* magazine, 1876. Recent anthropological research suggests that workers and peasants do not passively submit to domination, but resist in subtle but effective ways.

Chapter Ten

The Power of the People

In the United States during the Civil War, the Confederate army lost nearly a quarter of a million qualified whites to avoidance of conscription and to desertion. Although certainly not the major reason for the South's defeat, this was an important contributing factor (Scott 1985: 30). In Iran, the nonviolent refusal by Moslem fundamentalists of the westernization programs imposed by the Shah created a climate and structure that would help bring about the Shah's fall from power (Skalník 1989: 14). Among the Lusi of New Guinea, and in many other societies, revenge suicide can be an effective political strategy by women who are otherwise utterly powerless; suicide can mobilize support and direct community action against the woman's oppressor (Counts 1984). Throughout the world, despite attempts by powerful state governments to force assimilation, ethnic groups have been able to maintain and even strengthen their cultural identities (Castile and Kushner 1981). These are all examples of what political scientist James Scott calls *Weapons of the Weak* (1985).

A dominant focus in political anthropology has been how indigenous peoples have been crushed by state power. In books such as *Assault on Paradise* (Kottak 1983), *Victims of Progress* (Bodley 1982), and *Victims of the Miracle* (Davis 1977), the emphasis has been on the exploitation or destruction of tribal cultures. With the rise of the world systems perspective during the 1970s, the detrimental effects of colonialism became almost de rigueur in any study of native politics. It would be almost unconscionable to speak of the American Indians without mentioning their oppression by European conquerors. The underlying assumption, usually tacit, has been that power was identical to the state, and that the underclasses could do no more than submit, or that they alternated between violent revolution and passiveness. This is a legitimate perspective in many cases. However, anthropologists are increasingly beginning to look at the ways that people, such as cane cutters in Malaysia, fight back, nonviolently with whatever weapons they have at their disposal.

Even though the state claims a monopoly on the legitimate use of force, if power is defined as the ability to affect the decisions and actions of others, many forms of power are available to the people at the bottom of the state hierarchy. Some of these forms of power may be individual, as in hiding from military conscription or deserting an army; or they may be well organized, as in Mohandas Gandhi's or Martin Luther King's nonviolent protest.

Pierre Clastres, in his *Society Against the State* (1977) sees this type of power, disseminated among the people, as actually preventing state formation in tribal societies and chieftainships. In nonstate societies in times of war a strong leader may come to the fore, but in peacetime the very structure of kinship-based systems prevents any single person or elite group from assuming dominance. There is a constant pull back from the temptation of state-formation. A Tupinamba chief in Brazil might be unchallenged during time of war, but in peacetime would be carefully supervised by a council of elders. Geronimo spent thirty years trying to become the sole leader of the Apache but failed; as a young man he had been given authority to lead a revenge attack on a Mexican garrison. Once that revenge was accomplished, despite his military renown, he had a difficult time getting others to follow him on what was perceived as a personal quest. The Apache would allow no man to lord it over them. As Clastres puts it, "the history of peoples without history is the history of their struggle against the State" (p. 186).

However, once the state is there—and virtually all indigenous peoples today live in imposed states that they had little or no part in forming—new strategies for cultural survival and individual autonomy must be developed. Peter Skalník (1989: 9–11) lists some of these strategies. If a group has a valuable resource at their disposal, as the eighteenth-century Cree Indians had furs, they can force a reciprocity on the conquering power, demanding gifts and special treatment. Another tactic is to collaborate with the state and actually use the state's own policies against it, as the Malaysian *negris* accepted British-imposed party politics and then created pro-*negri* parties that prevented the colonial power from carrying out its policies. If an indigenous group is powerful enough, or far enough from the centers of state power, it may be left alone and the people may go about their business as though they were not even part of a state. A fairly drastic strategy is to avoid the state by moving away from the sources of oppression; the Old Believers in revolutionary Russia moved to China, then to Brazil, then to the United States, and finally to Canada in search of freedom from persecution. People might just wait a generation or two; once state pressures for assimilation have waned, they can return to traditional ways, often with a vengeance, as many Blackfoot Indians did when they resumed the once-banned Sun Dance religion. The power of people against the state may be on a much more massive scale. In his international best seller *The Other Path* (see Chapter 9), Hernando de Soto shows how the Peruvian economy has become dominated by an informal and illegal economy of squatter housing, gypsy transportation, and black-market exchange.

The following three case studies suggest only a few of the myriad ways that people at the bottom of the political hierarchy stake their claims to power.

EVERYDAY RESISTANCE IN MALAYSIA

The words *peasant resistance* are more likely to conjure up images of violent and bloody uprisings, such as the Tupac Amaru II rebellion in Peru or the Chinese revolution, than villagers sitting around the local bar gossiping about a stingy landlord. But, according to James C. Scott, in his book *Weapons of the Weak* (1985), this latter form of protest is the most common and, perhaps, the most successful, given the failure rate of revolutions and the repression that inevitably follows such failure. Such resistance is an ongoing, everyday process through which the peasantry struggles against exploitation by pilfering, lying, foot-dragging, slander, minor sabotage, and arson. Resistance may be more or less organized, but it is not linked to any wider political movements or ideologies. This is counter to the more commonly held view of peasants as alternating between mindless eruptions of violence and passive acceptance of their fate; peasants are never really quiescent, but their protest takes place, almost unnoticed, day in and day out.

The country of Malaysia is one of the Third World's more successful examples of export-led growth, with rapid increases in gross national product and in per capita income. As is normal in such processes, progress has been paid for at the cost of a growing maldistribution of wealth and income. Between 1960 and 1970 the incomes of the rural poor declined, while the rest of the people were moving ahead. For the next decade the poor showed a modest recovery of about 2.4 percent a year, but because their incomes were starting at such a low base level, the real increase was almost negligible. By the early 1980s, 44 percent of the rural population lived below Malaysia's already low official poverty line. There has been no suggestion of significant restructuring of property relations to solve the problem of the poor; rather, the government has turned to the soft options of providing roads, schools, clinics, piped water, electricity, mosques, community halls, and resettlement schemes.

Sedaka, a community of seventy families, was affected by a massive irrigation project that opened the area to green revolution inputs and the double-cropping of rice (where only one crop a year had been possible before). Though this did not lead to a significantly greater concentration of land, as has been the case in Latin America and India, those who already had large land holdings were in the best position to take advantage of the innovations. In addition, only the well-off have been able to obtain government aid and loans—which need never be repaid if one belongs to the Farmers' Association and the dominant political party. Wealth and power are increasingly accruing to the already wealthy and powerful.

Traditional rice growing is very labor intensive. The four stages—land preparation, transplanting, reaping, and threshing—were all done by hand. The landless and land-poor relied heavily or entirely on wages provided by paddy work. In the last two decades, however, tractors and combines have taken over most of this labor. Because of the increased value of the land, tenants without the capital to invest in green revolution technology have been displaced, and rents on land have risen considerably. The predictable result has been that while the rich have gotten richer, the poor have suffered the dual loss of access to the means of production and of work and income. The poor are also faced with surrendering what little status and dignity they previously had, as they must become more dependent on loans and charity from the rich.

In this rapid process of agricultural capitalism, a new ideological system consonant with the new political economy has not yet emerged either among the wealthy or the poor. To be sure, the earlier system had been exploitive, but it was based on a bond of mutual dependence between the land owners and their tenants and workers. Now, except for the transplanting process, which is still done by hand mainly by women, there is little need for human labor, and often it would be more profitable if tenants relinquished their claims on the land. In other words, the poor are no longer needed by the wealthy. Yet the wealthy must continue living in a community where everyone knows everyone else. They must not only maximize profits but also try to gain and retain status and leadership in a setting in which they no longer have structural claims on the larger part of the population.

The situation is potentially explosive. Early on, it almost did explode: combines were sabotaged and even burnt, and there was a brief, and ultimately futile, attempt at a boycott by women transplanters. However, there are many constraints against direct confrontation, not least of which is the atmosphere of routine repression that pervades Malaysia. An Internal Security Act provides for preventative arrest and proscribes some types of protest. There have been large-scale police roundups following demonstrations. More locally, and more subtly, however, violent confrontation has been prevented by the complex and overlapping class structure and by webs of kinship, friendship, and patronage that tie together all segments of the community. Also, the green revolution changes have come about piecemeal, over a period of decades, so that there was no single point at which resistance would have been naturally mobilized. Finally, the problem is not one of direct exploitation, which would make it easier to find a common enemy, a common target of protest; rather the poor have simply been removed from the productive process.

To understand how the class struggle takes place, we must look at it through the eyes of the participants and within the particular ideological context. Scott defines class resistance as any act by the poor intended to advance its own claims or to mitigate claims by a superordinate class. Such resistance is designed to prevent competition among the poor for jobs, land, and loans. It carefully avoids direct confrontation with the rich and is always couched in a language of deference and conformity (though seldom cringing, since the poor person's claim to status is also at stake).

The poor can humiliate the rich through malicious gossip, inventing derogatory nicknames, or by boycotting a feast or only showing up for a brief time. The refusal of loans or of charity, a prime value of Islam, can be the occasion for accusations (never made to the offender himself) of stinginess, arrogance, or conceit. This leads to a euphemization of relations between rich and poor, in which direct transactions are virtually always hiding something, virtually always inauthentic. The wealthy man universally known among the poor as Haji Broom, because he swept up all the land in his path, is never called such to his face. An employee who thinks himself underpaid thanks his employer but quickly spreads his complaint among family and friends. When asking for a loan or for charity, the poor always use a verb that suggests that what they seek is their moral right.

There are more concrete forms of resistance, of course. When threshing, one can fill up the sacks faster—important in piecework—if each bundle is not beaten enough to get all the rice out; this forces the owner to observe the process every minute. When working in water-logged fields not amenable to combines, one can always threaten to walk off the job if the wages are too low. There is constant grumbling and negotiating for higher wages and constant complaints that the paddy in which one is working is too deep in water or the grain immature. More to the point, thievery from the wealthy is constant, despite the smallness of the community. Fruit from trees, gunny sacks of rice, chickens, water cans, bicycles, water buffalo, and even motorcycles are stolen. Resistance may also be expressed in the killing of the livestock of the rich after claims that they are getting into crops or storage facilities.

Routine resistance is maintained by an imposed mutuality or sanctioned solidarity among the poor. There is unspoken agreement not to undercut each other in demands for wages or to offer higher rents for land. Competition is prevented among the poor by such sanctions as gossip, character assassination, ostracism, the threat of being excluded from information networks about jobs and credit, and by a subtle threat of violence.

Scott's analysis is contrary to Marx's attribution of peasant quiescence to mystification or false-consciousness, emerging from the elites' dom-ination of the symbolic, as well as physical, means of production. Marx believed that elite control of the media and other means of communication brainwashed the exploited into assuming elite values. Looked at from the point of view of the actors themselves, this is not true; the rich and poor—the winners and losers in the game—see the world very differently. The poor see themselves as pushed down by the rich. The rich see themselves as generous and kindly, doing what they can while still earning a living. There is, to be sure, a moral context of village life, which is a common set of expectations about class relations and about individual behavior. This moral context is, however, used by the poor to intimidate the rich, just as much as it is used by the rich to legitimize their power.

Far from being brainwashed, the peasants of Sedaka are aware of the limitations of their power, which is precisely why they resort to routine resistance rather than revolution. There is no use in attacking modern capitalism, which is the real cause of their present plight. Basic structures are notoriously difficult to change. Individual capitalists, however, can be attacked, though only behind a facade of deference and conformity.

SPHERES OF POLITICS IN MICRONESIA

The island of Ponape in Micronesia, as described by Glenn Petersen (1989), reveals how politics can take place in separate spheres, and how the assertion of traditional values can moderate colonial influences.

Despite its remoteness, Ponape, like the other islands of Micronesia, has had a long history of relations with the West. After a half-century of off-and-on contact, the island became a colony of Spain in 1886, followed by subjugation by the Germans, Japanese, and Americans. Formerly a trusteeship of the United States, the Federated States of Micronesia presently have an ambigious status of sovereignty coupled with U.S. control of military defense.

The official political structure imposed on Ponape thus represented centuries of historical development in Europe and the United States, and bore little relation to the indigenous political culture of the island. Under the trusteeship U.S. rule was autocratic (though not necessarily heavy-handed) because it was based on the absolute authority of the state and on a hierarchy of power similar to the hierarchy of municipal/state/federal authority in the United States. The imposed government of Micronesia consisted of a wide array of appointed and elected individuals and groups—governor, executives, a state legislature with elected representatives, legislative committees, courts, departments, agencies—each with its arena of power and each under the control of a higher officialdom. In addition there was a constitution, charters, legal codes, and so forth, all based on abstract principles of government and law.

The traditional Ponapean chieftainship system also recognizes hierarchy, but only in close conjunction with an opposite trend toward individual autonomy. Chiefs, who assume their positions through ranked lineages, cannot rest on their inherited statuses but must continually maintain their positions through a ceaseless round of feasting in which great quantities of food are redistributed to the community. At a feast, a chief is seated on a raised platform. He presents gifts to other chiefs according to their rank, which they in turn distribute among kin, friends, and followers. Since the yams, kava, pigs, and community service that bestow status are not in scarce supply, authority does not inhere in control of such resources but rather in the ability to produce and distribute them. Chieftainship is earned and maintained through social skills, resourcefulness, and hard work.

Under the trusteeship the ritual predominance of the chiefs did not translate into a predominance of power. The five paramount chiefs, representing the five municipalities, supposedly ruled through the section chiefs; in reality, there was little ruling to be done. Most aspects of life were thoroughly routinized. Special projects were organized by section chiefs, who could demand community participation, but if the project was too onerous the section chief was simply ignored. Most chiefly decision making revolved around organizing and supplying rituals and celebrations, but even here the threat of ostracism or ridicule by the community was a stronger sanction than chiefly commands. A generous chief could expect cooperation, but only within limits. While social and political hierarchy is firmly embedded in the culture, it is hierarchy without coercive power. In Ponape, says Petersen, "the locus of authority . . . is the community itself" (p. 29).

How was this traditional system maintained in a colonial situation, when the colonial concept of hierarchy and power was so totally different? Mainly the traditional system survived because it was confined to the sphere of community decision making, ritual, ceremony, and status, with which the imposed "electoral/bureaucratic system" did not involve itself. The chiefs did not make decisions nor try to enforce compliance in regard to modernization—schools, roads, public health, export cropping, and so forth. In other words, there were two spheres of politics, each with its own hierarchy: The first is a sphere of traditional face-to-face politics based in personal relations, and the second, a sphere of impersonal, legalistic politics based on abstract principles.

The two spheres were not entirely distinct. Many Ponapean natives achieved office within the bureaucracy and identified with the imported values. Even though they might consider the old ways illogical and inefficient, they remained a part of that culture. Similarly, the people themselves had no trouble functioning within the European political culture when that was practical.

Traditional concepts of authority may further insinuate themselves into the bureaucratic sphere as American influence wanes. In a 1983 plebiscite the people defiantly voted for full independence rather than an ongoing relationship with the United States, even though the latter would have meant a continued inflow of dollars. The absence of a foreign power may gradually lead to a retraditionalizing of the society, in which the conflicts between the two spheres of politics will be resolved in the direction of traditional concepts of hierarchy and autonomy.

LOCAL-LEVEL POWER IN NICARAGUA

Corporatism is a model of the state in which the government functions through a limited number of monopolistic interest groups that are recognized and sometimes created by the state itself. It is based on the idea that individuals gain their rights, their identities, and their privileges through group membership. Corporatism is often contrasted with pluralism, with its emphasis on the individual voter and its articulation of power via innumerable competing interest groups, such as unions, political parties, and lobbies. "Corporate" groups do not operate in such a laissez-faire political environment. There is only one interest group in each major occupational, vocational, or social category: factory workers, large-scale agriculturalists, or cattle ranchers. Each organization speaks for all of its members and, ideally, the government makes policy affecting that group only after close consultation with its leadership.

Though corporatism was widely proclaimed at the turn of the century as the system of the future, the two most notorious corporatist examples in Europe, fascist Italy and Nazi Germany, did not exactly inspire emulation. However, the corporatist model imported from Spain and Portugal has firmly taken root in Latin America, where it has been distinctly elitist, providing the wealthy sectors of society and sometimes urban labor with inputs into government while excluding the masses of poor. Two countries have made significant attempts to use the corporatist model to integrate the poor, Peru under the Velasco regime (1968–76) and Nicaragua under the Sandinista National Liberation Front (FSLN).

The Sandinistas, who ran Nicaragua from the ousting of the Somoza dictatorship in 1979 until their electoral defeat in 1990 were self-proclaimed Marxists, though the state they actually created borrowed heavily from indigenous Iberic-Latin corporatism. Mass organizations, some pre-existing from the Somoza era and others having evolved out of the revolutionary struggle, were integrated into the government from the outset. The original colegislative body, the Council of State, included six officially recognized corporatist groups, such as the Rural Workers Association, the National Union of Farmers and Ranchers, and AMNLAE, a women's organization. The largest of these groups, and thus awarded the most seats on the council, was an umbrella organization comprised of fifteen thousand Sandinista Defense Committees (CDS) with nearly six hundred thousand members.

Unlike other governing political parties in Latin America, the Sandinistas drew their support from the underclasses. Thus the Sandinista Defense Committees were seen as "the primary and elemental connection between our people and the revolution." The groups were hierarchically ordered by block, neighborhood (*barrio*), zone, region, and nation. At each level, leaders were chosen by vote, with block members voting for neighborhood leaders, neighborhood representatives voting for zonal leaders, and so on. The task of the CDSs was to oversee virtually every aspect of neighborhood life, including training and managing the health brigades, participating in Popular Health Councils, organizing literacy campaigns, finding housing, helping with rationing and food distribution, and fighting crime and counter-revolution (this latter task earned them a reputation in the American press as neighborhood spy organizations).

Built into the system were opportunities for corruption, especially given the low levels of training and education of the leaders. Licenses to run local government-subsidized food stores were handled by the CDSs, as were guaranty cards, distributed to each family to assure access to low-cost staples, such as sugar and rice. Licenses and guaranty cards could be withheld for political or personal reasons, or illegally sold. As early as 1982 one of the top Sandinista commanders sent a letter to all CDS coordinators condemning such abuses. However, the lack of regularly scheduled elections made it difficult to get rid of bad leaders.

Nevertheless, a study of five such organizations in Estelí (Lewellen 1989b) suggested problems of corruption were not as severe as often believed. The real problems—the problems that led to the dissolution of the Sandinista Defense Committees—had more to do with the structure of the system itself than with corruption. Though originally conceived as the representatives of the masses to the government, the CDSs increasingly became the representatives of the government to the masses. Instead of demands flowing up, demands flowed down, so that local members found themselves constantly involved in doing unpaid work for the government and in implementing government policy which they had little part in deciding. This was especially true as the U.S.-supported contra invasion increased in intensity. Between 1983 and 1987 national defense became virtually the entire focus of activity, to the detriment of projects of purely local value. This could be justified as long as the country was under attack. However, the contras were effectively defeated on the battlefield in 1987 when the bulk of fighters were driven out of Nicaragua (bloody harassment incursions run across the border from Honduras continued for three more years). With the cooling-down of the war, people wanted more autonomy, but the existing CDS structure would not permit it.

The people fought back in a very simple manner: they stopped participating. It is doubtful that there was ever any significant organized opposition at the grass-roots level. Rather, interest flagged as people were unable to see the concrete results of their efforts on their own lives. Where government depends on voluntary compliance, refusal to participate can be an extremely powerful weapon. This was not the only weapon, of course. Because the organizations were democratic, voting and complaining were equally employed. In one meeting of CDS coordinators in Estelí, fifteen minutes were spent discussing local achievements and four hours complaining about failures.

The result was that the local CDSs were officially dissolved, starting in 1988 (notably two years before the elections that ousted the Sandinistas). They did not simply disappear, however, but were gradually replaced by Communal Movements not tied to the Sandinista party and functionally autonomous; they had no obligations to any higher body, including the government. Their tasks were entirely local—health, roads, sewage, education, electricity, water, care of orphans and war widows, and so forth. In many communities the reorganization was welcomed by a resurgence of participation. Because they are no longer tied to a particular political party, the Communal Movements have continued after the Sandinista defeat, making Nicaragua the most organized country at the grass-roots level in Latin America.

The CDS experiment revealed three structural contradictions of any corporatist attempt to integrate the masses into the political processes: First, is what might be called the contradiction between verticality and horizontality. The state, which represents a broad alliance of interests, constantly attempts to impose a structure that provides top-down control, whereas the people themselves want autonomy. A second, closely related conflict, is that of national interest versus local interest. Organizing military conscription, local militia training, handling rationing, and store licensing can be onerous for people who lack such basics as electricity and running water. People may identify with national interests in a crisis or for a brief time, but ultimately local needs prevail. Finally, there is a conflict between elite leadership and popular leadership. While the CDSs were supposedly open to everyone, inevitably the leadership came from members of the FSLN. This led to much nonparticipation by those unsympathetic to the Sandinistas. Notably, these conflicts were ultimately resolved in favor of the neighborhoods, not the state.

Despite their many problems, the CDSs were a necessary precursor to the Communal Movements. It is doubtful that local level organizations would have been formed on such a scale without initial direct government involvement.

*   *   *

Such studies require a reconceptualization of the notion of power. They reveal that power belongs not only to the chiefs or to the state but also inheres in the general populace and the individual. Even within the most authoritative of polities, people find niches of autonomy and control, or they create them.

We should be wary of romanticizing these tactics. They are seldom very effective in bringing about the structural changes that would provide formal power to such people. But neither are they trivial. In their sum total they can make a real difference. As James Scott (1985: 36) puts it, "Just as millions of anthozoan polyps create, willy-nilly, a coral reef, so do thousands upon thousands of individual acts of insubordination and evasion create a political or economic barrier reef of their own."

SUGGESTED READINGS

Castile, George Pierre, and Gilbert Kushner, eds. *Persistent Peoples: Cultural Enclaves in Perspective* (Tucson: University of Arizona, 1981). Thirteen articles dealing with cultural enclavement, emphasizing the "continuity of common identity in resistance to absorption by a dominant surrounding culture." The studies, mostly from the Americas, range from Blacks and Mormons in the United States to Mayans and Pimas of Mexico. A variety of strategies are analyzed, from outright opposition to the state to collaboration and fusion.

Clastres, Pierre. *Society Against the State.* (New York: Urizen Books, 1977). Perhaps more philosophy than ethnography, Clastres questions the nature of political power and argues that the very structure of kin-based polities impedes the evolution of centralized state systems. Examples used for analysis are drawn from South American Indians, mainly the Tupi-Guarani of Brazil and Paraguay.

Scott, James C. *Weapons of the Weak: Everyday Forms of Peasant Resistance* (New Haven, Conn.: Yale University Press, 1985). Scott, a political scientist who spent two years of ethnographic fieldwork in Malaya, provides a minutely detailed examination of how the introduction of green revolution cropping has exacerbated class conflict in one small community. His focus is on the perceptions of the different actors in the struggle, and the tactics that peasants use to fight back.

Skalník, Peter ed. *Outwitting the State: Political Anthropology*, Vol. 7 (New Brunswick, N.J.: Transaction Publishers, 1989). From the title one would expect a focus on tactics and strategies for getting around state power, but the eight ethnographic selections in this book do not so much exemplify outwitting the state as learning to live with it while maintaining cultural identity. The examples represent a wide variety of cultures from the James Bay Cree to the Russian Old Believers. Skalník provides an introductory overview of the material and a classification of outwitting tactics.

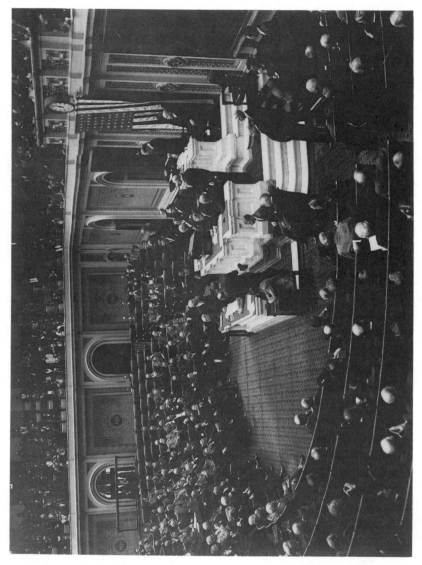

Even United States politics is no longer beyond the scrutiny of anthropologists. J. McIver Weatherford's *Tribes on the Hill* reveals how senators gather "clans" to bolster their power.

Chapter Eleven

Politics in Industrial Society

Nowhere has the line between political anthropology and political sociology become more blurred than in the studies of modernization and the formal political institutions of industrial society. Anthropology has been characterized traditionally by its subject matter—informal political structures in relatively closed preindustrial societies—and by its emphasis on participant observation as the primary method of research. Recently, however, anthropologists have increasingly turned their attention to the political integration (or nonintegration) of tribal groups in developing nations, and to such formal political structures as parties, governmental bureaucracies, and even multinational corporations. In such contexts, it may be impossible to gather information by immersing oneself in the culture. Indeed, a national political party may crosscut any number of cultural divisions, so that interviewing, questionnaires, and the study of documents may be the most useful techniques of research. While one can buy one's way into a Yanomamo village with a few machetes, the vice-president of a multinational corporation might be less amenable to such inducements, with the result that access to even the most basic information may be tightly restricted. Though freed from the threat of hepatitis or of having to eat grubs, the anthropologist faces an entirely new set of problems and must choose research according to the availability of information. One result is that the growing number of anthropological studies of modern political systems—although individually of high quality—seem catch-as-catch-can when viewed as a group.

Despite this lack of a theoretical common denominator, such studies usually do retain a distinctly anthropological flavor. Politics is not treated as analytically separate, but rather as embedded in a wider culture. Small segments, modern equivalents of the band or the tribal village, are investigated as representing the whole. The informal mechanisms that underlie formal organization are emphasized.

TRADITIONAL CULTURES IN MODERN STATES

The fate of traditional societies that find themselves encapsulated within modern states has been of continuing interest to anthropologists. Two of the earliest ethnographies ever written, Lewis Henry Morgan's 1877 book on the Iroquois and James Mooney's 1896 monograph on the Ghost Dance, were studies of American Indians in a reservation context. Most such studies, however, have been focused tightly on the group itself. This was especially true during the heyday of structural-functionalism when tribal groups were treated as if they were entirely autonomous. A more recent tendency is to bring the state itself to the fore as one of the actors in the drama, so that the key focus is on the interaction between the encapsulated group and the national government.

Political Ethnicity and Retribalization: The Hausa Case

Early modernization theorists believed that modernization inevitably leads to ethnic uniformity. Ostensibly, old tribal loyalties are shifted to the centralized nation-state, and politics itself becomes detribalized in the sense that factions and parties cross-cut local and ethnic divisions. In *Custom and Politics in Urban Africa* (1969), Abner Cohen shows that the case may be just the opposite; modernization may lead to a reformation and hardening of ethnic identity.

The Hausa of Nigeria are renowned traders who have developed a widespread reputation as shrewd businessmen, exploiters, troublemakers, and geniuses at their profession. There is a certain truth in at least the latter accusation, though their genius resides more in their trading network than in individual brilliance. The Hausa are neither pastoralists nor farmers, and therefore have had to make up in efficiency for what they lack in control over the production of the cattle and kola nuts they trade. The forest zone people of the South cannot raise their own meat because the tsetse fly kills off cattle within two weeks. The savanna people of the North put a high value on the kola nut but cannot grow this food themselves. Trading between these two ecological zones is a tricky business; because cattle die so quickly in the forest and the kola nut is highly perishable, one cannot just transfer these goods from one area to another and wait around for the best price. Information on supply and demand must be obtained before goods are moved. Nor can one depend on either traders or customers having money on hand when the actual transfer is made. The Hausa trading network has solved both these technical problems: information on market conditions moves rapidly through the system, and the Hausa have established a virtual monopoly on credit and trust in these business transactions. There is nothing primitive or small in such trading: millions of dollars worth of goods are involved, and the wealth and income of the vast majority of the Hausa are directly or indirectly derived from the dual trading of kola and cattle. Yet despite their sophisticated knowledge of banking, insurance, and legal documents, the Hausa quite rationally prefer traditional arrangements based on partnerships of trust and reciprocity.

Cohen's study focuses on the retribalization of the Hausa quarter of Sabo in the city of Ibadan. Only a few decades earlier, Sabo had been little more than a Hausa sector of a largely Yoruba village; but as Ibadan grew into a major city, Hausa influence was reduced. With independence after World War II, the central government of the newly liberated nation simultaneously emphasized party politics and condemned tribalism in an attempt to unify the country. These pressures combined to weaken the effectiveness of the traditional Hausa chiefs, and both outmarriage and the revolt of the young against tribal ways threatened to detribalize the Hausa altogether. The Hausa were not particularly self-conscious nor defensive about their tribal heritage, but they became increasingly aware that their trading network, and therefore their livelihood, depended on their ethnic cohesiveness.

The Hausa answer to this political and economic challenge was to reemphasize the tribal unit. The major tool in this process was the development of a Moslem religious brotherhood called Tijaniyia. The majority of Hausa had previously, like the Yoruba, been rather casual about their religion. The Tijaniyia practiced a highly puritanical mode of religion, which involved an intense form of community ritual that clearly set them off from the morally inferior non-Hausa. In addition, the Tijaniyia established a religious hierarchy that provided strong ritual leaders to fill the power vacuum left by the declining authority of the traditional chiefs. Through retribalization, Hausa ethnicity was politi-cized and used as a weapon in the struggle to maintain their monopoly on trade. The forces of modernization thus drove the Hausa to a degree of exclusiveness more radical than at any time in the past.

Cohen sees this tendency away from assimilation as a normal element in the modernization process. Indeed, retribalization and detribalization operate on the same groups simultaneously: a tribal group may integrate itself at one level through increased participation in the national economy and in factional or party politics, while emphasizing its cultural distinctiveness at another level.

Political ethnicity, or the deliberate use of ethnicity to attain political ends, should not be seen as a matter of conservatism or a striving for continuity. Although old structures and traditional beliefs may be given great emphasis, observation reveals that their functions have changed radically.

Political Adjustment in a Reservation Context: The Mapuche

In postcolonial Africa, modernization has brought many tribal groups into national politics. A more common effect of modernization is that native groups lose their previous political autonomy while being barred from national politics, as has been and continues to be the case with Native Americans in the United States. Where there exists clear political, technological, and economic domination, tribal politics may have to change substantially and continually to adapt to the whims of the dominating power. Native government is faced with contradictory mandates to provide for the needs of the community while at the same time satisfying the state. One solution, chosen by some Pueblo reservations in the United States, is simply to supply nominal chiefs to whatever council is required by the federal government, while keeping traditional arrangements separate. This is not possible, however, where there is a great degree of dependency on national government largesse or where the national government is extremely intrusive. L. C. Faron's (1967) ethnohistoric account of the Mapuche of Chile reveals tribal politics in an almost constant process of change in response to the varying policies of the Chilean government.

Traditionally, the Mapuche lacked any centralized political authority. The functioning social unit was the kin group, under the limited leadership of an elder called the *lonko*. During more than three hundred years of resistance to European invaders, a powerful military organization with strong war chiefs developed. By the mid-1800s, after a period of relatively peaceful defiance, the Mapuche grew increasingly restive as lands maintained through force of arms were eroded by fraudulent legal claims. Taking advantage of Chile's preoccupation with the War of the Pacific against Peru and Bolivia (1879–83), the Mapuche staged their last major uprising. They were soundly defeated, most of their lands were confiscated, and they were placed on relatively small reservations.

The Chilean government preferred to deal with each reservation through a single chief. This centralization of political authority was alien to the Mapuche, but there was sufficient precedent in the institution of strong military chiefs for a militarylike power to be transferred to a peacetime office. Of course, this meant drawing power away from both the *lonkos* and the lesser military leaders. The federal government reinforced this centralization of reservation power by directly providing the chief with three times as much land as anyone else, at a time when land was a scarce and valuable commodity. Moreover, the chief was given limited legal control of all reservation land, and so many government restrictions were funnelled through him that he ended up controlling, directly or indirectly, all of the wealth of the community. Anyone wishing to set up a household within the reservation had to seek permission of the chief. This made it extremely difficult to settle disputes, as of old, by moving to another area. There was no choice but to submit to the chief. In addition, the chiefs were given responsibility for mediating Chilean law for the Bureau of Indian Affairs, and for enforcing the customary law of the Mapuche. Such a concept of centralized power depended entirely on the reservation system and on the intrusion of the federal government into native politics.

By the 1950s, the reservation chief's kingly position had become an increasing irritation to the very national government that had created it in the first place. An extremely powerful chief is in a position not only to exploit his people but also to defend them from outside exploitation. In a deliberate attempt to break the power of these chiefs, the government began to bypass them and deal individually with the Mapuche as Chilean citizens. The predictable result was that the power of the chiefs declined almost as rapidly as it had arisen.

Some of the chief's powers reverted to the *lonkos,* whose authority nevertheless continued to be localized and traditional. With increasing interaction between the Mapuche and their wider social environment, however, and with increasing threats against their land, mediation was as necessary as ever. Even though the chief continued to represent the reservation (his leadership was recemented in times of real stress), a new mechanism of culture brokerage developed—the political pressure group. The *Corporación Araucana* formed to fight for maintenance of the reservations and for increased government assistance to the Indians. A smaller opposition group, the *Unión Araucana*, was conceived by the Capuchin missionaries to promote absorption of the Mapuche into Chilean society.

In sum, we find among the Mapuche a reactive and adaptive process beginning with authority vested in the elders of local kin groups, followed by the rise of war chiefs, the decline of the power of such chiefs, the emergence of strong reservation chiefs, and finally by the shift of authority into the hands of political action groups.

FORMAL POLITICAL INSTITUTIONS IN MODERN SOCIETY

Max Weber's now-classical studies of bureaucracy were written at a time when modern industrial organization and administration were still emerging from more personalistic forms of management. By contrast, the new systems seemed to be distinguished by cold scientific rationality, single-minded devotion to production and profit, and an almost inhuman mechanical efficiency. The nepotism and paternalism so highly valued in an earlier day gave way to a system of hiring based entirely on qualifications for specific jobs. The personal lives of workers were not to intrude into the work environment. The ideal system would seem to have been independent of individual personality altogether.

Despite vast differences in approach, the structural Durkheimian model, which displaced the Weberian model during the 1950s, presented an equally dehumanized image. Bureaucratic organizations were viewed as aggregates with structures and functions that transcended the individuals comprising them. It was sufficient to describe those structures and functions at the level of the organization itself, so that the individual worker could be virtually ignored.

Both models can still be defended, and continue to provide the theoretical basis for important studies of industrial-level organizations. In fact, many of the tendencies merely inchoate in Weber's time have solidified, as just a glance at the flow chart of authority within a major corporation shows. Yet something is missing—the same missing element in the structural-functionalist studies of preindustrial political systems, namely, the individual. Contrary to prediction, individuals have not simply become robots in gray flannel suits within corporations. Just the opposite seems to be the case. Vine Deloria, in his book *Custer Died For Your Sins* (1969), makes the remarkable observation that corporations may ultimately turn out to be the white man's form of tribalism, a way of creating the kinds of personal face-to-face group identifications that

Native Americans are trying to preserve. In any case, it requires only a slight shift of focus to see that behind the cold rationality and computerized structures are human beings who do indeed bring their lives and personalities to the job, and always have; who interact with each other in sometimes-not-entirely-rational ways; who form cliques and factions; and who are as liable to work around the formal rules as to work within them.

This, of course, is the stuff of which anthropology is made, and anthropologists have brought some refreshing perspectives to some hoary bureaucracies. Essentially, anthropologists have focused on two elements largely ignored by political scientists: First, they have described the *informal* groups—based on class, interests, age, and education—that function within formal organizations. Second, they have shown the relation between the organization, the individuals that comprise it, and the wider environment.

Bureaucracies may be described in degrees of rationality, in the Weberian sense of expressly defined goals and formal organization designed to implement these goals. A system that is rigidly rational, in which formal rules are dominant so that individual workers and administrators must act within set roles, may be successful in the short run but lacks the flexibility to adapt to changing conditions. At the opposite end of the spectrum is the organization in which informal rules prevail. Here members act as individuals, not as roles or offices, and decision making is based on a wide range of personalistic relations including consultation, friendship, intimacy, factionalism, competition, and outright hostility. A third possibility, more stable than either extreme, is a balance of both formal and informal mechanisms.

A bureaucracy is not a closed system; it must constantly interact and make adaptive adjustments to its environments if it is to survive. It must compete with other organizations for scarce resources, including power. It must provide services or products that impinge on the prerogatives of others, and it must defend its own field of interest against competitors. Individuals working for the organization are also involved in external personal and professional networks that divide their time and loyalties and influence their on-the-job decisions.

The anthropologist, by training and through the unique role of participant-observer, is in an excellent position to describe the everyday workings of such organizations, the informal rules that guide individual behavior, and the informational networks.

Bureaucracy and Antibureaucracy in Modern China

Martin King Whyte's (1980) analysis of the two faces of Communist rule in the People's Republic of China reveals how an inbuilt tendency toward rigid bureaucratic rationality can be balanced by officially sanctioned antibureaucratic activities.

Throughout the 1950s, China was portrayed in the West as the supreme example of bureaucratic totalitarianism. Using the Leninist-Stalinist model of socialism, Mao set out to assimilate every institution in Chinese society into one mammoth bureaucracy, organized around a highly complex system of ranks and wages. Between 1949 and 1958, the number of state cadres grew from 720,000 to 7,920,000 as agriculture was collectivized and powerful central bureaucracies were established to control mass communications, the arts, and foreign trade. With regard to labor, the Chinese outstripped their Soviet model; virtually all labor was allocated by the state, and there were considerably more attempts to organize the after-hours activities of the workers. Bureaucratic organization even penetrated to the neighborhood and family levels of society; street committees that formed in urban areas were subdivided, first into residence committees, and finally into small residence groups that jointly and separately were responsible for running local factories, for sanitation, for health, crime prevention, and the like.

All of this was seen as necessary if a country as vast and populous as China was to function as a national unit and realize stated economic goals. Only through such means could the nation avoid duplication of effort and local group rivalries, organize labor for large-scale projects, and assure some degree of equality in the distribution of goods and services.

Along with the growth of the Chinese bureaucracy, however, there developed a corresponding tendency toward antibureaucracy, that is, toward avoiding the negative effects of such a rigidly hierarchical scheme. In 1967, Mao Tse-tung himself castigated bureaucrats in general as conceited, complacent, ignorant, and endlessly competing for power and money. A major aspect of the Cultural Revolution of the mid-1960s was the disruption of the entrenched bureaucracy. Government officials had to leave office periodically to purify themselves of bourgeois tendencies through manual labor or political study. There have been numerous attempts to obtain more mass input into decision making. At various times wall posters have been used to expose the faults of superiors.

In addition, the Communist party itself mounts periodic campaigns to disrupt bureaucratic routine. The normal rules and procedures of administration may be denounced for hindering the enthusiasm and initiative of the masses. Central-level organizations may be moved and placed under local-level authorities; even entire factories, universities, and scientific institutions have been dismantled and relocated in relatively small towns.

Whyte views such obstructions as complementary rather than contradictory to Chinese bureaucratic organization. In a society which has idealized equality, bureaucracy poses three main dangers: first, such organization inevitably creates vested interests; second, it creates a system of hierarchical ranks that threatens to coalesce into a new class to replace the overthrown capitalist class; and finally, if all power is contained in the administrative hierarchy, the ordinary worker is disenfranchised from the decision-making process. By regularly reshuffling the bureaucracy and allowing it to be actively criticized by the masses—within limits, of course—China has been able to take advantage of modern bureaucratic organization while still holding on to its revolutionary ideals.

Primitive Politics on Capitol Hill

It was perhaps inevitable that the United States Congress should fall under the anthropologist's unflinching scrutiny. As a legislative assistant to Senator John Glenn, anthropologist J. McIver Weatherford was perfectly placed for the participant observation research that led to his book *Tribes on the Hill* (1981). The book is popularly written and somewhat more resolutely and self-consciously anthropological in its viewpoint than may be absolutely necessary. The author perceives little difference between the United States Congress and a primitive tribe in status rivalries, clan social structure, political socialization, and ritual. Each chapter begins with a description of some tribal practice—among the Iroquois, the Shavante of the Amazon Basin, the Kawelka of Highland New Guinea, the Aztec—which is then compared to the behavior of Congress. All this becomes somewhat perfunctory and a bit gimmicky, especially since the author is never clear when he is postulating a general principle of political behavior or using primitive tribes merely as analogies. Because some of the comparisons are rather farfetched, the latter would seem to be usually the case. However, once one gets past the pop anthropology, the author has much to say of real substance about the workings of the United States government at its highest levels. The real system is revealed to have only the most tenuous correspondence to the mythological civics-text system taught in high school.

A basic and universal aspect of politics is certainly the socialization of those who aspire to power. Senior senators have one absolute goal: to get reelected. Freshmen senators not only must pursue this goal against much greater odds than their elders, but they must also learn the rules of the power game as it is played in Washington. The Longworth Building, where freshmen senators have their offices, is described as resembling the bachelor hut among some tribal groups, where young men are conditioned for their place in the social hierarchy. Before they can earn their way across the street to the Sam Rayburn Building, where senior senators reside, the freshmen must build up a strong enough base of support both at home and in the Senate to get reelected a number of times. Meanwhile, they are constantly reminded of their lowly place in the pecking order; a favorite method used by seniors to keep freshmen in place is to consistently mispronounce their names, which even the greenest senators hold to be the most sacred parts of their personal *manas*. Freshmen are allowed short speeches on the Senate floor (usually to an empty house) and may give interviews to the home-state press without fear of being sanctioned by gossip or ostracism; but anything delivered to the national media must be extremely circumspect.

For senior senators, committee chairs may be the prime mechanism for wielding enormous power; for freshman senators, such offices are a means of creating an illusion of power for the folks back home. The committees to which the freshmen have access have impressive titles: the Subcommittee on Oversight of the Internal Revenue Service; the Economic Stabilization Committee; the Western Hemisphere Subcommittee of Foreign Relations. Unfortunately (or perhaps fortunately for the public), such committees are virtually powerless. By collecting subcommittees, however, novices gradually build up at least a modicum of power over authorization and appropriations. Equally important, each committee and subcommittee brings new staff that can be added to the senator's clan.

Weatherford divides senators into three categories based on their strategies for gaining and maintaining power: shamans, warlords, and godfathers. Different strategies are adaptive to different personalities and offer different political yields.

The shaman is a highly visible generalist whose major function is to allay people's fears of communism, big business, pollution, or the Mafia. Senator Edward Kennedy, the prototypal shaman, is endlessly quoted in the press and often the first on the scene. For example, during the Three Mile Island nuclear crisis, he was giving authoritative interviews before others had even established a position. According to Weatherford, however, Kennedy had never gotten a significant bill passed. The power

of such senators derives not from their ability to deliver results but from their skill in garnering and manipulating popular support. Other senators who fell into this category were Joseph McCarthy, Estes Kefauver, and Richard Nixon.

Warlords are those senators who try to establish a monopoly over one aspect of government and then extend that power outward to increase its scope. For example, Russell Long, as chairman of the Finance Committee, possessed a virtual monopoly on anything to do with taxation. Issues involving energy were largely in the hands of Senator Mark Hatfield, who assumed chairmanship of the Senate Appropriations Committee in 1981. Senator John Stennis of Mississippi sat on only two committees, Appropriations and Armed Services, but these were so powerful that Stennis was able to pass one of the biggest home-state boondoggles in history as a routine in-house operation. The Tennessee-Tombigbee Waterway is a $3 billion canal longer than the Panama Canal; it is parallel to and only 150 miles from the Mississippi River. Appropriations for this extravaganza, a virtual twin to the Mississippi, were passed in 1971 with few objections, because Stennis had the power to reduce or withdraw military bases in other senators' states.

In contrast to the highly visible shamans and finely focused warlords are the godfathers, who have mastered the art of manipulating power from behind the scenes. This is the most difficult of all roles; it requires an exquisitely tuned sense, not only of how the system works, but also of the personal habits, fears, soft spots, and ambitions of virtually all of the members of Congress. Lyndon Johnson was the supreme godfather. Former Speaker of the House Thomas O'Neill also assumed such a role.

Ultimately, the primary power units of Congress—virtual miniature governments within themselves—are not the individual senators and congresspersons but the *clans* that form around them. The larger and more influential the clan, the greater its power. Clans are comparable to large kinship groups in tribal communities; until Congress passed antinepotism rules in 1967 the core of the network might be actual kin. Even today a great deal of power is concentrated through family networks. The Byrds of Virginia; the Cabots, Lodges, and Kennedys of Massachusetts; the Tafts of Ohio; and the Roosevelts of New York—all have passed their power from generation to generation, some eventually establishing family power niches (e.g., the Udalls of Utah have focused on issues of environment and natural resources) or ideological niche (Kennedy liberalism, Goldwater conservatism). Intermarriage among the various congressional families often serves to ally clans and extend networks of power.

Although the basic component of the congressional clan is the staff, there are many ways to incorporate others. The clan network can be extended by building patron-client relations with bureaucrats who have, through the power of willful complacency, the ability to block legislation that has been enacted. Lobbies can also be incorporated into the clan network. Fifteen thousand registered lobbies and two thousand political action committees play a vital function in the government, not only in providing information on the particular issue being lobbied but also on what is going on in Congress. Congresspersons may even further extend their clans by establishing their own lobbies in the form of institutes, think tanks, or public affairs groups. Harlem congressman Adam Clayton Powell used his Tenants Protective Association, headquartered in Bimini in the Caribbean, to move large amounts of money. Senator Jesse Helms has been instrumental in the establishment of the Heritage Foundation, the Institute on Money and Inflation, the American Family Institute, the Center for a Free Society, and the Institute of American Relations.

The major thrust of Weatherford's analysis is that Congress has become so ritualized it hardly functions at all. As the Senate floor grew into a theatrical exhibition hall where impassioned rhetoric supplanted real decision making, most productive discussion and information gathering was shifted to closed committee meetings. The Legislative Reorganization Act of 1946 opened these committee hearings not only to the public and press, but also to the same kind of ritualistic showmanship as exists on the floor. As celebrities, Mafiosa, and Communists were paraded before the wise and judicious panels, the drama increased while the effectiveness of the panels decreased. Today, real decisions are made in private offices, over lunch, and in the hallways, leaving the more public arenas as showplaces for the government as it should be—that is, the government of the American myth.

The true goal of Congress, according to Weatherford, is to produce the *Congressional Record,* which is really nothing more than a repetition of the empty rhetoric displayed on the House and Senate floors, but in a form that can be mailed back home to show that the congressperson is doing the job. Rules allow changes to be entered into the published version so that a speech might seem more articulate than it actually was, and there is even a rule that allows entries of speeches that were never presented. Through such entries, senators can make themselves appear prime movers on certain bills, when actually they may have played no part whatsoever.

Congresspersons have become so involved in ritualistic posturing— giving speeches, attending benefits, soothing constituents, and the like—

that real power has shifted to the staffs who control the information flow, develop resolutions and bills, and write the speeches. "The greatest deliberative body in the world has become the greatest ceremonial body in the world, and the talents of its members are devoted less to deciding matters of national policy than to arranging and considering minute points of ceremony" (Weatherford 1981: 266).

TOWARD THE FUTURE

The journey from Evans-Pritchard's *The Nuer* to Weatherford's study of the United States Congress is long and convoluted, but there is a certain logical inevitability to it. From its beginnings in relatively closed-system analyses of folk cultures, political anthropology has spread outward in every direction; there has been an increase in complexity and scope, in relation both to theory and to the societies studied. Predictably, this has led not only to greater breadth and depth in political studies but also to increasing fragmentation. Indeed, there is little evidence that anthropologists writing on politics read each other's works; individual research often seems isolated, and there is often little building on earlier studies.

Despite the wide variety of approaches, there are some significant absences. The process approach and action theory have tended toward an increasing emphasis on cognition, decision making, and motivation. The materialist perspective has been left by the wayside. There are no end of analyses on how actors in political dramas manipulate symbols, rules, norms, or customs, but very little discussion is devoted to how they manipulate physical resources, or how they are affected by such resources. One of the more promising developments in social anthropology has been the application of ecological principles to show how various social forms are adaptive to changing environments; this orientation might be of great value in interpreting political behavior. Also, the trend in cultural anthropology toward increasing quantification has been largely ignored by political researchers.

With new political studies appearing regularly, it is to be expected that gaps will not remain for long. However, the crucial problem at this point is not to produce more narrowly focused ethnographies—though, of course, these are certainly valuable—but to draw together the material that already exists into some sort of cohesive framework.

The first major challenge, then, is to make political anthropology meaningful by incorporating the scores of isolated studies into some larger theory. The second major challenge is to make political anthropology relevant. In this regard, it would be a major deficiency to overlook what has come to be called action anthropology (to carefully distinguish it from the more benign action theory). It is almost inevitable that an anthropologist studying power in modern society should learn far more than he or she would really like to know about the effects of that power. Oppression is a nice word to bandy about at cocktail parties when trying to one-up a fellow liberal; it becomes a very ugly word when brought down to the level of real people suffering real hunger, real privation, and perhaps real torture and death. The emotional thresholds of individual anthropologists vary, so there is no way to determine the point at which pure research turns to active protest. Action anthropology is an attempt, usually futile, to confront the very powers we started studying with such illusions of objectivity and to try to redress, if only through exposure, some of the evils of modern interpretations of power. Cultural Survival, is perhaps the largest and best known of the specifically anthropological action groups; it is a combined resource center, pressure group, and communications network dedicated to the protection of traditional societies throughout the world. Although such groups belong to all of anthropology, indeed to all people, political anthropologists can play a key role in exposing and analyzing systems of repression, and equally important, in developing practical recommendations for change.

Whether political anthropology will duly become cohesive and relevant to the problems of change in the modern world is a moot question, but it can no longer fall back on the excuse that it is still a fledgling discipline. Some of the finest work of modern anthropology has already been accomplished under the rubric of political anthropology. There is certainly much to come.

SUGGESTED READINGS

Britan, Gerald M., and Ronald Cohen, eds. *Hierarchy and Society* (Philadelphia: Institute for the Study of Human Issues, 1980). Traditionally, anthropology has tended to examine informal political structures. In this book, a score of anthropologists turn their jaundiced eyes on formal bureaucracies only to discover that these work mainly through informal interactions. Organizations under scrutiny include a health center in the American Midwest, provincial government in Ethiopia, and the massive bureaucracy of the People's Republic of China. In a theoretical chapter, the editors summarize anthropological theory on formal organization and present their own model.

Huizer, Gerrit, and Bruce Mannhein, eds. *The Politics of Anthropology* (The Hague, Netherlands: Mouton, 1979). Anthropologists have always considered themselves the vanguard in the fight against sexism, racism, ethnocentrism, and colonialism. It is the basic premise of this book that anthropology itself is basically sexist, racist, ethnocentric, and colonialist. The editors do not settle for mere self-accusation, however, but include articles that seriously examine the problems and possibilities of a liberation anthropology.

Seaton, S. Lee, and H. J. M. Claessen, eds. *Political Anthropology* (The Hague, Netherlands: Mouton, 1979). This collection of papers, presented at a conference in Chicago, self-consciously attempts to present a state-of-the-art overview of its subject. It succeeds to the extent that it reveals that political anthropology remains a potpourri of unrelated theories and ethnographic analyses. The part titles—Centers and Peripheries, Authority and Power, and Political Culture—are sufficiently general to cover just about anything. Despite the lack of cohesion, many of the articles are of the highest quality. Several chapters deal with politics in industrial states.

Weatherford, J. McIver. *Tribes on the Hill* (New York: Rawson, Wade, 1981). As a member of Senator John Glenn's staff, author Weatherford was able to employ participant observation research in the halls of Congress. The results (summarized in this chapter) are presented in a lively and humorous manner aimed at, and deserving, a popular audience. Though it is sometimes difficult to separate Weatherford's black humor from his scholarship, as when he compares senators to cannibals, there is no ambiguity in his main theme: Congress is so caught up in performing primitive rituals that it can barely function at all.

Glossary

Action theory. A perspective within the **process approach** in which the focus is on the strategies of individuals for gaining and maintaining power.

Age-set system. In some societies, all those who undergo puberty initiation at the same time form a coherent group that passes through different statuses and roles together. In tribal societies, this can be an important pantribal sodality that overrides kinship loyalties and unites the wider group.

Arena. This term has no agreed-on meaning, but in the **process approach** and **action theory** it often delimits a small area within the political **field** in which competition between a few individuals or factions takes place. In F. G. Bailey's **game theory**, it is an area in which teams that agree on a common set of rules compete.

Band. The least complex level of sociocultural integration, associated with hunting-gathering societies. Characterized by small, fluid groups, egalitarianism, informal leadership, and bilateral kinship.

Bivocal symbolism. According to Abner Cohen, all true symbols serve both existential and political ends; that is, they are felt in a deeply personal way, but at the same time they maintain political continuity through reaffirming common myths and values.

Cargo cult. A type of **revitalization movement** that seeks to gain access to Western trade goods (*cargo* in Pidgin English) by supernatural means.

Chiefdom. The least complex form of centralized political system, usually found in cultures that base their subsistence on extensive agriculture or intensive fishing. Characterized by a ranking of individuals and lineages, inheritance of power within a dominant lineage, and maintenance of power through redistribution of wealth by a charismatic chief.

Complementary opposition. A system in which groups that are antagonistic at one level unite at another level to counter a military threat.

Consensual power. Leadership that derives from the assent of the people, rather than force alone. This assent may be based on tradition, respect for an office, or faith in the personal qualities of a leader.

Corporatism. A model of the state in which the government functions through a limited number of monopolistic interest groups.

Dependency theory. A broad paradigm that views the underdevelopment of the Third World as a result of the capitalist expansion of the First World. In contrast to **modernization theory**, dependency theory puts the emphasis on *external* factors of underdevelopment.

Dependent power. Power that is granted, allocated, or delegated by someone who holds **independent power**.

Diachronic study. An analysis of a society "in time," that is, in a historical or evolutionary context.

Environmental circumscription. A theory by Robert Carniero that **primary states** arose when population growth and other pressures within areas bounded by mountains or desert forced increasingly complex modes of political and social organization.

Factions. Informal, leader-follower political groups organized for a particular purpose and disbanding when that purpose is accomplished or defeated. See also **Pervasive factionalism** and **Segmentary factional political systems**.

Field. The basic unit of study in the **process approach**. Previous researchers tended to focus on a defined group, such as a tribe or community; a field, which is defined anew by each researcher, may cross the boundaries of different groups and may change over time. In Bailey's **game theory**, a field is more specifically defined as an area in which rival political structures interact, but without agreed-on rules between them.

Game theory. Introduced into political anthropology by F. G. Bailey, this approach seeks to discover the **normative rules** and **pragmatic rules** of political manipulation. Politics is viewed as a game composed of teams competing for prizes.

General systems theory. A relatively new and highly complex paradigm for the social sciences in which whole systems are viewed as adapting to changes in their internal and external environments through feedback mechanisms (see **Positive feedback** and **Negative feedback**). This orientation has been especially important in explaining the rise of primary states.

Hydraulic theory. A theory of state formation proposed by Karl Wittfogel. Canal irrigation required a division of classes into workers and administrators and tended to concentrate power in the hands of those who controlled the water supplies on which the community depended.

Independent power. A relation of dominance based on the direct capabilities of an individual, such as knowledge, skills, or personal charisma. In centralized societies, such power may attach to a particular office, such as that of king. See **Dependent power**.

Institutionalization of leadership. A theory by Elman Service that the development of centralized political organization can be explained by the perceived benefits of strong leadership and political continuity.

Intensification. As used by Marvin Harris, this refers to a fundamental process of cultural evolution by which population pressures combine with resource depletion to force improved means of producing food. Such technological changes in turn require new modes of social organization.

Legitimacy. A primary basis for **power** that derives from the people's expectations about the nature of power and how it should be attained, for example, by election in the United States or by holding redistributive feasts in Polynesia.

Male dominance. Control of productive resources and political power by men. Although widespread, cross-cultural studies show that male dominance is not universal.

Man the Hunter theory of evolution. The belief that the biological evolution of humans focused on the cooperative hunting of big game. The theory is presently disputed.

Matriarchy. Political control by women. Despite a widespread belief in primitive matriarchies, no such social system, either past or present, has ever been documented by anthropologists.

Mode of production. For Karl Marx, the way that production, especially labor, is organized. As reinterpreted by anthropologist Eric Wolf, the three main modes of production are: the *kin-ordered mode* typical of bands, tribes, and chiefdoms; the *tributary mode* in which an elite demands the products of labor as tribute; and the *capitalist mode* that directly buys and sells human labor.

Modernization theory. The assumption that the *internal* dynamics of a country are responsible for its development or underdevelopment. In some permutations, the emphasis is put on what a country is lacking, such as entrepreneurial spirit, technology, capital, and so forth. Other versions emphasize such dynamics as **internal colonialism** or the growth of a vast informal economy. Contrasts with **dependency theory**.

Negative feedback. Deviation-minimizing processes in which change in a system is limited by other elements of the system so that equilibrium is maintained (e.g., in hot weather the body is cooled by sweating to maintain a constant temperature). See **Positive feedback**.

Neo-evolutionism. A revival by Leslie White in the 1940s of nineteenth-century cultural evolutionary theory. Later theorists distinguished *general evolution—*

broad changes in cultural complexity, such as from band to tribal society—and *specific evolution,* the observable adaptational changes of particular societies.

Normative rules. In F. G. Bailey's **game theory,** the political rules that are publicly professed, such as honesty, fair play, and so forth. See, in contrast, **Pragmatic rules.**

Pervasive factionalism. A condition in which formal political structures have broken down or have become inoperative, and temporary **factions** arise to solve each problem as it appears.

Politics. One of those undefinable words that depends on the particular interests of the researcher. A good working definition is "the processes involved in determining and implementing public goals and . . . the differential achievement and use of power by the members of the group concerned with these goals" (Swartz, Turner, and Tuden 1966: 7).

Positive feedback. Deviation-amplifying processes. A slight initial kick starts a process of increasingly rapid change; it stops only when the system attains a new level of equilibrium or collapses. See **Negative feedback.**

Power. In its broadest sense, "an ability to influence the behavior of others and/or gain influence over the control of valued actions" (R. Cohen 1970: 31). In its purely political aspect, such influence would be limited to the public domain. This amorphous term is better defined by breaking it into its component parts: **independent power, dependent power, consensual power, legitimacy,** and **support.**

Pragmatic rules. In F. G. Bailey's **game theory,** those political rules that are concerned with gaining or maintaining power—that is, with winning the game, not with public display. See, in contrast, **Normative rules.**

Primary state. A state that developed independently of preexisting states. This occurred in six areas: Mesopotamia, the Nile Valley, the Indus Valley of India, the Yellow River Valley of China, Mesoamerica, and Peru.

Process approach. Sometimes referred to as process theory, though it is too amorphous to constitute a coherent theory. Originally a reaction against **structural-functionalism,** this approach emphasizes change and conflict.

Retribalization. The tendency for some tribal groups to become more cohesive, to protect economic and political interests, during the process of modernization.

Revitalization movement. A deliberate attempt by a group, usually in a situation of cultural collapse and/or subjugation by a foreign power, to create a better society. Such movements may seek apocalyptic transformation through supernatural means, try to recreate a golden age of the past, or expel all foreign influences. A **cargo cult** is a type of revitalization movement.

Secondary state. Any state that came into existence through the influence of preexisting states.

Segmentary factional political system. A system either without formal political structures or in which such structures have broken down, so that competition between **factions** becomes the normal mode of political decision making.

Segmentary lineage. A unilineal system based on small, local, relatively autonomous units that can be put together, building-block fashion, into increasingly larger structures for ritual or military purposes.

State. The most complex level of political integration. Found in societies whose subsistence is based on intensive agriculture, and characterized by leadership centered in an individual or elite group supported by a bureaucracy, suprakinship loyalties, class structure, and economic redistribution based on tribute or taxation.

Structural-functionalism. The dominant theoretical orientation of British anthropology during the 1930s and 1940s. **Synchronic analysis**, usually of groups treated as closed systems, showed how the various component institutions contributed to the equilibrium of the whole.

Support. A broad concept, including virtually anything that contributes to or maintains political **power**. Two basic supports are coercion (force) and **legitimacy**.

Synchronic study. A type of analysis, typical of the **structural-functionalists** and French structuralists, that treats societies as though they were outside of time, that is, without reference to historical context.

Tribe. A loosely defined term denoting a wide range of social organizations that exist between hunting-gathering **bands** and centralized systems. Associated with horticulture or pastoralism, charismatic leadership, unilineal kinship, and pantribal sodalities.

Tributary elite. The owners and managers of production, banking, and trade within periphery and semiperiphery countries; they really represent the interests of the core. See **World Capitalist System**.

World Capitalist System. According to Immanuel Wallerstein, the expansion of capitalism outward from Europe beginning in the sixteenth century created a single world economy, consisting of a core of developed nations, a periphery of underdeveloped countries that supply raw materials and cheap labor to the core, and an intermediary group of semiperipheral countries.

Bibliography

Abrahamson, Mark. 1969. "Correlates of Political Complexity." *American Sociological Review* 34:690–701.

Adams, Richard N. 1975. *Energy and Structure: A Theory of Social Power*. Austin: University of Texas Press.

———. 1977. "Power in Human Societies: A Synthesis." In *The Anthropology of Power*, ed. R. D. Fogelson and R. N. Adams. New York: Academic Press.

Adams, Robert McCormick. 1966. *The Evolution of Urban Society*. Chicago: Aldine.

Aronoff, Myron J. 1983. "Conceptualizing the Role of Culture in Political Change." In *Culture and Political Change: Political Anthropology*. Vol. 2, ed. M. J. Aronoff. New Brunswick, N.J.: Transaction Books.

———. 1984a. "Gush Emunin: The Institutionalization of a Charismatic, Messianic, Religious-Political Revitalization Movement in Israel." In *Religion and Politics, Political Anthropology*, Vol. 3, ed. M. J. Aronoff. New Brunswick, N.J.: Transaction Books.

———. 1984b. "Introduction." In *Religion and Politics, Political Anthropology*. Vol. 3, ed. M. J. Aronoff. New Brunswick, N.J.: Transaction Books.

Bailey, F. G. 1960. *Tribe, Caste and Nation*. Manchester: Manchester University Press.

———. 1968 "Parapolitical Systems." In *Local Level Politics*, ed. M. Swartz. Chicago: Aldine.

———. 1969. *Strategems and Spoils: A Social Anthropology of Politics*. New York: Schocken Books.

———. 1970. *Politics and Social Change*. Berkeley: University of California Press.

Balandier, Georges. 1970. *Political Anthropology*. New York: Random House.

Banton, Michael, ed. 1965. *Political Systems and the Distribution of Power*. London: Tavistock.

Barth, Frederick. 1959. *Political Leadership among the Swat Pathans*. London: Athalone.

Block, Maurice, ed. 1975. *Political Language and Oratory in Traditional Society*. New York: Academic Press.

Boas, Franz. 1894. *The Social Organization and Secret Societies of the Kwakiutl Indians*. United States National Museum Annual Report 1894.

Bodley, John N. 1982. *Victims of Progress*. 2d ed. Palo Alto, Calif.: Mayfield.

Boserup, Esther. 1965. *The Conditions of Agricultural Growth: The Economics of Agrarian Change under Population Pressure*. Chicago: Aldine.

Briggs, Jean L. 1970. *Never in Anger: Portrait of an Eskimo Family*. Cambridge, Mass.: Harvard University Press.

Britan, Gerald M., and Ronald Cohen. 1980. "Toward an Anthropology of Formal Organizations." In *Hierarchy and Society: Anthropological Perspectives on Bureaucracy*, ed. G. M. Britan and R. Cohen. Philadelphia: Institute for the Study of Human Issues.

Britan, Gerald M., and Ronald Cohen, eds. 1980. *Hierarchy and Society: Anthropological Perspectives on Bureaucracy*. Philadelphia: Institute for the Study of Human Issues.

Brown, Donald. 1991. *Human Universals*. New York: McGraw-Hill.

Brown, Judith K. 1975. "Iroquois Women: An Ethnohistoric Note." In *Toward an Anthropology of Women*, ed. R. R. Reiter. New York: Monthly Review Press. pp. 235–51.

Buckley, Walter, ed. 1968. *Modern Systems Research for the Behavioral Sciences: A Sourcebook*. Chicago: Aldine.

Buenaventura-Posso, Elisa, and Susan E. Brown. 1980. "Forced Transition from Egalitarianism to Male Dominance: The Bari of Colombia." In *Women and Colonization: Anthropological Perspectives*, ed. Mona Etienne and Eleanor Leacock. New York: Praeger.

Bujra, Janet M. 1973. "The Dynamics of Political Action: A New Look at Factionalism." *American Anthropologist* 75:132–52.

Burling, Robbins. 1974. *The Passage of Power: Studies in Political Succession*. New York: Academic Press.

Campbell, Bernhard G. 1979. *Humankind Emerging*. 2d ed. Boston: Little, Brown.

Carniero, Robert L. 1967. "On the Relationship between Size of Population and Complexity of Social Organization." *Southwestern Journal of Anthropology* 23:234–43.

———. 1970. "A Theory of the Origin of the State." *Science* 169:733–38.

———. 1978. "Political Expansion as an Expression of the Principle of Competitive Exclusion." In *Origins of the State: The Anthropology of*

Political Evolution, ed. R. Cohen and E. Service. Philadelphia: Institute for the Study of Human Issues.

Castile, George Pierre, and Gilbert Kushner, eds. 1981. *Persistent Peoples: Cultural Enclaves in Perspective*. Tucson: University of Arizona Press.

Chagnon, Napoleon. 1968. *Yanomamo: The Fierce People*. New York: Holt, Rinehart and Winston.

Chilcote, Ronald H. 1984. *Theories of Underdevelopment*. Boulder, Colo.: Westview Press.

Childe, V. Gordon. 1936. *Man Makes Himself.* London: Watts.

————. 1946. *What Happened in History*. New York: Penguin.

Claessen, Henri J. M. 1978. "The Early State: A Structural Approach." In *The Early State*, ed. J. M. Claessen and P. Skalník. The Hague, Netherlands: Mouton.

Claessen, Henri J. M., and Peter Skalník. 1978. "The Early State: Theories and Hypotheses." In *The Early State*, ed. H. J. M. Claessen and P. Skalník. The Hague, Netherlands: Mouton.

Claessen, Henri J. M., and Peter Skalník, eds. 1978. *The Early State*. The Hague, Netherlands: Mouton.

Clastres, Pierre. 1977. *Society Against the State*. New York: Urizen Books.

Codere, Helen. 1950. *Fighting with Property: A Study of Kwakiutl Potlatching and Warfare, 1792–1930*. Seattle: University of Washington Press.

————. 1957. "Kwakiutl Society: Rank without Class." *American Anthropologist* 59:473–86.

Cohen, Abner. 1969a. *Custom and Politics in Urban Africa: A Study of Hausa Migrants in a Yoruba Town*. Berkeley: University of California Press.

————. 1969b. "Political Anthropology: The Analysis of the Symbolism of Power Relations." *Man* 4:215–44.

————. 1974. *Two-Dimensional Man: An Essay on the Anthropology of Power and Symbolism in Complex Societies*. London: Routledge and Kegan Paul.

————. 1981. *The Politics of Elite Culture: Explorations in the Dramaturgy of Power in a Modern African Society*. Berkeley: University of California Press.

Cohen, Ronald. 1965. "Political Anthropology: The Future of a Pioneer." *Anthropological Quarterly* 38:117–31.

————. 1970. "The Political System." In *A Handbook of Method in Cultural Anthropology*, ed. R. Naroll and R. Cohen. Garden City, N.Y.: Natural History Press.

————. 1978a. "Introduction." In *Origins of the State: The Anthropology of Political Evolution*, ed. R. Cohen and E. Service. Philadelphia: Institute for the Study of Human Issues.

————. 1978b. "State Foundations: A Controlled Comparison." In *The Origin of the State: The Anthropology of Political Evolution*, ed. R. Cohen and E. Service. Philadelphia: Institute for the Study of Human Issues.

Cohen, Ronald, and John Middleton, eds. 1967. *Comparative Political Systems: Studies in the Politics of Pre-Industrial Societies*. Austin: University of Texas Press.

Cohen, Ronald, and Alice Schlegal. 1968. "The Tribe as a Socio-Political Unit: A Cross-Cultural Examination." In *Essays on the Problem of Tribe: Proceedings of the 1967 Annual Spring Meeting of the American Ethnological Society*, ed. J. Helm. Seattle: University of Washington Press.

Cohen, Ronald, and Elman Service, eds. 1978. *Origins of the State: The Anthropology of Political Evolution*. Philadelphia: Institute for the Study of Human Issues.

Colson, Elizabeth. 1968. "Political Anthropology: The Field." In *International Encyclopedia of the Social Sciences*. Vol. 12, ed. D. L. Sills. New York: Macmillan and Free Press.

————. 1974. *Tradition and Contract: The Problem of Order*. Chicago: Aldine.

Coontz, Stephanie, and Peta Henderson. 1986. "Property Forms, Political Power, and Female Labour in the Origins of Class and State Societies." In *Women's Work, Men's Property: The Origins of Gender and Class*, ed. S. Coontz and P. Henderson. London: Verso.

Counts, Dorothy Ayers. 1984. "Revenge Suicide by Lusi Women: An Expression of Power." In *Rethinking Women's Roles: Perspectives from the Pacific*, ed. D. O'Brien and S. W. Tiffany. Berkeley: University of California Press.

Dahlberg, Frances. 1981. "Introduction." In *Woman the Gatherer*, ed. F. Dahlberg. New Haven, Conn.: Yale University Press.

Damas, David. 1968. "The Diversity of Eskimo Societies." In *Man, The Hunter*, ed. R. B. Lee and I. DeVore. Chicago: Aldine.

Davenport, W. 1969. "The Hawaiian Cultural Revolution: Some Political and Economic Considerations." *American Anthropologist* 71:1–20.

Davis, Shelton H. 1977. *Victims of the Miracle: Development and the Indians of Brazil*. Cambridge: Cambridge University Press.

Deloria, Vine. 1969. *Custer Died for Your Sins*. New York: Avon.

de Soto, Hernando. 1989. *The Other Path: The Invisible Revolution in the Third World*. New York: Harper and Row.

Draper, Patricia. 1985. "Two Views of Sex Differences in Socialization." In *Male-Female Differences: A Bio-Cultural Perspective*, ed. R. L. Hall. New York: Praeger.

Drucker, P., and Robert F. Heizer. 1967. *To Make My Name Good: A Reexamination of the Southern Kwakiutl Potlatch*. Berkeley: University of California Press.

Duley, Margot I., and Karen Sinclair. 1986. "Male Dominance: Myth or Reality?" In *The Cross-Cultural Study of Women*, ed. M. Duley and M. Edwards. New York: The Feminist Press.

Dumond, D. E. 1965. "Population Growth and Cultural Change." *Southwestern Journal of Anthropology* 21:302–24.

Easton, David. 1953. *The Political System*. New York: Knopf.

———. 1959. "Political Anthropology." In *Biennial Review of Anthropology, 1958*. Stanford: Stanford University Press.

Eisenstadt, S. N. 1959. "Primitive Political Systems: A Preliminary Comparative Analysis." *American Anthropologist* 61:200–20.

———. 1963. *The Political Systems of Empire*. Glencoe, Ill.: Free Press.

———. 1966. *Modernization: Protest and Change*. Englewood Cliffs, N.J.: Prentice Hall.

———. 1967. "Transformation of Social, Political, and Cultural Orders in Modernization." In *Comparative Political Systems*, ed. R. Cohen and J. Middleton. Austin: University of Texas Press.

———. 1970. "Social Change and Development." In *Readings in Social Evolution and Development*, ed. S. N. Eisenstadt. Oxford: Pergamon Press.

———. 1973. "Varieties of Political Development: The Theoretical Challenge." In *Building States and Nations*, ed. S. N. Eisenstadt and S. Rokkan. Beverly Hills: Sage.

———. 1990. "Functional Analysis in Anthropology and Sociology: An Interpretive Essay." *Annual Review of Anthropology, 1990*, 19: 243–60.

Engels, Frederick. [1891] 1972. *The Origin of the Family, Private Property and the State*. Reprint, ed. E. B. Leacock. New York: International Publishers.

Estioko-Griffin, Agnes, and P. Bion Griffin. 1981. "Woman the Hunter: The Agta." In *Woman the Gatherer*, ed. F. Dahlberg. New Haven, Conn.: Yale University Press.

Evans-Pritchard, E. E. 1940a. *The Nuer*. Oxford: Oxford University Press.

———. 1940b. "The Nuer of the Southern Sudan." In *African Political Systems*, ed. M. Fortes and E. E. Evans-Pritchard. Oxford: Oxford University Press.

———. 1965. *The Position of Women in Primitive Societies and Other Essays in Social Anthropology*. London: Faber and Faber.

Faron, L. C. 1967. "The Mapuche Reservation as a Political Unit." In *Comparative Political Systems*, ed. R. Cohen and J. Middleton. Austin: University of Texas Press.

Flannery, Kent. 1968. "Archeological Systems Theory and Early Mesoamerica." In *Anthropological Archeology in the Americas*, ed. B. Meggers. Washington, D.C.: Anthropological Society of Washington.

Fogelson, R. D., and Richard N. Adams, eds. 1977. *The Anthropology of Power: Ethnographic Studies from Asia, Oceania, and the New World*. New York: Academic Press.

Fortes, Meyer, and E. E. Evans-Pritchard, eds. 1940. *African Political Systems*. Oxford: Oxford University Press.

Fox, Robin. 1967. *Kinship and Marriage*. Middlesex: Penguin.

Frazer, James G. [1890] 1900. *The Golden Bough*. 3 vols. London: Macmillan.

Freeman, L. C., and R. F. Winch. 1957. "Societal Complexity: An Empirical Test of a Typology of Societies." *American Journal of Sociology* 62:461–66.

Fried, Morton H. 1967. *The Evolution of Political Society*. New York: Random House.

———. 1968. "On the Concepts of 'Tribe' and 'Tribal Society.' " In *Essays on the Problem of Tribe: Proceedings of the 1967 Annual Spring Meeting of the American Ethnological Society*, ed. J. Helm. Seattle: University of Washington Press.

———. 1978. "The State, the Chicken, and the Egg: Or, What Came First?" In *Origins of the State*, ed. R. Cohen and E. Service. Philadelphia: Institute for the Study of Human Issues.

Friedl, Ernestine. 1975. *Women and Men: An Anthropologist's View*. New York: Holt, Rinehart and Winston.

———. [1978] 1990. "Society and Sex Roles." In *Conformity and Conflict: Readings in Cultural Anthropology*. 7th ed., ed. J. Spradley and D. W. McCurdy. Glenview, Ill.: Scott, Foresman.

Fulton, Richard. 1972. "The Political Structure and Function of Poro in Kpelle Society." *American Anthropologist* 74:1218–33.

Gailey, Christine Ward. 1987. *Kinship to Kingship: Gender Hierarchy and State Formation in the Tongan Islands*. Austin: University of Texas Press.

Gluckman, Max. 1940. "The Kingdom of the Zulu of South Africa." In *African Political Systems*, ed. M. Fortes and E. E. Evans-Pritchard. Oxford: Oxford University Press.

———. 1955. *Custom and Conflict in Africa*. New York: Barnes and Noble.

———. 1960. *Order and Rebellion in Tribal Africa*. Glencoe, Ill.: Free Press.

———. 1965. *Politics, Law and Ritual in Tribal Society*. Oxford: Basil Blackwell.

Gluckman, Max, and Fred Eggan. 1965. "Introduction." In *Political Systems and the Distribution of Power*, ed. M. Banton. London: Tavistock.

Goody, Jack, ed. 1966. *Succession to High Office*. Cambridge: Cambridge University Press.

Haas, Jonathan. 1982. *The Evolution of the Prehistoric State*. New York: Columbia University Press.

Hall, John R. 1985. "Apocalypse at Jonestown." In *Magic, Witchcraft, and Religion: An Anthropological Study of the Supernatural*, ed. A. C. Lehmann and James E. Meyers. Palo Alto, Calif.: Mayfield Publishing.

Hammond, Dorothy, and Alta Jablow. 1976. *Women in Cultures of the World*. Menlo Park, Calif.: Cummings Publishing.

Harner, Michael. 1970. "Population Pressure and the Social Evolution of Agriculturalists." *Southwestern Journal of Anthropology* 26:67–86.

Harris, Marvin. 1968. *The Rise of Anthropological Theory*. New York: Thomas Crowell Co.

———. 1974. *Cows, Pigs, Wars and Witches*. New York: Vintage.

———. 1977. *Cannibals and Kings: The Origins of Culture*. New York: Vintage.

Helm, J., ed. 1968. *Essays on the Problem of Tribe: Proceedings of the 1967 Annual Spring Meeting of the American Ethnological Society*. Seattle: University of Washington Press.

Hoebel, E. Adamson. 1940. *The Political Organization and Law Ways of the Comanche Indians*. American Anthropological Association Memoir 54.

———. 1960. *The Cheyenne: Indians of the Great Plains*. New York: Holt, Rinehart and Winston.

Hopkins, Terance, and Immanuel Wallerstein, eds. 1982. *World System Analysis: Theory and Methodology*. Beverly Hills: Sage.

Horowitz, Irving Louis. 1984. "Religion, the State, and Politics." In *Religion and Politics, Political Anthropology*. Vol. 3, ed. M. J. Aronoff. New Brunswick, N.J.: Transaction Books.

Huizer, Gerrit, and Bruce Mannheim, eds. 1979. *The Politics of Anthropology: From Colonialism and Sexism toward a View from Below*. The Hague, Netherlands: Mouton.

Hunt, Eva, and Robert C. Hunt. 1978. "Irrigation, Conflict and Politics: A Mexican Case." In *Origins of the State*, ed. R. Cohen and E. Service. Philadelphia: Institute for the Study of Human Issues.

Izmirlian, Harry, Jr. 1969. "Structural and Decision-Making Models: A Political Example." *American Anthropologist* 71:1062–73.

Janssen, Jacobus J. 1978. "The Early State in Ancient Egypt." In *The Early State*, ed. H. J. M. Claessen and P. Skalník. The Hague, Netherlands: Mouton.

Johnson, Allen W., and Timothy Earle. 1987. *The Evolution of Human Societies: From Foraging Group to Agrarian State*. Stanford, Calif.: Stanford University Press.

Jolly, Clifford J., and Fred Plog. 1976. *Physical Anthropology and Archeology*. 2d ed. New York: Knopf.

Kertzer, David I. 1988. *Ritual, Politics and Power*. New Haven, Conn.: Yale University Press.

Kottak, Conrad Phillip. 1983. *Assault on Paradise: Social Change in a Brazilian Village*. New York: Random House.

Kuper, Adam. 1973. *Anthropologists and Anthropology: The British School, 1922–1972*. New York: Pica Press.

Kuznets, Simon. 1955. "Economic Growth and Income Inequality." *American Economic Review* 45 (March):1–28.

Lanternari, Vittorio. 1963. *The Religions of the Oppressed: A Study of Modern Messianic Cults*. New York: New American Library.

Leach, Edmund R. 1954. *Political Systems of Highland Burma*. Boston: Beacon
    Press.
————. 1961. *Rethinking Anthropology*. London: Athlone Press.
Leacock, Eleanor B. 1979. "Lewis Henry Morgan on Government and Prop-
    erty." In *New Directions in Political Economy: An Approach from
    Anthropology*, ed. M. B. Leons and F. Rothstein. Westport, Conn.:
    Greenwood Press.
————. 1981. *Myths of Male Dominance: Collected Articles on Women
    Cross-Culturally*. New York: Monthly Review Press.
Leibowitz, Lila. 1975. "Perspectives on the Evolution of Sex Differences." In
    Toward an Anthropology of Women, ed. R. R. Reiter. New York:
    Monthly Review Press.
Levinson, David, and Martin J. Malone. 1980. *Toward Explaining Human
    Culture: A Critical Review of the Findings of Worldwide Cross-Cultural
    Research*. New Haven, Conn.: HRAF Press.
Lewellen, Ted C. 1978. *Peasants in Transition: The Changing Economy of the
    Peruvian Aymara*. Boulder, Colo.: Westview Press.
————. 1979. "Deviant Religion and Cultural Evolution: The Aymara Case."
    Journal for the Scientific Study of Religion 18:243–51.
————. 1981. "Political Anthropology." In *The Handbook of Political Behav-
    ior*. vol. 3. ed. S. Long. New York: Plenum.
————. 1989a. "Holy and Unholy Alliances: The Politics of Catholicism in
    Revolutionary Nicaragua." *Journal of Church and State* 31:15–33.
————. 1989b. "Penny Corporatism: Control and Autonomy in Neighborhood
    Political Organization in Revolutionary Nicaragua." Paper presented at
    the American Anthropological Association Annual Meeting, Washing-
    ton, D.C., November 1989.
Lewis, Herbert. 1968. "Typology and Process in Political Evolution." In *Essays
    on the Problem of Tribe: Proceedings of the 1967 Annual Spring
    Meeting of the American Ethnological Society*, ed. J. Helm. Seattle:
    University of Washington Press.
Little, Kenneth. 1965. "The Political Function of Poro." *Africa* 35:349–65.
Lloyd, Peter C. 1965. "The Political Structure of African Kingdoms: An
    Explanatory Model." In *Political Systems and the Distribution of
    Power*, ed. M. Banton. London: Tavistock.
Logan, N., and W. Sanders. 1976. "The Model." In *The Valley of Mexico*, ed.
    E. Wolf. Albuquerque: University of New Mexico Press.
Lomax, Alan, and C. M. Arensberg. 1977. "A Worldwide Evolutionary
    Classification of Cultures by Subsistence Systems." *Current Anthro-
    pology* 18:659–708.
Lomax, Alan, and Norman Berkowitz. 1972. "The Evolutionary Taxonomy of
    Culture." *Science* 177:228–39.
Lott, Bernice. 1987. *Women's Lives: Themes and Variations in Gender Learn-
    ing*. Monterey, Calif.: Brooks/Cole Publishing.

Lowie, Robert H. [1927] 1962. *The Origin of the State*. New York: Russell and Russell.

―――. [1920] 1970. *Primitive Society*. New York: Liveright.

MacCormack, Carol P. 1980. "Nature, Culture and Gender: A Critique." In *Nature, Culture and Gender*, ed. C. P. MacCormack and M. Strathern. Cambridge: Cambridge University Press.

Maine, Henry. [1861] 1887. *Ancient Law: Its Connection with the Early History of Society and Its Relation to Modern Ideas*. London: J. Murray.

Mair, Lucy P. 1962. *Primitive Government*. Baltimore: Penguin.

Malinowski, Bronislaw. 1922. *Argonauts of the Western Pacific*. New York: Dutton.

Marquet, Jacques. 1971. *Power and Society in Africa*. New York: McGraw-Hill.

Marshall, Lorna. 1967. "!Kung Bushman Bands." In *Comparative Political Systems*, ed. R. Cohen and J. Middleton. Austin: University of Texas Press.

Mason, J. Alden. 1957. *The Ancient Civilisations of Peru*. Middlesex: Penguin.

McLean, John. 1889. "The Blackfoot Sun Dance." *Proceedings of the Canadian Institute*, ser. 3, vol. 4:231–37.

Middleton, John. 1960. *Lugbara Religion: Ritual and Authority among an East African People*. London: Oxford University Press.

―――. 1966. "The Resolution of Conflict among the Lugbara of Uganda." In *Political Anthropology*, ed. M. Swartz, V. Turner, and A. Tuden. Chicago: Aldine.

Middleton, John, and David Tate, eds. 1958. *Tribes without Rulers*. London: Routledge and Kegan Paul.

Mitchell, Clyde. 1964. "Foreword." In *The Politics of Kinship: A Study of Social Manipulation among the Lakeside Tonga*, by J. van Velsen. Manchester: Manchester University Press.

Mooney, James. [1896] 1973. *The Ghost Dance Religion and Wounded Knee*. New York: Dover Publications, Inc.

Moore, Henrietta. 1988. *Feminism and Anthropology*. Minneapolis: University of Minnesota Press.

Morawetz, David. 1977. *Twenty-five Years of Economic Development 1950 to 1975*. Baltimore: Johns Hopkins University Press.

Morgan, Lewis Henry. 1877. *Ancient Society*. New York: Henry Holt.

Morgen, Sandra. 1989. "Gender and Anthropology: Introductory Essay." In *Gender and Anthropology: Critical Reviews for Research and Teaching*, ed. S. Morgen. Washington, D.C.: American Anthropological Association.

Mukhopadhyay, Carol C., and Patricia J. Higgens. 1988. "Anthropological Studies of Women's Status Revisited, 1977–1987." *Annual Review of Anthropology 1988* 17:461–95.

Murdock, George Peter. 1949. *Social Structure*. New York: Macmillan.

————. 1959. "Evolution in Social Organization." In *Evolution and Anthropology: A Centennial Appraisal*, ed. B. Meggers. Washington, D.C.: Anthropological Society of Washington.

————. 1973. "Measurement and Cultural Complexity." *Ethnology* 12:379–92.

Murdock, George Peter, and Suzanne F. Wilson. 1972. "Settlement Patterns and Community Organization: Cross-Cultural Codes 2." *Ethnology* 11:254–95.

Murra, John V. 1958. "On Inca Political Structure." In *Systems of Political Control and Bureaucracy in Human Societies: Proceedings of the 1958 Annual Spring Meeting of the American Ethnological Society*. Seattle: University of Washington Press.

Nicholas, Ralph W. 1965. "Factions: A Comparative Analysis." In *Political Systems and the Distribution of Power*, ed. M. Banton. London: Tavistock.

————. 1966. "Segmentary Factional Political Systems." In *Political Anthropology*, ed. M. Swartz, V. Turner, and A. Tuden. Chicago: Aldine.

O'Brien, Denise. 1984. " 'Women Never Hunt': The Portrayal of Women in Melanesian Ethnography." In *Rethinking Women's Roles: Perspectives from the Pacific*. Berkeley: University of California Press.

Ornstein, Henry. 1980. "Asymmetrical Reciprocity: A Contribution to the Theory of Political Legitimacy." *Current Anthropology* 21:69–91.

Ortner, Sherry B. 1974. "Is Female to Male as Nature Is to Culture?" In *Woman, Culture and Society*, ed. M. Z. Rosaldo and L. Lamphere. Stanford: Stanford University Press.

Ortner, Sherry B., and Harriet Whitehead. 1981. "Introduction: Accounting for Sexual Meanings." In *Sexual Meanings: The Cultural Construction of Gender and Sexuality*, ed. S. Ortner and H. Whitehead. Cambridge: Cambridge University Press.

Otterbein, Keith P. 1971. "Comment on 'Correlates of Political Complexity.' " *American Sociological Review* 36:113–14.

Packard, Randall M. 1981. *Chiefship and Cosmology: An Historical Study of Political Competition*. Bloomington: Indiana University Press.

Paige, Jeffrey M. 1974. "Kinship and Polity in Stateless Societies." *American Journal of Sociology* 80:301–20.

Parker, Seymour, and Hilda Parker. 1979. "The Myth of Male Superiority: Rise and Demise." *American Anthropologist* 18:289–309.

Patterson, Thomas C. 1971. "The Emergence of Food Production in Central Peru." In *Prehistoric Agriculture*, ed. S. Struever. Garden City, N.Y.: Natural History Press.

Petersen, Glenn. 1989. "Ponapean Chieftainship in the Era of the Nation-State." In *Outwitting the State: Political Anthropology*, Vol. 7. ed. P. Skalník. New Brunswick, N.J.: Transaction Publishers.

Pfeiffer, John E. 1977. *The Emergence of Society: A Prehistory of the Establishment*. New York: McGraw-Hill.

Price, Barbara J. 1978. "Secondary State Formation: An Explanatory Model." In *Origins of the State*, ed. R. Cohen and E. Service. Philadelphia: Institute for the Study of Human Issues.

————. 1979. "Turning States' Evidence: Problems in the Theory of State Formation." In *New Directions in Political Economy: An Approach from Anthropology*, ed. M. B. Icons and F. Rothstein. Westport, Conn.: Greenwood Press.

Radcliffe-Brown, A. R. 1940. "Preface." In *African Political Systems*, ed. M. Fortes and E. E. Evans-Pritchard. Oxford: Oxford University Press.

Rappaport, Roy. 1968. *Pigs for the Ancestors: Ritual in the Ecology of a New Guinea People*. New Haven, Conn.: Yale University Press.

Rosaldo, Michelle Z. 1974. "Women, Culture and Society: A Theoretical Overview." In *Woman, Culture and Society*, ed. M. Z. Rosaldo and L. Lamphere. Stanford: Stanford University Press.

Ross, Marc Howard. 1986. "Female Political Participation: A Cross-Cultural Explanation." *American Anthropologist* 88:843–58.

Rostow, W. W. 1960. *The Stages of Economic Growth*. Cambridge: Cambridge University Press.

Sacks, Karen. 1979. *Sisters and Wives: The Past and Future of Sexual Equality*. Westport, Conn.: Greenwood Press.

Sahlins, Marshall. 1969. "The Segmentary Lineage and Predatory Expansion." *American Anthropologist* 63:332–45.

Sahlins, Marshall, and Elman Service. 1960. *Evolution and Culture*. Ann Arbor: University of Michigan Press.

Schapera, Isaac. 1967. *Government and Politics in Tribal Societies*. New York: Schocken Books.

Schlegel, Alice. 1977. "Toward a Theory of Sexual Stratification." In *Sexual Stratification: A Cross-Cultural View*, ed. A. Schlegel. New York: Columbia University Press.

Schwartz, Norman B. 1969. "Goal Attainment through Factionalism: A Guatemalan Case." *American Anthropologist* 63:332–45.

Scott, James C. 1985. *Weapons of the Weak: Everyday Forms of Peasant Resistance*. New Haven, Conn.: Yale University Press.

Seaton, S. Lee. 1978. "The Early State in Hawaii." In *The Early State*, ed. H. J. M. Claessen and P. Skalník. The Hague, Netherlands: Mouton.

Seaton, S. Lee, and Henri J. M. Claessen, eds. 1979. *Political Anthropology: The State of the Art*. The Hague, Netherlands: Mouton.

Service, Elman R. 1962. *Primitive Social Organization: An Evolutionary Perspective*. 2d ed. New York: Random House.

————. 1975. *Origins of the State and Civilization: The Processes of Cultural Evolution*. New York: W. W. Norton.

———. 1978. "Classical and Modern Theories of Government." In *Origins of the State: The Anthropology of Political Evolution*, ed. R. Cohen and E. Service. Philadelphia: Institute for the Study of Human Issues.

Shannon, Thomas Richard. 1989. *An Introduction to the World-System Perspective*. Boulder, Colo.: Westview.

Sharp, Henry S. 1981. "The Null Case: The Chipewyan." In *Woman the Gatherer*, ed. F. Dahlberg. New Haven, Conn.: Yale University Press.

Shepherd, George W., Jr. 1987. *The Trampled Grass: Tributary States and Self-Reliance in the Indian Ocean Zone of Peace*. Westport, Conn.: Greenwood Press.

Siegel, B. J., and A. R. Beals. 1960. "Pervasive Factionalism." *American Anthropologist* 62:394–417.

Silverblatt, Irene. 1988. "Women in States." *Annual Review of Anthropology 1988* 17:427–60.

Skalník, Peter. 1989. "Outwitting the State: An Introduction." In *Outwitting the State: Political Anthropology. Vol. 7.*, ed. P. Skalník. New Brunswick, N.J.: Transaction Publishers.

Slocum, Sally. 1975. "Woman the Gatherer: Male Bias in Anthropology." In *Toward an Anthropology of Women*, ed. R. R. Reiter. New York: Monthly Review Press.

Smith, Michael G. 1968. "Political Anthropology: Political Organization." In *International Encyclopedia of the Social Sciences*. Vol. 12, ed. D. L. Sills. New York: Macmillan and the Free Press.

Southall, Aidan W. 1953. *Alur Society*. Cambridge: W. Heffer and Sons.

———. 1965. "A Critique of the Typology of States and Political Systems." In *Political Systems and the Distribution of Power*, ed. M. Banton. London: Tavistock.

———. 1974. "State Formation in Africa." In *Annual Review of Anthropology*. vol. 3, ed. B. J. Siegel. Palo Alto, Calif.: Annual Reviews, Inc.

Southwold, Martin. 1966. "Succession to the Throne in Buganda." In *Succession to High Office*, ed. J. Goody. Cambridge: Cambridge University Press.

Spier, Leslie. 1921. *The Sun Dance of the Plains Indians: Its Development and Diffusion*. American Museum of Natural History Anthropological Papers, vol. 16, pt. 7.

Spiro, Melford E. 1965. "A Typology of Social Structure and the Patterning of Social Distributions: A Cross-Cultural Study." *American Anthropologist* 67:1097–1119.

Stavrianos, L. S. 1981. *Global Rift: The Third World Comes of Age*. New York: William Morrow.

Stem, Bernhard J. 1931. *Lewis Henry Morgan: Social Evolutionist*. Chicago: University of Chicago Press.

Stevenson, Robert R. 1968. *Population and Political Systems in Tropical Africa*. New York: Columbia University Press.

Steward, Julian. 1949. "Cultural Complexity and Law: A Trial Formulation of the Development of Early Civilizations." *American Anthropologist* 51:1–27.

———. 1955. *Theory of Culture Change: The Methodology of Multilinear Evolution.* Urbana: University of Illinois Press.

Swartz, Marc. 1968. *Local-Level Politics.* Chicago: Aldine.

Swartz, Marc, Victor Turner, and Arthur Tuden, eds. 1966. *Political Anthropology.* Chicago: Aldine.

Textor, Robert B. 1967. *A Cross-Cultural Summary.* New Haven: HRAF Press.

Tuden, Arthur, and Catherine Marshall. 1972. "Political Organization: Cross-Cultural Codes 4." *Ethnology* 11:436–64.

Turner, Victor. 1957. *Schism and Continuity in an African Society.* Manchester: Manchester University Press.

Upham, Steadman. 1990. "Analog or Digital?: Toward a Generic Framework for Explaining the Development of Emergent Political Systems." In *The Evolution of Political Systems*, ed. Steadman Upham. Cambridge: Cambridge University Press.

van Velsen, J. 1964. *The Politics of Kinship: A Study in Social Manipulation among the Lakeside Tonga.* Manchester: Manchester University Press.

Vincent, Joan. 1978. "Political Anthropology: Manipulative Strategies." In *Annual Review of Anthropology.* vol. 7, ed. B. J. Siegal. Glencoe, Calif.: Annual Reviews, Inc.

———. 1990. *Anthropology and Politics: Visions, Traditions, and Trends.* Tucson: University of Arizona Press.

Voget, Fred W. 1975. *A History of Ethnology.* New York: Holt, Rinehart and Winston.

Wallace, Anthony F. C. 1972. *The Death and Rebirth of the Seneca.* New York: Vintage.

———. 1985. "Nativism and Revivalism." In *Magic, Witchcraft, and Religion: An Anthropological Study of the Supernatural*, ed. A. C. Lehmann and J. E. Meyers. Palo Alto, Calif.: Mayfield Publishing.

Wallerstein, Immanuel. 1974. *The Modern World-System I: Capitalist Agriculture and the Origins of the European World-Economy in the Sixteenth Century.* New York: Academic Press.

———. 1980. *The Modern World-System II: Mercantalism and the Consolidation of the European World-Economy, 1600–1750.* New York: Academic Press.

———. 1989. *The Modern World-System III: The Second Era of Great Expansion of the Capitalist World-Economy, 1730–1840s.* New York: Academic Press.

Weatherford, J. McIver. 1981. *Tribes on the Hill.* New York: Rawson, Wade.

Webster, Paula. 1975. "Matriarchy: A Vision of Power." In *Toward an Anthropology of Women*, ed. R. R. Reiter. New York: Monthly Review Press.

Wenke, Robert I. 1980. *Patterns in Prehistory: Mankind's First Three Million Years*. New York: Oxford University Press.

Weyer, E. M. 1959. "The Structure of Social Organization among the Eskimo." In *Comparative Political Systems*, ed. R. Cohen and J. Middleton. Austin: University of Texas Press.

White, Leslie. 1943. "Energy and the Evolution of Culture." *American Anthropologist* 45:335–56.

———. 1949. *The Science of Culture*. New York: Grove.

———. 1959. *The Evolution of Culture*. New York: McGraw-Hill.

Whyte, Martin King. 1978. *The Status of Women in Preindustrial Societies*. Princeton, N.J.: Princeton University Press.

———. 1980. "Bureaucracy and Anti-Bureaucracy in the People's Republic of China." In *Hierarchy and Society: Anthropological Perspectives on Bureaucracy*, ed. Gerald M. Britan and Ronald Cohen. Philadelphia: Institute for the Study of Human Issues.

Winkler, Edwin A. 1970. "Political Anthropology." In *Biennial Review of Anthropology, 1969*. Stanford: Stanford University Press.

Wirsing, Rolf. 1973. "Political Power and Information: A Cross-Cultural Study." *American Anthropologist* 75:153–70.

Wissler, Clark. 1918. *The Sun Dance of the Blackfoot Indians*. Anthropological Papers of the American Museum of Natural History, vol. 16, pt. 3.

Wittfogel, Karl. 1957. *Oriental Despotism: A Comparative Study of Total Power*. New Haven: Yale University Press.

Wolf, Eric R. 1982. *Europe and the People Without History*. Berkeley: University of California Press.

Wolf, Eric R., and Edward Hansen. 1972. *The Human Condition in Latin America*. New York: Oxford University Press.

Worsley, Peter M. 1985. "Cargo Cults." In *Magic, Witchcraft, and Religion: An Anthropological Study of the Supernatural*, ed. A. C. Lehmann and J. E. Meyers. Palo Alto, Calif.: Mayfield Publishing.

Wright, Henry T. 1977. "Recent Research on the Origin of the State." In *Annual Review of Anthropology, 1977*, ed. B. J. Siegel. Palo Alto, Calif.: Annual Reviews, Inc.

———. 1978. "Toward an Explanation of the Origin of the State." In *Origins of the State: The Anthropology of Political Evolution*. Philadelphia: Institute for the Study of Human Issues.

Index

ABOUT THE AUTHOR

TED C. LEWELLEN is Associate Professor of Anthropology at the University of Richmond, Virginia. His focus on political anthropology began over ten years ago with the research for and subsequent publication of *Peasants in Transition* (1978). He also has published numerous articles and book chapters on political anthropology in different cultures.